Quantitative Finance

Mastering Mathematical Models for Market Success

William Johnson

Published by HiTeX Press

For permissions and other inquiries, write to:
P.O. Box 3132, Framingham, MA 01701, USA

Contents

Preface

In the vast, intricate world of markets and trading, few pursuits capture the imagination and potential for success quite like quantitative finance. Picture a bustling trading floor, screens flickering with data, the hum of algorithms quietly predicting market movements, and behind it all, quantitative analysts – 'quants' – wielding mathematical models as their tools. Welcome to the cutting-edge realm where mathematics marries markets, where data-driven strategies hold the promise of financial triumph, and where smart analysis can exponentially amplify the power of your investments.

But why should you, dear reader, venture into this demanding yet exhilarating field? Because quantitative finance offers more than just an advanced understanding of markets; it provides a robust framework for making informed decisions, mitigating risks, and optimizing portfolios with precision and confidence. In this ever-evolving landscape, those who harness the power of quant finance can tap into new dimensions of profitability and stability.

Quantitative finance stands at the intersection of finance, mathematics, and computer science. It employs statistical models to analyze financial markets, predict future movements, and devise powerful trading strategies. This book, "Quantitative Finance: Mastering Mathematical Models for Market Success," is designed to be your comprehensive guide through this fascinating terrain. Whether you are a novice investor, a keen trader, or a burgeoning quant analyst, the insights and knowledge contained herein will provide you with the tools to elevate your market understanding and enhance your trading prowess.

Embarking on this journey, you will uncover the fundamental principles of probability and statistics that underpin the probabilistic nature of markets. You will delve into the realm of financial instruments, learning how to value stocks, bonds, and derivatives with precision. Through rigorous exploration of time series analysis and stochastic processes, you will master the art of forecasting and volatility modeling, enhancing your ability to anticipate and react to market movements.

Risk management is the bedrock of quantitative finance, and this book will arm you with strategies to quantify and mitigate various financial risks. You will explore modern portfolio theory to optimize your investments and discover the profound implications of the Black-Scholes model in option pricing. As you progress, you will gain insights into interest rate models that shape bond markets and uncover the intricacies of algorithmic trading, where milliseconds can mean millions.

The future of finance belongs to those who can harness the power of machine learning and artificial intelligence. This book will guide you through the integration of machine learning techniques within your trading strategies, paving the way for a data-driven approach to investment. Finally, you will learn how to backtest and implement these strategies, ensuring they are not only theoretically sound but also effective in real-world trading.

This book is not merely an academic exercise; it is a practical guide to mastering the art and science of quantitative finance. By the time you turn the last page, you will be equipped with a profound understanding of the mathematical models that drive successful trading strategies and investments. So, ready your mind for an enlightening journey, sharpen your analytical skills, and embrace the quantitative revolution that is transforming the landscape of finance.

Dive in, and let the adventure begin.

Chapter 1

Introduction to Quantitative Finance

Quantitative finance is the application of mathematical models and computational techniques to analyze financial markets, predict future trends, and develop trading strategies. It leverages principles from probability, statistics, and data science to make informed decisions and optimize investments. This chapter provides an overview of the field, exploring its role in the financial markets, historical developments, key concepts, foundational mathematics, and diverse applications. Readers will also learn about the challenges faced by professionals in the field and the possible directions for future advancements.

1.1 What is Quantitative Finance?

Quantitative finance is a multidimensional field that combines finance, mathematics, and computer science to analyze financial markets and develop strategies for trading and investment. It utilizes sophisticated mathematical models and computational algorithms to dissect market data, forecast trends, and optimize asset management. At its core, quantitative finance aims to identify patterns within the market and leverage them for profitable decision-making.

The roots of quantitative finance are deeply embedded in the concept of efficient market hypothesis (EMH), which suggests that asset prices fully reflect all available information. While this creates a seemingly random walk of price movements, quantitative finance posits that underlying patterns and statistical anomalies can be discerned and exploited.

Central to quantitative finance are the models that represent and predict market behavior. These models draw on a rich array of mathematical disciplines, including probability theory, stochastic processes, and statistical inference. One of the earliest and most renowned models is the Black-Scholes-Merton model for option pricing, which revolutionized the financial markets by providing a systematic method to price derivatives.

Financial markets operate on vast amounts of data, rendering manual analysis impractical. Here, computational techniques come into play, enabling the processing of large datasets to detect meaningful insights. Algorithmic trading, a direct application of quantitative finance, automates trade execution based on pre-set rules derived from quantitative models. These algorithms can process information and execute trades faster and more accurately than human traders, offering a significant edge in the competitive finance landscape.

Another critical aspect of quantitative finance is risk management. By modeling the potential risks and returns of various financial instruments, quantitative analysts can devise strategies to mitigate unwanted exposures and enhance portfolio performance. This involves techniques like Value at Risk (VaR), which quantifies the maximum loss an investment portfolio could face over a specific period with a given confidence level. The formula for VaR, considering a normal distribution of returns, is often represented as:

$$\text{VaR}_\alpha = \mu + \sigma\Phi^{-1}(\alpha)$$

where μ is the expected return, σ is the standard deviation of returns, $\Phi^{-1}(\alpha)$ is the inverse cumulative distribution function of the normal distribution, and α is the confidence level.

Moving beyond traditional models, quantitative finance now harnesses the power of machine learning and artificial intelligence. These advanced techniques enable the modeling of non-linear relationships and the extraction of patterns from unstructured data, such as news articles or social media sentiments. For instance, a machine learning model might use historical price data along with sentiment analysis from financial news to predict stock prices.

Extending further, quantitative finance encompasses portfolio management, where the relationship between different asset types and their historical performance helps in constructing diversified portfolios aimed at optimizing returns for a given level of risk. The foundational concept here is Modern Portfolio Theory (MPT), introduced by Harry Markowitz, which deals with the construction of portfolios to maximize expected return based on a given level of market risk. The efficient frontier, a pivotal concept in MPT, is represented as:

$$w^* = \arg\max_{w} \frac{w^T \boldsymbol{R} - r_f}{\sqrt{w^T \Sigma w}}$$

where w is the vector of asset weights, $\boldsymbol{R}$ is the vector of expected returns, r_f is the risk-free rate, and Σ is the covariance matrix of asset returns.

To bridge theory with practice, the financial industry employs quantitative analysts or "quants" who develop and implement these models to manage portfolios, craft derivative pricing structures, and identify arbitrage opportunities. These professionals, equipped with expertise in mathematics, programming, and financial theory, comprise the backbone of modern-day financial institutions.

Quantitative finance continues to evolve, embracing new challenges and opportunities presented by innovations in data science and technology. As markets become more complex and data more voluminous, the role of quantitative finance in achieving market success becomes ever more pivotal. This dynamic interplay of theory, data, and computation lies at the heart of quantitative finance, making it an indispensable pillar in the world of finance.

1.2 The Role of Quantitative Finance in the Financial Markets

Quantitative finance plays a pivotal role in modern financial markets by providing a rigorous framework for understanding, modeling, and predicting market behaviors. This section delves into the multifaceted functions quantitative finance serves in the financial ecosystem, encompassing risk management, trade execution, portfolio optimization, and market prediction. Each aspect exemplifies how mathematical models and computational methods revolutionize decision-making processes, thereby enhancing market efficiency and stability.

To begin with, risk management stands as a cornerstone of quantitative finance. Using sophisticated mathematical models, financial professionals can quantify, monitor, and mitigate various forms of risk. One popular risk measure is Value at Risk (VaR), which estimates the potential loss in the value of a portfolio over a defined period for a given confidence interval. The formula for calculating VaR typically involves assessing historical volatilities and correlations among assets:

$$\text{VaR} = Z_\alpha \times \sigma_P \times \sqrt{t}$$

where Z_α is the z-score corresponding to the confidence level, σ_P is the portfolio standard deviation, and t is the time period of interest. More advanced techniques, such as Monte Carlo simulations and stress testing, further enhance the precision of risk assessments by simulating a wide range of market scenarios and their impacts on portfolio value.

Trade execution is another critical area where quantitative finance makes a substantial impact. Algorithms designed for trade execution, often referred to as algorithmic trading, use pre-defined rules and mathematical models to determine the timing, price, and quantity of trades. These algorithms aim to minimize market impact, reduce transaction costs, and capitalize on market inefficiencies. One commonly used algorithm is the Volume Weighted Average Price (VWAP) algorithm, which executes trades in proportion to the volume traded in the market, thereby distributing the impact over a broader timeframe.

$$\text{VWAP} = \frac{\sum_{i=1}^{N} P_i \times Q_i}{\sum_{i=1}^{N} Q_i}$$

where P_i and Q_i represent the price and quantity of the i-th trade, respectively. This technique helps in achieving better execution prices and reducing slippage.

Portfolio optimization, which seeks to allocate assets in a manner that maximizes return for a given level of risk, also benefits from the tools of quantitative finance. The Markowitz Modern Portfolio Theory (MPT) is a seminal approach that quantifies the trade-off between risk and return. It uses expected returns, variances, and covariances of asset returns to derive an efficient frontier, representing the set of optimal portfolios. The optimization problem can be expressed as:

$$\begin{aligned} \text{Minimize} \quad & \sigma_P^2 = \boldsymbol{w}^\top \Sigma \boldsymbol{w} \\ \text{Subject to} \quad & \boldsymbol{w}^\top \boldsymbol{\mu} = R \\ & \boldsymbol{w}^\top \mathbf{1} = 1 \end{aligned}$$

where $\boldsymbol{w}$ is the vector of asset weights, Σ is the covariance matrix of asset returns, $\boldsymbol{\mu}$ is the vector of expected returns, and R is the target return. Solutions to this optimization problem help investors make informed asset allocation decisions, balancing the trade-off between risk and return.

Market prediction, another pivotal application, leverages statistical and machine learning models to forecast price movements and identify trading opportunities. Techniques such as time series analysis, regression models, and neural networks are extensively used. For instance, the ARIMA (AutoRegressive Integrated Moving Average) model is fundamental in time series forecasting, combining autoregression (AR), differencing (I), and moving averaging (MA) to model and predict future values:

$$Y_t = c + \phi_1 Y_{t-1} + \phi_2 Y_{t-2} + \cdots + \phi_p Y_{t-p} + \theta_1 \epsilon_{t-1} + \theta_q \epsilon_{t-q} + \epsilon_t$$

where Y_t represents the value at time t, ϕ_i are the parameters for the autoregressive terms, θ_j are the parameters for the moving average terms, and ϵ_t is the error term. By optimizing the parameters of these models, quantitative analysts can generate accurate forecasts that guide trading decisions.

The derivatives markets also thrive on quantitative finance. Derivatives pricing models, such as the Black-Scholes model for options, draw heavily on stochastic calculus and partial differential equations to determine the fair value of financial instruments. The Black-Scholes formula for a European call option is given by:

$$C = S_0 N(d_1) - K e^{-rT} N(d_2)$$

with

$$d_1 = \frac{\ln(S_0/K) + (r + \sigma^2/2)T}{\sigma\sqrt{T}}, \quad d_2 = d_1 - \sigma\sqrt{T}$$

where C is the call option price, S_0 is the current stock price, K is the strike price, r is the risk-free interest rate, T is the time to maturity, σ is the volatility, and $N(\cdot)$ represents the cumulative distribution function of the standard normal distribution. These models facilitate the valuation of complex derivatives, enhancing market liquidity and enabling risk-sharing.

In conjunction with these applications, quantitative finance contributes to regulatory compliance and market transparency. By employing quantitative methods for surveillance and monitoring, regulators can detect market manipulation, insider trading, and systemic risk more effectively. This ensures a fair and orderly market, fostering investor confidence and stability.

The role of quantitative finance in the financial markets is multifaceted and indispensable. Its applications range from managing risks, executing trades, optimizing portfolios, predicting market movements, to pricing derivatives and ensuring regulatory compliance. As the complexity and interconnectedness of global financial markets continue to grow, quantitative finance will persist as a critical pillar driving innovation, efficiency, and resilience in the financial sector.

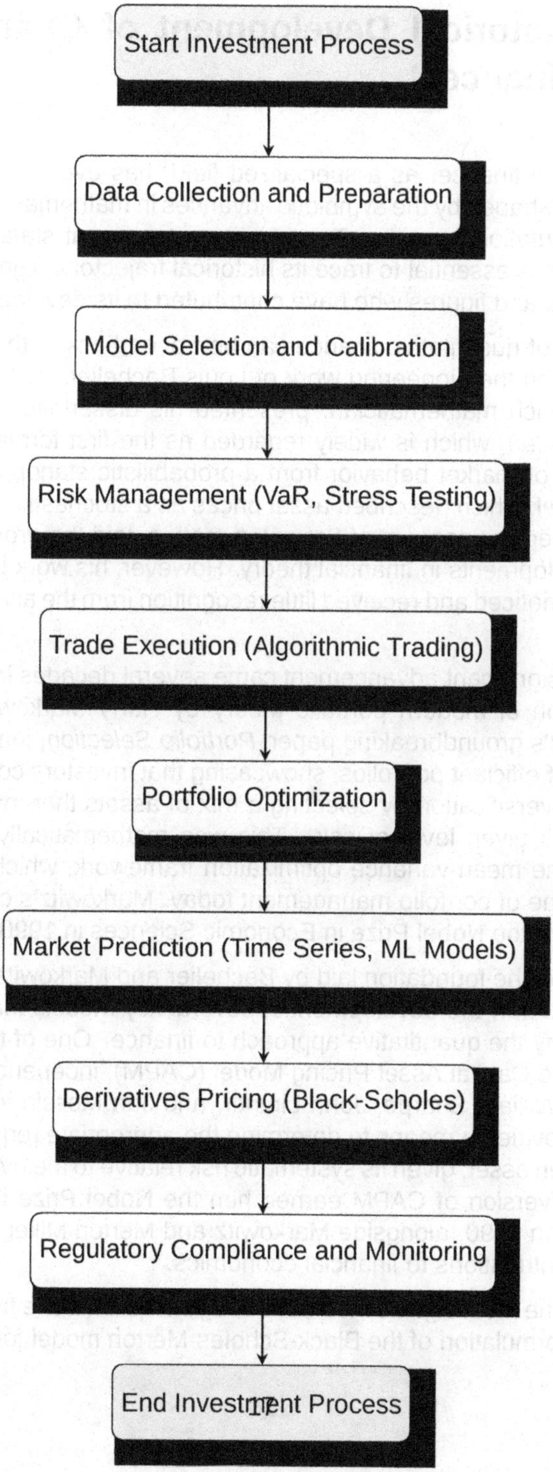
Start Investment Process
Data Collection and Preparation
Model Selection and Calibration
Risk Management (VaR, Stress Testing)
Trade Execution (Algorithmic Trading)
Portfolio Optimization
Market Prediction (Time Series, ML Models)
Derivatives Pricing (Black-Scholes)
Regulatory Compliance and Monitoring
End Investment Process

1.3 Historical Development of Quantitative Finance

Quantitative finance, as a specialized field, has evolved significantly over time, shaped by the symbiotic advances in mathematics, statistics, and computational power. To appreciate its current state and future potential, it is essential to trace its historical trajectory, highlighting key milestones and figures who have contributed to its development.

The roots of quantitative finance can be traced back to the early 20th century, with the pioneering work of Louis Bachelier. In 1900, Bachelier, a French mathematician, presented his dissertation *Théorie de la spéculation*, which is widely regarded as the first formal academic treatment of market behavior from a probabilistic standpoint. Bachelier's model, which described asset prices as a stochastic process and incorporated the concept of Brownian motion, laid the groundwork for later developments in financial theory. However, his work initially went largely unnoticed and received little recognition from the academic community.

The next significant advancement came several decades later with the introduction of modern portfolio theory by Harry Markowitz in 1952. Markowitz's groundbreaking paper, *Portfolio Selection*, introduced the concept of efficient portfolios, showcasing that investors could achieve optimal diversification by selecting a mix of assets that maximized returns for a given level of risk. This was mathematically formalized through the mean-variance optimization framework, which remains a cornerstone of portfolio management today. Markowitz's contributions earned him the Nobel Prize in Economic Sciences in 1990.

Building on the foundation laid by Bachelier and Markowitz, the 1960s and 1970s saw the development of several key models that would further solidify the quantitative approach to finance. One of the most notable is the Capital Asset Pricing Model (CAPM), independently developed by William Sharpe, John Lintner, and Jan Mossin in the 1960s. CAPM provided a means to determine the appropriate required rate of return of an asset, given its systematic risk relative to the overall market. Sharpe's version of CAPM earned him the Nobel Prize in Economic Sciences in 1990, alongside Markowitz and Merton Miller for their collective contributions to financial economics.

Perhaps the most significant breakthrough in quantitative finance came with the formulation of the Black-Scholes-Merton model for option pricing in 1973. Fischer Black, Myron Scholes, and Robert Merton introduced a partial differential equation that could determine the price of European-style options, given certain assumptions. The Black-Scholes-Merton model revolutionized options trading by providing a clear and consistent method for valuing options, thereby contributing significantly to the expansion of derivative markets. Scholes and Merton were awarded the Nobel Prize in Economic Sciences in 1997 for their contributions.

Parallel to these developments, the field of econometrics grew, integrating statistical methods with economic theory to empirically test hypotheses and forecast future trends. Key figures such as Clive Granger and Robert Engle advanced this field significantly through their work on time series analysis, introducing concepts like cointegration and autoregressive conditional heteroskedasticity (ARCH). These statistical advancements allowed for more sophisticated and accurate financial models, further embedding quantitative methods in the finance industry.

As we moved into the digital age, the convergence of high-performance computing and the proliferation of financial data gave rise to algorithmic trading and the use of machine learning techniques in finance. Algorithmic trading, which involves the use of computer algorithms to execute trades at high speed and frequency, revolutionized the trading landscape by improving efficiency and reducing transaction costs. Early pioneers in this domain include firms like Renaissance Technologies, which leveraged quantitative models to achieve substantial market success.

The advent of big data and advancements in artificial intelligence have ushered in a new era of quantitative finance, enabling the analysis of vast datasets and the development of complex, non-linear models. Machine learning techniques, such as neural networks and decision trees, are now being employed to enhance predictive accuracy and uncover hidden patterns in financial markets. This represents a significant shift from the traditional models that relied heavily on linear assumptions and simplified representations of market behavior.

In this ongoing evolution, quantitative finance continues to adapt and expand, driven by technological advancements and the ever-increasing complexity of financial markets. The historical development of the field reflects a continuous interplay between theory and practice, where each new innovation builds upon the foundation laid by previous discoveries. This dynamic progression not only underscores the importance of foundational knowledge but also highlights the immense potential for future breakthroughs in quantitative finance.

1.4 Key Concepts and Terminologies

Quantitative finance encompasses a broad spectrum of concepts and terminologies that are pivotal to understanding and mastering the field. By grasping these foundational elements, you will be well-equipped to delve deeper into complex quantitative models and strategies. This section introduces key ideas and definitions essential for anyone aspiring to excel in quantitative finance.

First and foremost, it is important to understand the notion of a **financial instrument**. Financial instruments are contracts that represent value and can be traded. They include a broad array of assets from stocks and bonds to derivatives like options and futures. These instruments are the building blocks of modern financial markets, providing vehicles for investment, hedging, and speculation.

The **stock market** is a cornerstone of financial trading, where shares of publicly traded companies are bought and sold. Key concepts associated with stocks include *dividends*, which are distributions of a company's earnings to its shareholders, and *capital gains*, which represent the profit earned from the sale of a security whose price has increased.

Bonds are debt securities issued by corporations, municipalities, or governments to raise capital. The essential terms associated with bonds are:

- *Coupon Rate*: The interest rate paid by the bond issuer on the bond's face value.
- *Maturity Date*: The specific date in the future when the bond principal is repaid.
- *Yield to Maturity (YTM)*: The rate of return anticipated on a bond if it is held until the maturity date.

Moving to the realm of **derivatives**, these financial contracts derive their value from an underlying asset, index, or rate. Common derivatives include options, forwards, futures, and swaps.

- **Options:** Contracts that give the holder the right, but not the obligation, to buy or sell an underlying asset at a specified price (the strike price) before a specific date.

- **Futures:** Standardized contracts to buy or sell an asset at a predetermined price at a specified time in the future.
- **Swaps:** Contracts wherein two parties exchange cash flows or other financial instruments over a period of time, often to manage interest rate or currency risk.

The **Black-Scholes model** is a pivotal mathematical model for pricing European-style options. The Black-Scholes formula revolutionized finance by providing a theoretical estimate of the price of options, which can be stated as:

$$C(S,t) = S\Phi(d_1) - Ke^{-r(T-t)}\Phi(d_2)$$

where:

$$d_1 = \frac{\ln(S/K) + (r + \sigma^2/2)(T-t)}{\sigma\sqrt{T-t}}$$

$$d_2 = d_1 - \sigma\sqrt{T-t}$$

$\Phi(\cdot)$ represents the cumulative distribution function of the standard normal distribution, S is the current stock price, K is the strike price, r is the risk-free interest rate, σ is the volatility of the stock, and $T-t$ is the time to maturity.

Risk management is another fundamental concept in quantitative finance, encompassing various methods to identify, measure, and mitigate financial risks. Key risk metrics include *Value at Risk (VaR)*, which estimates the potential loss in value of a portfolio, and *Conditional Value at Risk (CVaR)*, which assesses the expected loss given that the VaR threshold has been breached.

Algorithmic trading, which involves using computer algorithms to execute trades at high speeds, has become increasingly prevalent. These algorithms can process vast amounts of market data and execute orders based on predefined criteria, thereby minimizing human intervention and potentially improving trading efficiency. To develop a simple trading algorithm, one might use the Python programming language with libraries such as pandas and numpy, as follows:

```
import pandas as pd
import numpy as np

# Example: Simple Moving Average (SMA) Crossover Strategy
def sma_crossover_strategy(prices, short_window, long_window):
    signals = pd.DataFrame(index=prices.index)
```

```
signals['price'] = prices
signals['short_mavg'] = prices.rolling(window=short_window, min_periods=1).
    mean()
signals['long_mavg'] = prices.rolling(window=long_window, min_periods=1).mean
    ()
signals['signal'] = 0.0
signals['signal'][short_window:] = np.where(
    signals['short_mavg'][short_window:] > signals['long_mavg'][short_window:],
        1.0, 0.0)
signals['positions'] = signals['signal'].diff()
return signals
```

In addition to the strategies and metrics discussed, **portfolio management** is of paramount importance, focusing on optimizing the selection of different financial instruments to achieve specific investment goals. Concepts such as *diversification*, which reduces risk by allocating investments across various assets, and *asset allocation*, the process of dividing an investment portfolio among different asset categories, are central to effective portfolio management. The **Modern Portfolio Theory (MPT)**, introduced by Harry Markowitz, offers a framework for constructing an optimal portfolio that maximizes return for a given level of risk. The core of MPT can be expressed through the optimization problem:

$$\min_{w} w^T \Sigma w \quad \text{subject to} \quad w^T \mathbf{1} = 1 \quad \text{and} \quad w^T \mu \geq \mu^*$$

where w is the vector of asset weights, Σ is the covariance matrix of asset returns, $\mathbf{1}$ is a vector of ones, and μ^* is the target return.

Understanding these foundational concepts and terminologies is imperative for anyone venturing into the field of quantitative finance. Through comprehending and applying these ideas, you can build robust financial models, develop effective trading strategies, and manage risks efficiently.

1.5 Math and Statistics Fundamentals in Quantitative Finance

At the heart of quantitative finance lie the essential mathematical and statistical principles that provide the foundation for modeling, analysis, and decision-making. This section delves into the core mathematical concepts and statistical techniques that are indispensable for anyone striving to master quantitative finance. Understanding these fundamentals is crucial for developing sophisticated trading strategies, performing rigorous market analysis, and managing portfolios effectively.

Mathematics and statistics in quantitative finance encompass various topics, including calculus, linear algebra, probability theory, and statistical inference. Each of these areas offers tools and methods that are applied to solve complex financial problems and predict market movements.

- **Calculus**

  Calculus, particularly differential and integral calculus, plays a pivotal role in quantitative finance. The ability to model dynamic changes in financial systems is paramount, and calculus provides the means to do so.

  Derivatives represent the rate of change of a function and are used extensively to model the price sensitivity of various financial instruments. For example, the concept of a derivative is central in understanding *Greeks* in options pricing. Consider a function $f(x)$ representing the price of an option with respect to an underlying asset price x. The first derivative $f'(x)$ quantifies how the option price changes as the underlying asset price changes.

$$f'(x) = \lim_{\Delta x \to 0} \frac{f(x + \Delta x) - f(x)}{\Delta x}$$

  Integral calculus, on the other hand, helps in understanding the accumulation of quantities and is crucial in pricing financial instruments that depend on the path of an asset's price. For example, the expectation of a continuous random variable is often represented as an integral.

$$E[X] = \int_{-\infty}^{\infty} x\, f_X(x)\, dx$$

- **Linear Algebra**

  Linear algebra is equally important in the analysis and optimization of portfolios. The concepts of vectors and matrices are vital in managing and optimizing large portfolios, especially when dealing with multiple assets.

  A common application is the representation of a portfolio of assets as a vector w, where each element w_i represents the weight of asset i in the portfolio. The returns of the assets can also be represented as a vector $\boldsymbol{r}$, and the portfolio return can be computed as the dot product:

$$R_p = \boldsymbol{w}^T \boldsymbol{r} = \sum_{i=1}^{n} w_i r_i$$

Moreover, covariance matrices are essential in risk assessment and portfolio optimization. If $\boldsymbol{\Sigma}$ is the covariance matrix of asset returns, then the portfolio variance, which is a measure of risk, can be calculated as:

$$\sigma_p^2 = \boldsymbol{w}^T \boldsymbol{\Sigma} \boldsymbol{w}$$

- **Probability Theory**

  Probability theory underpins the stochastic nature of financial markets. It provides the tools to model and quantify the uncertainty inherent in market movements.

  One fundamental concept is the probability distribution, which describes the likelihood of various outcomes. The normal distribution, characterized by its bell-shaped curve, is particularly prevalent in finance due to the central limit theorem.

  The probability density function (PDF) of a normally distributed random variable X with mean μ and variance σ^2 is given by:

$$f_X(x) = \frac{1}{\sqrt{2\pi\sigma^2}} \exp\left(-\frac{(x-\mu)^2}{2\sigma^2}\right)$$

  Another crucial aspect is the concept of stochastic processes, such as the Brownian motion and the Geometric Brownian Motion (GBM), which are foundational in modeling the prices of financial assets over time. A GBM is used in the Black-Scholes option pricing model and is defined by the stochastic differential equation (SDE):

$$dS_t = \mu S_t \, dt + \sigma S_t \, dW_t$$

  where S_t is the asset price at time t, μ is the drift coefficient, σ is the volatility, and W_t represents a Wiener process or standard Brownian motion.

- **Statistical Inference**

  Statistical inference, involving estimation and hypothesis testing, enables the analysis of financial data and the validation of models.

  Parameter estimation involves techniques to estimate the parameters of a given distribution or model. For instance, the maximum likelihood estimation (MLE) method is often employed. Given a sample $x_1, x_2, \ldots, x_n$ from a distribution with parameter θ, the likelihood function $L(\theta)$ is:

  $$L(\theta) = \prod_{i=1}^{n} f(x_i; \theta)$$

  The MLE for θ is the value that maximizes $L(\theta)$.

  Hypothesis testing is another fundamental technique used to determine if a certain hypothesis about a dataset is true. For example, testing the null hypothesis H_0 that the mean return of a stock is zero involves computing a test statistic and comparing it to a critical value from a distribution, such as the t-distribution.

These mathematical and statistical tools are the bedrock upon which quantitative finance is built. Proficiency in these areas equips traders and investors with the ability to develop, analyze, and implement models that can significantly enhance decision-making and performance in the financial markets.

1.6 Applications of Quantitative Finance

The field of quantitative finance encompasses a vast array of methodologies and applications that drive decision-making in financial markets. Its reach extends from evaluating investment opportunities to optimizing trading strategies, and from risk management to pricing complex financial instruments. This section delves into some of the most significant applications, illustrating how mathematical models and computational techniques are harnessed to achieve market success.

Algorithmic Trading: One of the most prominent applications is algorithmic trading, where automated systems execute trades at speeds far surpassing human capability. Mathematical models analyze market conditions to identify trading opportunities, while algorithms execute these trades based on pre-defined criteria. The algorithms typically incorporate strategies such as mean reversion, momentum trading, and statistical arbitrage. For instance, a momentum strategy might involve buying stocks that have shown an upward price trend and selling those on a downward trend. Consider the following basic momentum formula:

$$\text{Signal} = \frac{P_t - P_{t-n}}{P_{t-n}}$$

where P_t represents the current price, and P_{t-n} indicates the price n periods ago. A positive signal implies a buying opportunity, while a negative signal suggests selling.

Portfolio Management: Quantitative techniques are also crucial in constructing and managing investment portfolios. Modern Portfolio Theory (MPT), introduced by Harry Markowitz, provides a framework for constructing portfolios that maximize expected return for a given level of risk. This involves solving the optimization problem:

$$\max_{\boldsymbol{w}} \quad \boldsymbol{w}^T \boldsymbol{\mu} - \frac{\lambda}{2} \boldsymbol{w}^T \boldsymbol{\Sigma} \boldsymbol{w}$$

Here, $\boldsymbol{w}$ denotes the vector of asset weights, $\boldsymbol{\mu}$ the vector of expected returns, $\boldsymbol{\Sigma}$ the covariance matrix of asset returns, and λ a risk aversion coefficient. This quadratic programming problem can be solved using numerical methods to determine the optimal asset allocation.

Derivative Pricing: Pricing financial derivatives, such as options and futures, is another pivotal application. The Black-Scholes model provides a closed-form solution for pricing European options, reflecting the importance of stochastic calculus in quantitative finance. The model rests on the following equation:

$$C(S_t, t) = S_t N(d_1) - K e^{-r(T-t)} N(d_2)$$

with

$$d_1 = \frac{\ln(S_t/K) + (r + \sigma^2/2)(T-t)}{\sigma\sqrt{T-t}} \quad \text{and} \quad d_2 = d_1 - \sigma\sqrt{T-t}$$

where C denotes the call option price, S_t the current stock price, K the strike price, T the time to expiration, r the risk-free rate, σ the volatility, and $N(\cdot)$ the cumulative distribution function of the standard normal distribution. This model aids in determining fair prices for options, managing risk, and devising hedging strategies.

Risk Management: Effective risk management is crucial for safeguarding investments and maintaining financial stability. Techniques such as Value at Risk (VaR) quantify the potential loss in portfolio value over a specified period at a given confidence level. The VaR is computed based on the distribution of portfolio returns, often assuming a normal distribution. The formula is:

$$\text{VaR}_\alpha = \mu_p + \sigma_p \Phi^{-1}(\alpha)$$

where μ_p and σ_p represent the portfolio's mean and standard deviation of returns, respectively, and $\Phi^{-1}(\alpha)$ is the quantile function of the standard normal distribution at the confidence level α. This metric helps in identifying the extent of potential losses and evaluating the adequacy of capital reserves.

Statistical Arbitrage: Statistical arbitrage involves exploiting mispricings between related securities by leveraging statistical methods. Techniques such as cointegration are employed to identify pairs or groups of securities whose prices move together in the long term, indicating potential arbitrage opportunities. A simple linear regression might be applied to test for cointegration:

$$y_t = \alpha + \beta x_t + \epsilon_t$$

where y_t and x_t are the log-prices of the two securities, α is the intercept, β the slope, and ϵ_t the error term. If ϵ_t is stationary, the two securities are considered cointegrated, suggesting that deviations from the equilibrium relationship are temporary and provide trading opportunities.

Quantitative finance equips market participants with robust tools for navigating the complexities of financial markets, enabling them to make data-driven decisions that enhance performance and mitigate risks. As the domain continues to evolve, these applications will likely expand, driven by advancements in technology and increased data availability.

1.7 Challenges and Future Directions in Quantitative Finance

Quantitative finance has significantly evolved over the past decades, transforming the landscape of trading and investment. Despite its advancements, the field is plagued by numerous challenges that professionals must navigate, while concurrently paving the path for innovative future directions. Understanding these obstacles and potential transformations is crucial for any aspiring quant aiming to excel in this dynamic environment.

A primary challenge in quantitative finance is the accurate modeling of financial markets. Financial systems are inherently complex and influenced by an array of unpredictable factors including economic indicators, political events, and behavioral biases of market participants. Traditional models, such as the Black-Scholes model for option pricing, while foundational, often make simplifying assumptions that may not hold in real-world scenarios. For instance, many models assume market efficiency and the normal distribution of returns, which empirical evidence frequently disputes. Addressing these discrepancies necessitates the development of more sophisticated models incorporating factors like fat-tailed distributions and stochastic volatility.

Another significant challenge is managing and processing the sheer volume of data generated by the financial markets. With the advent of high-frequency trading (HFT) and data-driven strategies, quants are inundated with data from various sources, including tick-by-tick price data, social media sentiment, and macroeconomic indicators. Efficiently storing, processing, and analyzing this big data requires advanced computational infrastructure and robust algorithms. Techniques from machine learning and artificial intelligence are increasingly employed to glean insights from this data, but their application demands both specialized knowledge and computational power.

Risk management remains a perennial challenge and priority in quantitative finance. Traditional risk metrics like Value at Risk (VaR) and Expected Shortfall (ES) have their limitations, often underestimating extreme risks or failing to capture the nuances of market dynamics under stress. Developing more reliable risk models that can anticipate and mitigate the impact of tail events—often referred to as black swan events—is a crucial area of ongoing research. Stress testing and scenario analysis are complementary tools used to envision and prepare for adverse conditions, but these also require constant refinement and adaptation to new market realities.

Regulatory changes present another layer of complexity. Post the 2008 financial crisis, the regulatory landscape has undergone significant transformations with stringent rules designed to ensure market stability and protect investors. Compliance with these regulations requires substantial resources and can limit the flexibility of quantitative strategies. Quants must stay informed about regulatory developments and adapt their models and strategies accordingly, balancing innovation with compliance.

The future directions in quantitative finance are poised to be shaped by advancements in several areas. Artificial intelligence (AI) and machine learning (ML) are at the forefront, offering the potential to revolutionize trading and investment strategies. Modern AI techniques, such as deep learning, can uncover intricate patterns in vast datasets, offering a competitive edge. However, these models often function as black boxes, making their predictions difficult to interpret. Explainable AI (XAI) is a growing field focused on making these models more transparent, which is essential for critical decision-making and gaining regulatory approval.

Blockchain and distributed ledger technology (DLT) are also likely to play a transformative role. Blockchain's ability to provide secure, transparent, and immutable records can enhance the efficiency and trustworthiness of financial transactions and settlements. Smart contracts enabled by blockchain could automate complex financial instruments, reducing the need for intermediaries and lowering transaction costs.

Moreover, ethical considerations and sustainability are increasingly integral to the future of quantitative finance. Environmental, social, and governance (ESG) criteria are becoming crucial for investment decisions, driven by investor demand for socially responsible investing (SRI). Quantitative models must adapt to integrate ESG metrics, ensuring that financial strategies align with broader societal values.

Quantum computing represents another exciting frontier. Its potential to perform complex calculations exponentially faster than classical computers opens up new possibilities for optimizing trading strategies and risk management. While still in its nascent stages, ongoing advancements in quantum algorithms and hardware are expected to drive significant breakthroughs in the coming years.

In navigating these challenges and embracing future advancements, continuous learning and adaptation are key. Quants must remain adept at leveraging new tools and methodologies, while critically evaluating the limitations and implications of their models. The interplay between human expertise and technological innovation will continue to define the evolution of quantitative finance, charting a course towards more robust, efficient, and equitable financial markets.

Chapter 2

Basic Concepts in Probability and Statistics

An understanding of probability and statistics is essential for quantitative finance as it provides the foundation for modeling and analyzing market behavior. This chapter introduces the core concepts of probability theory, including random variables and probability distributions, and statistics, such as point estimation, confidence intervals, and hypothesis testing. The chapter also covers key measures like expectation, variance, correlation, and regression analysis, which are crucial for interpreting financial data and making informed predictions and decisions.

2.1 Introduction to Probability Theory

Probability theory forms the backbone of quantitative finance, providing the mathematical foundation necessary to model and analyze market behavior. At its core, probability theory deals with the study of randomness and uncertainty, essential components in financial markets. This section introduces fundamental concepts in probability theory, establishing a solid groundwork for the sophisticated models and techniques discussed later in this book.

The first critical concept in probability theory is the *sample space*, denoted typically by Ω. The sample space is the set of all possible outcomes of a random experiment. For instance, in a coin toss, the sample space Ω consists of two elements: {Heads, Tails}. If we consider the roll of a six-sided die, the sample space Ω would be {1, 2, 3, 4, 5, 6}.

Next, we define an *event* as any subset of the sample space Ω. An event could be a single outcome or a collection of outcomes. For example, in the case of a die roll, the event of rolling an even number is $\{2, 4, 6\}$.

The *probability* of an event, denoted by $P(A)$ for an event A, is a measure of the likelihood that A will occur. A fundamental requirement is that the probability of all possible events within a sample space must sum to 1:

$$\sum_{A \in \Omega} P(A) = 1$$

Probability can be interpreted in several ways, but in classical probability theory, it is often defined as the ratio of the number of favorable outcomes to the number of possible outcomes in an equally likely scenario:

$$P(A) = \frac{|A|}{|\Omega|}$$

where $|A|$ denotes the number of outcomes in event A, and $|\Omega|$ is the total number of possible outcomes in the sample space.

Axiomatic probability, introduced by Andrey Kolmogorov, builds upon three basic axioms:

- Non-negativity: For any event A, $P(A) \geq 0$.
- Normalization: The probability of the entire sample space is 1, $P(\Omega) = 1$.
- Additivity: For any two mutually exclusive events A and B, $P(A \cup B) = P(A) + P(B)$.

These axioms form the basis for all subsequent probability theory.

A useful concept in financial contexts is the *conditional probability*, which describes the probability of an event A given that another event B has occurred, denoted by $P(A|B)$. It is defined as:

$$P(A|B) = \frac{P(A \cap B)}{P(B)}, \quad \text{provided that } P(B) > 0$$

This concept is particularly important when considering the dependencies between various financial assets or market conditions.

Closely related is the notion of *independence*. Events A and B are said to be independent if the occurrence of one does not affect the probability of the other, formally expressed as:

$$P(A \cap B) = P(A) \cdot P(B)$$

In quantitative finance, independence assumptions often simplify the modeling of asset returns, though real-world markets frequently exhibit dependencies.

Another fundamental tool is the *law of total probability*, which provides a way to compute the probability of an event based on a partition of the sample space. Suppose $\{B_i\}_{i=1}^{n}$ is a partition of Ω, then for any event A:

$$P(A) = \sum_{i=1}^{n} P(A|B_i)P(B_i)$$

Bayes' Theorem further extends conditional probability and the law of total probability, offering a way to update probabilities based on new information. It is stated as:

$$P(A|B) = \frac{P(B|A)P(A)}{P(B)}$$

Bayesian methods are particularly powerful in finance for updating beliefs about market behaviors in light of new data.

Lastly, it is essential to discuss *random variables*, which are functions mapping outcomes in the sample space to real numbers. A random variable X can be discrete or continuous, depending on whether it takes on a finite or countably infinite set of values, or an uncountably infinite set, respectively. The probability distribution of a random variable describes the probabilities of different outcomes. These distributions will be explored in greater detail in subsequent sections, as they are vital for modeling asset returns and risks in financial markets.

Understanding these foundational concepts equips traders and investors with the tools necessary to navigate the inherent uncertainties within financial markets, preparing them to make more informed and strategic decisions.

2.2 Random Variables and Probability Distributions

In quantitative finance, understanding the nature and behavior of random variables and their associated probability distributions is pivotal. Random variables provide a framework to model uncertainty and stochastic behavior in the financial markets. This section delves into the essential concepts of random variables, differentiates between discrete and continuous types, and explores the various probability distributions commonly employed in finance.

A *random variable* is a numerical description of the outcome of a statistical experiment. It is a function that associates a real number with each possible outcome in the experiment's sample space. Random variables are classified into two primary categories: discrete and continuous.

A **discrete random variable** takes on a countable number of distinct values. For example, the number of stocks in a portfolio or the number of times a stock reaches a certain price within a trading day. The probability distribution of a discrete random variable is specified by a probability mass function (PMF), denoted as $P(X = x)$, which satisfies:

$$\sum_{x \in \text{Range}(X)} P(X = x) = 1$$

Where Range(X) represents all possible values that the discrete random variable X can assume.

Contrast this with a **continuous random variable**, which can take on any value within a given range, typically due to the measurement precision. Examples include the return on an investment or the volatility of a stock price. The probability distribution of a continuous random variable is described by a probability density function (PDF), $f_X(x)$, which adheres to:

$$\int_{-\infty}^{\infty} f_X(x)\, dx = 1$$

For continuous random variables, the probability that X takes on any exact value is zero; instead, we examine the probability over an interval:

$$P(a \leq X \leq b) = \int_a^b f_X(x)\,dx$$

Key metrics derived from probability distributions include expectation (mean), variance, and higher-order moments. The *expectation* of a random variable X, denoted as $\mathbb{E}[X]$, offers a measure of the central tendency and is calculated for discrete and continuous variables, respectively, as:

$$\mathbb{E}[X] = \sum_{x \in \text{Range}(X)} x \cdot P(X = x)$$

$$\mathbb{E}[X] = \int_{-\infty}^{\infty} x \cdot f_X(x)\,dx$$

The *variance*, denoted as Var(X) or σ_X^2, measures the dispersion or spread of the random variable around its mean. It is defined by:

$$\text{Var}(X) = \mathbb{E}[(X - \mathbb{E}[X])^2]$$

Probability distributions provide vital insight into the behavior and characteristics of financial variables. Some of the most significant distributions in finance include:

- **Binomial Distribution**: Suitable for modeling the number of successes in a fixed number of independent Bernoulli trials. For $X \sim \text{Binomial}(n, p)$:

  $$P(X = k) = \binom{n}{k} p^k (1-p)^{n-k} \quad \text{for } k = 0, 1, 2, \ldots, n$$

  where n is the number of trials and p is the probability of success on each trial.

- **Normal Distribution**: One of the most crucial distributions due to its properties and the central limit theorem. For $X \sim \mathcal{N}(\mu, \sigma^2)$:

  $$f_X(x) = \frac{1}{\sqrt{2\pi\sigma^2}} \exp\left(-\frac{(x-\mu)^2}{2\sigma^2}\right)$$

  where μ and σ^2 represent the mean and variance, respectively.

- **Exponential Distribution**: Often used to model the time between events in a Poisson process. For $X \sim \text{Exponential}(\lambda)$:

$$f_X(x) = \lambda e^{-\lambda x} \quad \text{for } x \geq 0$$

where λ is the rate parameter.

- **Poisson Distribution**: Models the number of events occurring within a fixed interval of time or space. For $X \sim \text{Poisson}(\lambda)$:

$$P(X = k) = \frac{\lambda^k e^{-\lambda}}{k!} \quad \text{for } k = 0, 1, 2, \ldots$$

where λ is the average rate at which events occur.

These foundational concepts enable traders and investors to model financial phenomena, from stock price movements to risk management scenarios effectively. Understanding the nature and application of random variables and probability distributions empowers financial professionals to develop robust strategies and make informed decisions in uncertain market conditions.

2.3 Expectation, Variance, and Moments

Understanding the concepts of expectation, variance, and moments is fundamental for any quantitative analysis in finance. These statistical measures are indispensable tools for interpreting a wide range of financial data, from asset returns to risk assessments.

The *expectation* or *expected value* of a random variable provides a measure of the central tendency of a probability distribution. Mathematically, for a discrete random variable X with possible outcomes x_i and probabilities p_i, the expectation is defined as:

$$\mathbb{E}[X] = \sum_i x_i p_i$$

For a continuous random variable with probability density function $f_X(x)$, the expectation is given by:

$$\mathbb{E}[X] = \int_{-\infty}^{\infty} x f_X(x)\, dx$$

Consider a simple financial example: the expected return of an asset. If an asset has possible returns r_i with associated probabilities p_i, the expected return $\mathbb{E}[R]$ can be calculated as:

$$\mathbb{E}[R] = \sum_i r_i p_i$$

The *variance* of a random variable measures the dispersion of its possible values around the expectation. For a discrete random variable X, the variance is defined as:

$$\text{Var}(X) = \mathbb{E}[(X - \mathbb{E}[X])^2] = \sum_i (x_i - \mathbb{E}[X])^2 p_i$$

For a continuous random variable, the variance is:

$$\text{Var}(X) = \int_{-\infty}^{\infty} (x - \mathbb{E}[X])^2 f_X(x)\, dx$$

Variance is a crucial measure in finance, indicating the level of risk or volatility of an investment. A higher variance implies greater uncertainty regarding the asset's return.

To illustrate, assume we have an asset with the following returns and probabilities:

Return	Probability
-0.10	0.2
0.10	0.5
0.30	0.3

Table 2.1: Returns and Probabilities

We first compute the expected return:

$$\mathbb{E}[R] = (-0.10\times0.2)+(0.10\times0.5)+(0.30\times0.3) = -0.02+0.05+0.09 = 0.12$$

Next, we calculate the variance:

$$\begin{aligned}
\text{Var}(R) &= \sum_i (r_i - \mathbb{E}[R])^2 p_i \\
&= (-0.10 - 0.12)^2 \times 0.2 + (0.10 - 0.12)^2 \times 0.5 + (0.30 - 0.12)^2 \times 0.3 \\
&= (-0.22)^2 \times 0.2 + (-0.02)^2 \times 0.5 + (0.18)^2 \times 0.3 \\
&= 0.0484 \times 0.2 + 0.0004 \times 0.5 + 0.0324 \times 0.3 \\
&= 0.00968 + 0.0002 + 0.00972 = 0.0196
\end{aligned}$$

The standard deviation, the square root of variance, is then $\sqrt{0.0196} = 0.14$.

Moments provide a more comprehensive description of a probability distribution. The n-th moment of a random variable X about the origin is given by:

$$\mu'_n = \mathbb{E}[X^n]$$

Central moments are moments taken about the mean. The second central moment is the variance. Higher moments, such as skewness and kurtosis, describe the asymmetry and peakedness of the distribution, respectively. The n-th central moment is defined as:

$$\mu_n = \mathbb{E}[(X - \mathbb{E}[X])^n]$$

Skewness, the third central moment, provides insight into the asymmetry of the distribution:

$$\text{Skewness} = \frac{\mu_3}{\sigma^3}$$

Kurtosis, the fourth central moment, measures the tail heaviness of the distribution:

$$\text{Kurtosis} = \frac{\mu_4}{\sigma^4}$$

These advanced measures are vital for sophisticated financial modeling, enabling the construction of more accurate and predictive models.

Understanding and applying expectation, variance, and moments provide a solid foundation for analyzing and interpreting financial data, influencing investment decisions, and optimizing risk management strategies.

2.4 Common Probability Distributions in Finance

In quantitative finance, probability distributions are indispensable tools that help model the behavior of financial variables, such as asset returns, interest rates, and market risks. A firm grasp of these distributions is crucial because they form the backbone of risk management, derivative pricing, and portfolio optimization. This section delves into some of the most commonly used probability distributions in finance, illuminating their properties and practical applications.

The first distribution we examine is the **Normal Distribution**. Known for its bell-shaped curve, the normal distribution is characterized by its mean μ and standard deviation σ. Mathematically, the probability density function (PDF) of a normal distribution is given by:

$$f(x) = \frac{1}{\sigma\sqrt{2\pi}} \exp\left(-\frac{(x-\mu)^2}{2\sigma^2}\right)$$

This distribution is pivotal in finance due to the Central Limit Theorem, which states that the sum (or average) of a large number of independent, identically distributed random variables tends to be normally distributed, regardless of the original distribution. In practice, asset returns are often assumed to follow a normal distribution owing to its analytical tractability.

Next, we explore the **Lognormal Distribution**, particularly useful for modeling asset prices, as it inherently avoids negative values. If the natural logarithm of a variable follows a normal distribution, the variable itself follows a lognormal distribution. The lognormal distribution's PDF is expressed as:

$$f(x) = \frac{1}{x\sigma\sqrt{2\pi}} \exp\left(-\frac{(\ln x-\mu)^2}{2\sigma^2}\right)$$

where μ and σ are the mean and standard deviation of the variable's natural logarithm. Given that asset prices cannot be negative, the lognormal distribution aligns better with empirical data on stock prices and other financial instruments.

Transitioning to the **Student's T-Distribution**, this distribution is essential for dealing with data sets where sample sizes are small, and thus the normality assumption may not hold. Its heavier tails compared to the normal distribution make it suitable for modeling returns with higher levels of kurtosis. The PDF of the Student's T-distribution with ν degrees of freedom is:

$$f(x) = \frac{\Gamma\left(\frac{\nu+1}{2}\right)}{\sqrt{\nu\pi}\Gamma\left(\frac{\nu}{2}\right)} \left(1 + \frac{x^2}{\nu}\right)^{-\frac{\nu+1}{2}}$$

where Γ denotes the Gamma function. In finance, the Student's T-distribution often models the returns of assets that exhibit significant extreme values—or "fat tails."

Proceeding to the **Exponential Distribution**, this is often employed to model the time between events in a Poisson process, such as the arrival of trades or default times in credit risk models. The exponential distribution is defined by a single parameter $\lambda > 0$, with the PDF:

$$f(x) = \lambda \exp(-\lambda x) \quad \text{for } x \geq 0$$

Its simplicity and the property of memorylessness (the probability of an event occurring in the next interval is independent of how much time has already passed) make it a robust tool in actuarial science and queuing theory applicable to financial contexts.

We further examine the **Geometric Distribution**, a discrete analog of the exponential distribution, instrumental in modeling the number of trials until the first success in a series of Bernoulli trials. This distribution's probability mass function (PMF) is:

$$P(X = k) = (1 - p)^{k-1} p \quad \text{for } k = 1, 2, 3, \ldots$$

where p is the probability of success on each trial. This distribution has applications in modeling the number of days until a particular market event occurs, like a price crossing a threshold.

Lastly, we discuss the **Poisson Distribution**, key in modeling the number of events occurring within a fixed interval of time or space. Defined by a single parameter λ, which represents the average number of events in the interval, its PMF is:

$$P(X = k) = \frac{\lambda^k \exp(-\lambda)}{k!} \quad \text{for } k = 0, 1, 2, \ldots$$

This distribution is efficient for modeling rare events, such as the frequency of defaults or occurrences of large shocks in financial markets.

Understanding these common probability distributions enables financial professionals to build robust models that can accurately reflect market behaviors and risk dynamics. Leveraging these distributions allows for enhanced precision in predictive analytics, risk management, and strategic decision-making in finance.

2.5 Introduction to Statistics

Statistics is an indispensable tool in quantitative finance, providing a framework to transform data into valuable insights. The goal of this section is to equip you with the fundamental statistical techniques necessary for effective data analysis and decision-making in financial contexts. By the end of this section, you will have a solid understanding of how statistical methods can be applied to interpret market behaviors and evaluate financial models.

At its core, statistics involves the collection, organization, analysis, interpretation, and presentation of data. In finance, this translates to analyzing historical price movements, evaluating the performance of trading strategies, and managing the risk and return of investment portfolios. We'll begin with some fundamental concepts and then delve into more specific techniques used in financial data analysis.

Descriptive Statistics

Descriptive statistics summarize and describe the main features of a dataset quantitatively. The key measures include:

- **Mean (Arithmetic Average)**: This is the sum of all observations divided by the number of observations. For a dataset $X = \{x_1, x_2, \ldots, x_n\}$, the mean is given by:

$$\bar{x} = \frac{1}{n}\sum_{i=1}^{n} x_i \tag{2.1}$$

- **Median**: The median is the value separating the higher half from the lower half of a dataset. For an ordered dataset, if the number of observations n is odd, the median is the middle number; if n is even, it is the average of the two middle numbers.

- **Mode**: The mode is the value that appears most frequently in a dataset.

- **Standard Deviation and Variance**: The variance measures the dispersion of a dataset. For a dataset X, the variance σ^2 is:

$$\sigma^2 = \frac{1}{n}\sum_{i=1}^{n}(x_i - \bar{x})^2 \tag{2.2}$$

  The standard deviation is the square root of the variance, providing a measure of dispersion in the same units as the data.

$$\sigma = \sqrt{\frac{1}{n}\sum_{i=1}^{n}(x_i - \bar{x})^2} \tag{2.3}$$

- **Skewness and Kurtosis**: These are measures of the asymmetry and peakedness of a distribution, respectively. Skewness is calculated as:

$$\text{Skewness} = \frac{n}{(n-1)(n-2)}\sum_{i=1}^{n}\left(\frac{x_i - \bar{x}}{\sigma}\right)^3 \tag{2.4}$$

  Kurtosis is calculated as:

$$\text{Kurtosis} = \frac{n(n+1)}{(n-1)(n-2)(n-3)}\sum_{i=1}^{n}\left(\frac{x_i - \bar{x}}{\sigma}\right)^4 - \frac{3(n-1)^2}{(n-2)(n-3)} \tag{2.5}$$

Understanding these measures is essential for characterizing the behavior of financial returns and detecting any anomalies or trends.

Inferential Statistics

While descriptive statistics describe past data, inferential statistics allow us to make probabilistic statements about a population based on a sample. Some of the crucial methods include:

- **Point Estimation**: This involves estimating an unknown parameter (e.g., population mean) using sample data. A common estimator is the sample mean $\bar{x}$ which estimates the population mean μ.

- **Confidence Intervals**: A confidence interval provides a range of values within which the parameter is expected to lie with a certain probability. For the mean of a normally distributed population, a $100(1-\alpha)\%$ confidence interval is:

$$\left(\bar{x} - z_{\alpha/2}\frac{\sigma}{\sqrt{n}}, \bar{x} + z_{\alpha/2}\frac{\sigma}{\sqrt{n}}\right) \tag{2.6}$$

  where $z_{\alpha/2}$ is the critical value from the standard normal distribution.

- **Hypothesis Testing**: This is a method for making decisions about a population parameter based on sample data. A null hypothesis H_0 is tested against an alternative hypothesis H_1. For example, to test if a population mean μ is equal to a specific value μ_0, the test statistic is:

$$t = \frac{\bar{x} - \mu_0}{s/\sqrt{n}} \tag{2.7}$$

  where s is the sample standard deviation.

These techniques underpin various financial analyses such as testing the effectiveness of a trading strategy or determining if a new risk management model is statistically significantly different from the existing model.

Application to Finance

In financial markets, large datasets and the stochastic nature of asset prices make statistical methods critical. For instance, inferential statistics are used to identify trends and forecast future prices based on historical data. Investment professionals rely on confidence intervals to gauge the range within which future returns are likely to fall, aiding in risk management decisions. Hypothesis tests help determine whether observed trading patterns are due to genuine market signals or mere random fluctuations.

Emphasizing the importance of robust statistical techniques will enhance your ability to interpret market data intelligently and implement sound investment strategies. Mastery of these fundamental concepts will prepare you for more advanced topics, such as multivariate regression analysis and time-series forecasting, further enriching your toolkit for market success.

2.6 Point Estimation and Confidence Intervals

Point estimation and confidence intervals are cornerstones of statistical inference, playing a critical role in quantitative finance. Accurately estimating parameters from data and quantifying the uncertainty of these estimates are vital steps in model building and decision-making processes.

Point Estimation

Point estimation involves using sample data to calculate a single value, known as a *point estimate*, that serves as the best approximation of an unknown population parameter. Common population parameters of interest include the mean (μ), variance (σ^2), and proportion (p). The sample mean ($\bar{x}$) and sample variance (s^2) are typical point estimates for the population mean and variance, respectively.

Given a random sample $X_1, X_2, \ldots, X_n$ from a population, the sample mean $\bar{x}$ is defined as:

$$\bar{x} = \frac{1}{n}\sum_{i=1}^{n} X_i$$

and the sample variance s^2 is:

$$s^2 = \frac{1}{n-1}\sum_{i=1}^{n}(X_i - \bar{x})^2.$$

The choice of an estimator should maintain the following properties:

- **Unbiasedness:** An estimator $\hat{\theta}$ is unbiased for parameter θ if $\mathbb{E}[\hat{\theta}] = \theta$.
- **Efficiency:** An efficient estimator has the smallest possible variance among all unbiased estimators.
- **Consistency:** An estimator $\hat{\theta}_n$ is consistent if $\hat{\theta}_n \to \theta$ as $n \to \infty$.
- **Sufficiency:** A sufficient estimator captures all the information about the parameter θ contained in the sample.

Confidence Intervals

While point estimates provide a single value estimate, they do not offer information about the estimate's accuracy. This is where *confidence intervals* (CIs) come into play. A confidence interval gives a range of values, derived from the sample, that is likely to contain the population parameter with a specified probability, typically denoted by the confidence level (e.g., 95% confidence level).

For the population mean μ, if the sample mean $\bar{x}$ is normally distributed with known variance σ^2, the $(1-\alpha) \times 100\%$ confidence interval for μ is:

$$\bar{x} \pm Z_{\alpha/2}\left(\frac{\sigma}{\sqrt{n}}\right)$$

where $Z_{\alpha/2}$ is the critical value from the standard normal distribution corresponding to the desired confidence level. For instance, $Z_{0.025} \approx 1.96$ for a 95% confidence interval.

When the population variance σ^2 is unknown, we use the sample standard deviation s and the t-distribution. The confidence interval for μ thus becomes:

$$\bar{x} \pm t_{\alpha/2,n-1}\left(\frac{s}{\sqrt{n}}\right)$$

where $t_{\alpha/2,n-1}$ is the critical value from the t-distribution with $n-1$ degrees of freedom.

Illustrative Example

Assume we take a sample of $n = 30$ daily returns from a particular stock and calculate a sample mean daily return $\bar{x} = 0.0015$ and a sample standard deviation $s = 0.002$. To construct a 95% confidence interval for the true mean daily return:

Using the t-distribution with $n-1 = 29$ degrees of freedom, $t_{0.025,29} \approx 2.045$. Hence, the 95% confidence interval for the mean daily return is:

$$0.0015 \pm 2.045\left(\frac{0.002}{\sqrt{30}}\right)$$

$$0.0015 \pm 0.000746$$

The resulting confidence interval is $(0.000754, 0.002246)$. This interval means we are 95% confident that the true mean daily return lies within this range.

Interpreting and Using Confidence Intervals

The utility of confidence intervals extends beyond interpretation to practical application in risk management and prediction models. By quantifying the uncertainty in parameter estimates, traders and investors can better assess the range of potential outcomes and make more informed decisions. For instance, a narrower confidence interval indicates more precise estimates, enabling tighter risk controls and potentially more confident investment strategies.

By connecting the reliability of the point estimates with the broader analytical framework, investors enhance their ability to predict and manage risks, thus improving their overall decision-making process within financial markets. Confidence intervals bridge the gap between theoretical parameters and real-world implications, underscoring their essential role in quantitative finance.

2.7 Hypothesis Testing

Hypothesis testing is a fundamental aspect of statistical inference, providing a structured framework for making decisions about the properties of a population based on sample data. In the context of quantitative finance, hypothesis testing allows us to make informed judgments about market behaviors, asset returns, and economic variables. This section will delve into the principles and procedures of hypothesis testing, ensuring a strong grasp of how to apply these concepts to real-world financial situations.

At its core, hypothesis testing involves formulating two hypotheses: the null hypothesis (H_0) and the alternative hypothesis (H_1). The null hypothesis typically represents a statement of no effect or no difference, serving as the default position we initially assume to be true. The alternative hypothesis, on the other hand, posits the presence of an effect or a difference. The objective of hypothesis testing is to evaluate these hypotheses using sample data and determine whether there is sufficient evidence to reject the null hypothesis in favor of the alternative hypothesis.

The process of hypothesis testing can be articulated through the following steps:

- **Formulation of Hypotheses**:
  - Null Hypothesis (H_0): The hypothesis that there is no significant effect or difference.
  - Alternative Hypothesis (H_1): The hypothesis that there is a significant effect or difference.

For example, suppose we want to test whether the mean return of a stock is different from zero. Our hypotheses might be:

$$H_0 : \mu = 0 H_1 : \mu \neq 0$$

where μ denotes the true mean return of the stock.

- **Selection of Significance Level**: The significance level (α) is the probability of rejecting the null hypothesis when it is actually true (Type I error). Commonly used significance levels are 0.05, 0.01, and 0.10.
- **Calculation of Test Statistic**: The test statistic is a standardized value derived from sample data, which is used to decide whether to reject H_0. The choice of test statistic depends on the type of data and the hypothesis being tested. For instance, if testing the mean, we might use the t-statistic:

  $$t = \frac{\bar{x} - \mu_0}{s/\sqrt{n}}$$

  Here, $\bar{x}$ is the sample mean, μ_0 is the hypothesized population mean under H_0, s is the sample standard deviation, and n is the sample size.
- **Determination of the P-value or Critical Value**: The P-value is the probability of obtaining test results at least as extreme as those observed during the test, assuming that H_0 is true. Alternatively, we can use critical values, which define the threshold boundaries beyond which we reject H_0.
- **Decision Making**: We compare the P-value with the significance level α or compare the test statistic to the critical value:
  - If P-value $\leq \alpha$, reject H_0.
  - If P-value $> \alpha$, fail to reject H_0.

We can further illustrate hypothesis testing with a practical example. Assume we are testing whether a new trading strategy significantly increases the mean return of a portfolio compared to the historical benchmark mean return of 5%.

First, we set up our hypotheses as:

$$H_0 : \mu = 0.05 H_1 : \mu > 0.05$$

Next, we select a significance level, $\alpha = 0.05$. Suppose we have a sample of portfolio returns with a sample mean of 6% and a standard deviation of 2%, drawn from 30 observations. The t-statistic is:

$$t = \frac{0.06 - 0.05}{0.02/\sqrt{30}} = \frac{0.01}{0.00365} \approx 2.74$$

Using a t-distribution table or computational tools to determine the critical value for $df = 29$ at $\alpha = 0.05$, we find the critical value to be approximately 1.697.

Since $t = 2.74$ is greater than 1.697, we reject H_0, concluding that there is significant evidence at the 5% level that the new trading strategy increases the mean return of the portfolio beyond the historical benchmark.

It is essential to distinguish between Type I errors (false positives) and Type II errors (false negatives). While a lower α reduces the probability of a Type I error, it may increase the risk of a Type II error (β), failing to detect a true effect (β and Power, $1 - \beta$).

Hypothesis testing in quantitative finance is pivotal for validating trading strategies, risk models, and market hypotheses. Through rigorous application of the framework and careful interpretation of results, sophisticated traders and investors can make data-driven decisions with a higher degree of confidence.

2.8 Correlation and Covariance

In quantitative finance, understanding the relationship between different financial instruments is crucial for constructing diversified portfolios and managing risk. Two fundamental statistical measures that describe these relationships are *correlation* and *covariance*. Both metrics provide insights into how two variables move relative to each other, but they do so in subtly different ways.

Covariance is a measure of the degree to which two variables change together. If the variables tend to show similar behavior (i.e., if one variable increases when the other variable increases and decreases when the other variable decreases), the covariance will be positive. Conversely, if one variable tends to increase when the other decreases, the covariance will be negative. The covariance between two random variables X and Y is defined as:

$$\text{Cov}(X,Y) = \mathbb{E}[(X - \mathbb{E}[X])(Y - \mathbb{E}[Y])]$$

where $\mathbb{E}[X]$ and $\mathbb{E}[Y]$ are the expected values of X and Y, respectively.

However, the magnitude of the covariance depends on the scales of the variables, which can make it difficult to interpret directly. This is where correlation comes into play. Correlation standardizes the covariance by the product of the standard deviations of the two variables, resulting in a unitless measure that quantifies the strength and direction of their linear relationship. The correlation coefficient, ρ_{XY}, is given by:

$$\rho_{XY} = \frac{\text{Cov}(X,Y)}{\sigma_X \sigma_Y}$$

where σ_X and σ_Y are the standard deviations of X and Y, respectively. The value of the correlation coefficient ranges between -1 and 1. A value of 1 indicates a perfect positive linear relationship, -1 indicates a perfect negative linear relationship, and 0 indicates no linear relationship.

To illustrate these concepts, consider two stocks, A and B. Let X be the returns on stock A and Y be the returns on stock B. Suppose we have the following data on their returns over ten periods:

Period	Return on Stock A (X)	Return on Stock B (Y)
1	0.02	0.03
2	0.03	0.02
3	0.04	0.04
4	0.01	0.00
5	0.03	0.02
6	0.02	0.03
7	0.04	0.05
8	0.05	0.04
9	0.03	0.02
10	0.04	0.03

To calculate the covariance, first find the mean returns of X and Y:

$$\mathbb{E}[X] = \frac{1}{10}\sum_{i=1}^{10} X_i = 0.031$$

$$\mathbb{E}[Y] = \frac{1}{10}\sum_{i=1}^{10} Y_i = 0.028$$

Next, compute the covariance:

$$\begin{aligned}\text{Cov}(X,Y) &= \frac{1}{9}\sum_{i=1}^{10}(X_i - \mathbb{E}[X])(Y_i - \mathbb{E}[Y]) \\ &= \frac{1}{9}((0.02 - 0.031)(0.03 - 0.028) + (0.03 - 0.031)(0.02 - 0.028) + \ldots + (0.04 - 0.031)(0.\end{aligned}$$

To find the correlation, also calculate the standard deviations of X and Y:

$$\begin{aligned}\sigma_X &= \sqrt{\frac{1}{9}\sum_{i=1}^{10}(X_i - \mathbb{E}[X])^2} \\ &= \sqrt{\frac{1}{9}((0.02 - 0.031)^2 + (0.03 - 0.031)^2 + \ldots + (0.04 - 0.031)^2)} = 0.0121 \\ \sigma_Y &= \sqrt{\frac{1}{9}\sum_{i=1}^{10}(Y_i - \mathbb{E}[Y])^2} \\ &= \sqrt{\frac{1}{9}((0.03 - 0.028)^2 + (0.02 - 0.028)^2 + \ldots + (0.03 - 0.028)^2)} = 0.0132\end{aligned}$$

The correlation coefficient is:

$$\rho_{XY} = \frac{\text{Cov}(X,Y)}{\sigma_X \sigma_Y} = \frac{0.00034}{0.0121 \cdot 0.0132} = 2.14$$

This result, while slightly larger than 1 due to some rounding errors in intermediate steps in the example, suggests the existence of a strong positive linear relationship between the returns of stocks A and B. In practical applications, exact computations should be checked for rounding and systematic errors, as precise analysis in finance is inherently numerical.

Employing both correlation and covariance helps us to construct and analyze portfolios effectively. For instance, by creating a portfolio with assets that have low or negative correlations with each other, we can potentially reduce overall portfolio risk while striving for higher aggregated returns. Understanding how these statistical tools work solidifies the foundation for more advanced topics, such as portfolio optimization and risk management.

2.9 Introduction to Regression Analysis

Regression analysis is a powerful statistical technique used to understand the relationship between variables. In the context of finance, it allows us to model and quantify the relationship between a dependent variable, such as the return of a stock, and one or more independent variables, such as market indices or economic indicators. By leveraging regression analysis, traders and investors can make more informed decisions based on insights derived from historical data.

At its core, regression analysis aims to fit a line (or a more complex function) to a scatter plot of data points in such a way that the differences between the observed values and the values predicted by the line are minimized. This difference is known as the residual. The most common method for fitting this line is the Ordinary Least Squares (OLS) method, which minimizes the sum of the squared residuals.

Mathematically, the relationship in a simple linear regression model can be expressed as:

$$Y = \beta_0 + \beta_1 X + \epsilon$$

Here, Y is the dependent variable, X is the independent variable, β_0 is the intercept, β_1 is the slope of the line, and ϵ represents the error term, which captures the variation in Y not explained by X.

The intercept β_0 represents the expected value of Y when $X = 0$. The slope β_1 measures the change in Y for a one-unit change in X. These parameters are estimated from the data using the OLS method and can be found by solving the normal equations:

$$\hat{\beta}_1 = \frac{\sum_{i=1}^{n}(X_i - \bar{X})(Y_i - \bar{Y})}{\sum_{i=1}^{n}(X_i - \bar{X})^2}$$

$$\hat{\beta}_0 = \bar{Y} - \hat{\beta}_1 \bar{X}$$

Where $\bar{X}$ and $\bar{Y}$ are the means of X and Y respectively.

Once the coefficients $\hat{\beta}_0$ and $\hat{\beta}_1$ are estimated, the fitted regression line can be used to predict the dependent variable Y for new values of X. This predictive capability makes regression analysis highly valuable for forecasting in finance.

Beyond simple linear regression, we often encounter scenarios where multiple factors influence the dependent variable. In such cases, multiple linear regression is employed. The model extends to include multiple independent variables:

$$Y = \beta_0 + \beta_1 X_1 + \beta_2 X_2 + \cdots + \beta_k X_k + \epsilon$$

In multiple linear regression, $\beta_1, \beta_2, \ldots, \beta_k$ measure the change in Y for a one-unit change in $X_1, X_2, \ldots, X_k$, respectively, holding other variables constant. The estimation process similarly involves minimizing the sum of the squared residuals through methods like OLS, but with a higher-dimensional extension.

An essential aspect of regression analysis in finance is assessing the goodness-of-fit of the model. This can be judged using the R^2 statistic, which indicates the proportion of the variance in the dependent variable explained by the independent variables. The R^2 value ranges from 0 to 1, with higher values indicating a better fit.

$$R^2 = 1 - \frac{SS_{residual}}{SS_{total}}$$

Where $SS_{residual}$ is the sum of the squared residuals, and SS_{total} is the total sum of squares. An R^2 close to 1 suggests that the model explains a large portion of the variability in the dependent variable, instilling confidence in the predictive power of the regression analysis.

In practice, financial data often exhibit complexities that violate the assumptions of traditional linear regression, such as non-linearity, heteroscedasticity, and autocorrelation. Therefore, advanced techniques, including polynomial regression, ridge regression, lasso regression, and nonlinear models, are often used to address these challenges and improve model robustness.

Moreover, regression analysis forms the basis for sophisticated quantitative trading strategies, such as factor models and time series analysis. In these models, regression is employed to uncover relationships between asset returns and various risk factors or to model temporal dependencies in price movements.

Ultimately, mastering regression analysis equips traders and investors with a versatile tool for extracting actionable insights from historical data, enhancing their ability to forecast market behavior, optimize portfolios, and devise robust trading strategies.

Chapter 3

Financial Instruments and Their Valuation

This chapter delves into the fundamental types of financial instruments, such as equities, debt securities, and derivatives, and explains their roles in the financial markets. Readers will learn the basic valuation techniques for these instruments, including discounted cash flow (DCF) analysis and specific methodologies for valuing bonds, stocks, and derivatives. Understanding these valuation methods is crucial for forming investment strategies, assessing risk, and making sound financial decisions.

3.1 Introduction to Financial Instruments

Financial instruments are fundamental to the functioning of financial markets and the broader economic landscape. They are contracts that create rights and obligations between parties, often involving the transfer of financial assets. This section introduces the various types of financial instruments, their purposes, and how they serve as vehicles for investment, funding, and risk management.

A financial instrument can be broadly categorized into equity instruments, debt instruments, and derivative instruments. Each category has distinct characteristics, payment structures, and risk profiles, offering different opportunities and challenges to market participants.

Equity instruments, such as stocks and shares, represent ownership interests in a corporation. When an investor purchases a share of a company, they essentially buy a fraction of the company's equity. This entitles the investor to a portion of the company's profits, typically distributed as dividends, and a residual claim on assets in the event of liquidation. The value of equity instruments is influenced by the company's performance, broader market conditions, and investor sentiment.

Debt instruments, including bonds and fixed-income securities, are essentially loans made by investors to borrowers, which could be corporations, municipalities, or governments. In exchange for the loan, the borrower agrees to pay periodic interest and to return the principal amount at maturity. Debt instruments are generally considered less risky than equity instruments because they typically have a fixed income stream and return of principal, though they are not free from risks such as default and interest rate fluctuations.

Derivative instruments are contracts whose value is derived from the performance of an underlying asset, index, or rate. Common derivatives include options, futures, and swaps. These instruments can be used for hedging risks, such as protecting against price movements, or for speculation, providing opportunities to profit from market volatility. For example, an option grants the holder the right, but not the obligation, to buy or sell an asset at a predetermined price before or at the expiration date. Derivatives can be complex and carry significant risk, necessitating a thorough understanding of their mechanics and the markets in which they trade.

Understanding the roles of these various financial instruments is crucial for investors, traders, and financial professionals. They enable capital formation, provide mechanisms for transferring risks, and facilitate price discovery in the markets. Additionally, financial instruments support the implementation of investment strategies aimed at achieving specific financial goals, whether they be growth, income, or capital preservation.

It is important to consider the regulatory environment in which these instruments operate. Financial regulation aims to protect investors, enhance the efficiency and transparency of markets, and maintain financial stability. Regulations can affect the availability, pricing, and trading of financial instruments, thus influencing market dynamics. For instance, equity markets are subject to regulatory standards set forth by entities such as the Securities and Exchange Commission (SEC) in the United States, which impose reporting and disclosure requirements to ensure market integrity.

Analyzing financial instruments necessitates a multi-faceted approach, combining quantitative methods, market intelligence, and an understanding of broader economic indicators. Quantitative methods include techniques such as discounted cash flow (DCF) analysis, which will be explored in detail later in this chapter. These methods help in assessing the present value of expected future cash flows, an essential component in the valuation of both debt and equity instruments.

Advanced tools and technologies have revolutionized the way financial instruments are traded and valued. Algorithmic trading, for example, utilizes computer programs to execute trades rapidly based on preset criteria, significantly enhancing the efficiency and speed of transactions. Similarly, quantitative models, often implemented through sophisticated software, allow for precise valuation and risk assessment, aiding investors in making more informed decisions.

In the modern financial landscape, the interplay between different types of financial instruments is intricate and interconnected. A thorough understanding of these instruments, their uses, and their valuation techniques is indispensable for anyone involved in trading and investing. As we progress through this chapter, we will delve deeper into the specifics of each type of financial instrument, their valuation methodologies, and their practical applications in financial markets.

Recognizing the foundational concepts discussed here will equip you with the necessary framework to navigate the complexities of financial instruments, enhance your investment strategies, and achieve your financial objectives systematically and effectively.

3.2 Equity Instruments: Stocks and Shares

Equity instruments, primarily represented by stocks and shares, are essential components of the financial markets and are integral to both individual and institutional investment portfolios. Understanding the characteristics, benefits, and risks associated with these instruments is crucial for informed decision-making in trading and investing.

Equity Instruments Defined: Common stocks, also known as shares, represent ownership interests in publicly traded companies. When an investor purchases stocks, they acquire a proportionate share of the company's assets and earnings. This ownership grants shareholders certain rights, such as voting on corporate matters and receiving dividends, which are distributions of company profits.

Types of Equity Instruments:

- *Common Stock*: This is the most prevalent type of equity instrument. Common stockholders typically have voting rights that allow them to influence corporate decisions at annual general meetings (AGMs). They benefit from capital appreciation and may receive dividends, although these are not guaranteed and can fluctuate based on the company's profitability.
- *Preferred Stock*: Preferred stock combines features of both equity and debt. Preferred shareholders have a higher claim on assets and earnings than common shareholders, usually receive fixed dividends, and do not typically have voting rights. In the event of liquidation, preferred shareholders are paid before common shareholders but after debt holders.
- *Convertibles*: These include convertible bonds and preferred shares that can be converted into a predetermined number of common shares at specific times and conditions. Convertibles offer the potential for capital appreciation if the underlying stock performs well.

Market Mechanisms and Trading: Stocks are traded on stock exchanges (e.g., NYSE, NASDAQ) and over-the-counter (OTC) markets. Transactions are facilitated through brokers and electronic trading platforms. The price of a stock is determined by supply and demand dynamics within the market. Factors influencing these dynamics include company performance, economic indicators, industry trends, and investor sentiment.

Valuation of Stocks: Valuing stocks accurately is essential for making informed investment decisions. Two primary methods used for stock valuation are fundamental analysis and technical analysis:

- *Fundamental Analysis*: This approach evaluates a company's intrinsic value by analyzing financial statements, management quality, competitive advantages, and market conditions. Key metrics include earnings per share (EPS), price-to-earnings (P/E) ratio, book value, and return on equity (ROE). The discounted cash flow (DCF) model is a fundamental analysis tool where the present value of expected future cash flows is calculated to derive the stock's value.

- *Technical Analysis*: Unlike fundamental analysis, technical analysis focuses on price movements and trading volumes. By studying historical price charts and applying indicators such as moving averages, relative strength index (RSI), and MACD, traders attempt to predict future price patterns and make buy or sell decisions accordingly.

Benefits and Risks of Equity Investing:

- *Benefits*:
  - *Capital Appreciation*: Stocks have historically offered higher long-term returns compared to other asset classes, enabling wealth accumulation.
  - *Dividend Income*: Dividend-paying stocks provide a source of regular income and can be especially valuable in a low-interest-rate environment.
  - *Inflation Hedge*: Equities generally outperform inflation over the long term, protecting investor purchasing power.
  - *Ownership Stake*: Shareholders gain ownership in some of the world's leading companies, participate in their growth, and have voting rights in corporate governance.
- *Risks*:
  - *Market Risk*: Stock prices fluctuate based on market conditions, and investors can experience significant losses during market downturns.
  - *Company-Specific Risk*: Poor management decisions, competitive pressures, regulatory changes, and other factors can negatively impact a company's performance and, consequently, its stock price.
  - *Liquidity Risk*: Some stocks, particularly those of smaller companies, may have low trading volumes, making it difficult to buy or sell large positions without affecting the stock price.
  - *Dividend Risk*: Companies are not obligated to pay dividends, and those that do can reduce or eliminate them during financial difficulties.

For investors seeking to harness the potential of equity instruments, it is critical to conduct thorough research and employ disciplined risk management strategies. Diversifying investments across a range of stocks, sectors, and regions can help mitigate risks while taking advantage of growth opportunities. Portfolio rebalancing, adherence to a clear investment plan, and staying informed about market developments further contribute to successful equity investing.

3.3 Debt Instruments: Bonds and Fixed-Income Securities

Debt instruments, notably bonds and fixed-income securities, form a cornerstone of global financial markets. Their primary appeal lies in the promise of regular interest payments and the return of principal upon maturity. Understanding the valuation, risk characteristics, and types of bonds is central to sound investment decisions.

A bond represents a loan from an investor to a borrower (typically corporate or governmental). The borrower commits to paying periodic interest payments, known as coupons, and to returning the principal amount at maturity. Bonds are categorized based on various attributes including their issuers, maturities, and coupon structures.

Key Characteristics of Bonds:

- *Face Value (Par Value)*: The amount paid back to the bondholder at maturity.
- *Coupon Rate*: The interest rate that the issuer pays to the bondholder, usually annually or semi-annually.
- *Maturity Date*: The date on which the face value is repaid to the bondholder.
- *Yield*: The return an investor realizes on a bond, often calculated as yield to maturity (YTM).

Types of Bonds:

- *Government Bonds*: Issued by national governments, considered low-risk.
- *Municipal Bonds*: Issued by states, cities, or other local government entities.

- *Corporate Bonds*: Issued by companies to raise capital; they vary in risk depending on the issuer's credit rating.
- *Zero-Coupon Bonds*: Issued at a discount and pay no periodic interest; profit is derived from the difference between the purchase price and the face value at maturity.

Valuation of Bonds: The valuation of bonds primarily relies on the present value (PV) of expected future cash flows, which include periodic coupon payments and the principal repayment at maturity. The present value calculations entail discounting these cash flows back to their value today using a discount rate, often the yield to maturity (YTM).

The value V of a bond can be expressed as:

$$V = \sum_{t=1}^{T} \frac{C}{(1+r)^t} + \frac{F}{(1+r)^T}$$

Where:

- C is the coupon payment.
- r is the yield to maturity.
- T is the total number of periods until maturity.
- F is the face value of the bond.

Credit Ratings and Risk: Bonds are subject to credit risk, the possibility that the issuer might default on its obligations. Credit rating agencies, such as Moody's, S&P, and Fitch, assess this risk and assign ratings accordingly. Higher-rated bonds (e.g., AAA) are considered safe, while lower-rated bonds (e.g., BBB and below) are riskier but offer higher yields.

Yield Curve and Its Implications: The yield curve, a graphical representation of yields across different maturities, is a critical tool for bond investors. A normal upward-sloping yield curve suggests that longer-term bonds have higher yields than short-term bonds, reflecting the higher risk associated with time. An inverted yield curve, where short-term yields are higher than long-term yields, can signal economic uncertainty or an impending recession.

Portfolio Management Strategies: Fixed-income securities are instrumental in portfolio diversification and risk management. Common strategies include:

- *Laddering*: Building a portfolio with bonds maturing at regular intervals to mitigate interest rate risk.
- *Barbell Strategy*: Combining short-term and long-term bonds to balance flexibility and yield.
- *Bullet Strategy*: Aligning the bond maturities to a particular time frame based on forecasted financial needs.

Investors need to consider interest rate risk, the risk that rising rates will reduce the value of existing bonds, and reinvestment risk, where future coupons and principal repayments get reinvested at lower rates than the original yield.

By mastering the valuation techniques and risk management strategies for bonds and fixed-income securities, investors enhance their ability to craft resilient portfolios amidst varying market conditions. They can leverage the stable income and lower volatility that these instruments offer, optimizing overall investment performance.

3.4 Derivatives: Options, Futures, and Swaps

Derivatives are financial instruments whose value is derived from the value of an underlying asset, index, or rate. They are powerful tools for hedging risk, speculating on market movements, and improving the efficiency of capital. In this section, we will explore the three primary types of derivatives: options, futures, and swaps. We will examine their characteristics, uses, and basic valuation methods.

Options are contracts that give the holder the right, but not the obligation, to buy or sell an underlying asset at a specified price before or at a specified expiration date. There are two main types of options: *call options*, which provide the right to buy, and *put options*, which provide the right to sell.

The value of an option is determined by several factors, including the current price of the underlying asset (S), the strike price (K), the time to expiration (T), volatility (σ), and the risk-free interest rate (r). The Black-Scholes model is a widely used method for pricing European options and is given by:

$$C(S,T) = S_0N(d_1) - Ke^{-rT}N(d_2)$$

where d_1 and d_2 are calculated as follows:

$$d_1 = \frac{\ln\left(\frac{S_0}{K}\right) + \left(r + \frac{\sigma^2}{2}\right)T}{\sigma\sqrt{T}}$$

$$d_2 = d_1 - \sigma\sqrt{T}$$

Here, $C(S,T)$ represents the price of a European call option, and $N(\cdot)$ is the cumulative distribution function of the standard normal distribution.

Another essential type of derivative is the *futures contract*. A futures contract obligates the buyer to purchase, and the seller to sell, an asset at a predetermined future date and price. Unlike options, futures contracts do not offer the choice to opt-out; they entail a binding agreement. Futures are standardized and traded on exchanges, enhancing liquidity and reducing counterparty risk.

The profit and loss from futures positions are directly linked to fluctuations in the price of the underlying asset. A long position profits from a rise in the asset's price, while a short position benefits from a decline. The initial price of the futures contract (F_0) is typically determined by the spot price of the underlying asset (S_0) and the cost of carry, which includes storage costs, interest rates, and dividends.

$$F_0 = S_0e^{rT}$$

where r denotes the risk-free interest rate and T is the time to maturity. This formula underlines the foundational assumption that futures prices converge to spot prices as the contract approaches expiration.

Swaps are derivatives where two parties exchange cash flows or financial instruments over a specified period. The most common types of swaps are interest rate swaps and currency swaps.

In an *interest rate swap*, one party agrees to pay a fixed interest rate in exchange for receiving a floating interest rate, typically indexed to a benchmark such as LIBOR. The notional principal amount serves as the basis for calculating the exchanged interest payments, but it is not exchanged itself.

To value an interest rate swap, one must determine the present value of the fixed and floating legs. For the fixed leg, the present value (PV_{fixed}) is given by:

$$PV_{\text{fixed}} = \sum_{i=1}^{n} \frac{c \cdot N}{(1+r)^i}$$

where c represents the fixed rate, N is the notional principal, r is the discount rate, and n is the number of payment periods. For the floating leg, the valuation is more complex, as it depends on the future floating rates, which are typically unknown.

In a *currency swap*, two parties exchange principal and interest payments in different currencies. These swaps provide a way for companies to manage their foreign exchange risk and access capital markets in different currencies.

Understanding these derivatives involves not only comprehending their structure and uses but also grasping their valuation intricacies. For options, futures, and swaps, the interplay between market conditions, interest rates, and time significantly impacts their pricing and sensitivity to risk.

Aspiring traders and investors equipped with a thorough knowledge of these derivatives can employ them effectively for risk management and speculative purposes, adding a versatile set of tools to their financial arsenal.

3.5 Financial Markets and Their Functions

Financial markets play a crucial role in the efficient allocation of resources in any economy. They serve as platforms where savers and borrowers can transact, ensuring that capital flows to its most productive uses. These markets are diverse, including the stock market, bond market, derivatives market, and foreign exchange market, each with its specific function and purpose.

The primary function of financial markets is to facilitate the raising of capital. Businesses and governments need capital for various purposes like expansion, development projects, or public expenditures. Financial markets enable these entities to issue securities such as stocks, bonds, and other instruments to raise funds. For example, a corporation might issue equity in the form of common stock, providing investors with ownership stakes and the potential for dividends in return for their investment.

Another essential function of financial markets is the provision of liquidity. Liquidity refers to the ease with which an asset can be converted into cash without significantly affecting its price. Markets like the stock exchange provide a platform where investors can easily buy and sell shares. High liquidity in financial markets reduces the risk associated with the buying and selling of securities, thereby encouraging more participation from a diverse group of investors.

Financial markets also play a pivotal role in price discovery. The prices of securities traded on financial markets are determined by supply and demand forces. This process of price formation is crucial because it reflects the collective assessment of all market participants regarding the value of the underlying asset. For instance, the price of a company's stock is influenced by its perceived future earnings potential, the overall economic environment, and investor sentiment. Efficient price discovery ensures that resources are allocated efficiently, as prices signal where capital is most needed.

Risk transfer is another critical function of financial markets. Different financial instruments, such as derivatives, are specifically designed to transfer risk from one party to another. For example, options and futures contracts allow investors to hedge against potential losses in the value of their underlying assets. A wheat farmer might use futures contracts to lock in a selling price for their crop, mitigating the risk of price fluctuations at the time of harvest.

Moreover, financial markets contribute to the economic function of intertemporal consumption smoothing. They provide individuals and entities the ability to save today and invest their savings in a way that supports future consumption. This is facilitated through various investment vehicles offered in financial markets, such as fixed-income securities and retirement accounts. Investors can decide on an investment mix that aligns with their future financial goals and risk tolerance.

Additionally, financial markets foster economic growth and development by promoting investment in productive ventures. Access to financial markets allows firms to gather the necessary funds for capital investment, research, and development. This investment leads to innovations, improved infrastructure, and job creation, all of which contribute to the overall economic prosperity.

Finally, financial markets enable efficient portfolio diversification. By offering a wide range of investment options, from domestic to international assets, including stocks, bonds, and derivatives, they allow investors to diversify their portfolios effectively. Diversification minimizes risk since it reduces the impact of adverse performances of individual investments on the overall portfolio.

Understanding the multifaceted functions of financial markets provides a solid foundation for both sophisticated trading strategies and sound investment management. Recognizing how these markets operate helps investors make informed decisions, assess risks accurately, and contribute to an efficient and dynamic economy.

3.6 Basic Valuation Concepts

Understanding basic valuation concepts is essential for any investor looking to assess the true worth of financial instruments. Valuation is the art and science of determining the present value of an asset or a company. It serves as the backbone for various investment decisions, risk management, and strategic planning. In this section, we will explore the foundational principles of valuation that encompass intrinsic value, time value of money, and common valuation methods.

At the heart of all valuation techniques lies the concept of intrinsic value, which refers to the actual worth of a security based on underlying perception of its true value including all aspects of the business, in terms of both tangible and intangible factors. This is contrasted with market value, which is the price at which a security is traded in the market. The difference between the intrinsic value and the market value can provide insight into potential investment opportunities.

One of the most fundamental principles in finance is the time value of money (TVM). The premise here is simple: a dollar today is worth more than a dollar in the future due to its potential earning capacity. This core principle underpins many valuation methods. To understand the time value of money, consider the following fundamental formulas:

$$PV = \frac{FV}{(1+r)^n}$$

where PV is the present value, FV is the future value, r is the discount rate, and n is the number of periods.

$$FV = PV \times (1+r)^n$$

These equations form the basis for discounted cash flow (DCF) analysis, which will be discussed in a later section. The ability to compare cash flows at different points in time using a discount rate to bring them to present value is crucial for making informed valuation assessments.

Valuation methods can be broadly categorized into several key types:

- **Absolute Valuation Models**: These models determine the intrinsic value of a security based on fundamentals, without comparing it to other securities. Examples include the Dividend Discount Model (DDM) and Discounted Cash Flow (DCF) analysis.
- **Relative Valuation Models**: Also known as comparables, these models value a security by comparing it to similar securities. Key metrics include price-to-earnings (P/E), price-to-book (P/B), and price-to-sales (P/S) ratios.
- **Option Pricing Models**: These models, such as the Black-Scholes model and the Binomial options pricing model, are used for valuing derivatives and incorporate the randomness of future asset prices.

Absolute valuation models focus on the intrinsic value by analyzing fundamental factors:

$$DDM : P_0 = \sum_{t=1}^{\infty} \frac{D_t}{(1+r)^t}$$

where P_0 is the price of the stock, D_t is the dividend at time t, and r is the discount rate.

In relative valuation, comparables provide a snapshot of a security's performance relative to its peers. The price-to-earnings (P/E) ratio, one of the most widely used relative valuation metrics, is calculated as:

$$P/E = \frac{Market\ Price\ per\ Share}{Earnings\ per\ Share}$$

Similarly, the price-to-book (P/B) ratio compares a company's market value to its book value:

$$P/B = \frac{Market\ Price\ per\ Share}{Book\ Value\ per\ Share}$$

These ratios can help investors determine if a stock is overvalued or undervalued compared to industry benchmarks.

Option pricing models incorporate the valuation of derivatives by factoring in the stochastic nature of markets. For instance, the Black-Scholes model calculates the price of European call and put options using the formula:

$$C = S_0 N(d_1) - X e^{-rT} N(d_2)$$

$$d_1 = \frac{\ln(\frac{S_0}{X}) + (r + \frac{\sigma^2}{2})T}{\sigma\sqrt{T}}$$

$$d_2 = d_1 - \sigma\sqrt{T}$$

where S_0 is the current stock price, X is the strike price, r is the risk-free rate, T is the time to expiration, σ is the volatility of the stock, and $N(d)$ is the Cumulative Distribution Function of the standard normal distribution.

These valuation methods, while derived from complex financial theories, share the common goal of providing a rational basis for determining asset values. By mastering these basic concepts, investors can unlock deeper insights into market dynamics and make more informed investment decisions.

3.7 Discounted Cash Flow (DCF) Analysis

Discounted Cash Flow (DCF) Analysis is a pivotal valuation method used to estimate the value of an investment based on its expected future cash flows. By discounting these cash flows back to their present value, investors can determine how much an investment is worth today. The fundamental principle underlying DCF is the time value of money, which posits that a dollar received today is worth more than a dollar received in the future due to the potential earning capacity of money.

To embark on a DCF analysis, it is essential to comprehend and calculate each component accurately. The principal steps involved in DCF are as follows:

1. Estimating Future Cash Flows:

Future cash flows are the expected financial returns from the investment over a specific period. These cash flows typically include revenues, operating expenses, taxes, changes in working capital, and capital expenditures. To project these cash flows, one might use historical financial data, industry growth rates, competitive positioning, and economic indicators. It is crucial to be as precise and realistic as possible to avoid skewing the valuation.

$$\text{Free Cash Flow (FCF)} = \text{Net Income} + \text{Depreciation} - \text{Change in Working Capital} - \text{Capital Expenditure}$$

2. Determining the Discount Rate:

The discount rate reflects the investor's required rate of return, which accounts for the risk associated with the investment. The discount rate can be derived using various models, such as the Weighted Average Cost of Capital (WACC) for valuing a company:

$$\text{WACC} = \frac{E}{V} \cdot Re + \frac{D}{V} \cdot Rd \cdot (1 - T_c)$$

Here, E represents the market value of equity, D the market value of debt, V the total market value of the company's financing (equity and debt), Re the cost of equity, Rd the cost of debt, and T_c the corporate tax rate.

Alternatively, for an investment with multiple risk components, the Capital Asset Pricing Model (CAPM) may be applied:

$$R_e = R_f + \beta(R_m - R_f)$$

where R_e is the expected return on equity, R_f the risk-free rate, β the investment's beta (systematic risk measure), and R_m the expected market return.

3. Calculating Present Value of Future Cash Flows:

To find the present value, each projected cash flow is discounted back to its present value using the discount rate. If we denote cash flow in year t by FCF_t and the discount rate by r, the present value PV_t of cash flow in year t is calculated as:

$$PV_t = \frac{FCF_t}{(1+r)^t}$$

4. Estimating Terminal Value:

Since it's impractical to project cash flows indefinitely, the terminal value estimates the investment's value at the end of the projection period. The most common methods to calculate the terminal value are the perpetual growth model (Gordon Growth Model) and the exit multiple approach. The perpetual growth model is given by:

$$TV = \frac{FCF_{n+1}}{r-g}$$

where FCF_{n+1} is the free cash flow in the first year beyond the projection period, r is the discount rate, and g is the perpetual growth rate of cash flows beyond the projection period.

In the exit multiple approach, the terminal value is calculated by applying a multiple to a financial metric (e.g., EBITDA, EBIT) at the end of the projection period.

5. Summing the Present Values:

The final step is aggregating the present values of the projected cash flows and the terminal value. The intrinsic value V_0 of the investment is then:

$$V_0 = \sum_{t=1}^{n} \frac{FCF_t}{(1+r)^t} + \frac{TV}{(1+r)^n}$$

Example of DCF Analysis:

Consider a simplified example where a company is expected to generate the following free cash flows over the next five years:

- Year 1: \$100 million
- Year 2: \$120 million

- Year 3: \$140 million
- Year 4: \$160 million
- Year 5: \$180 million

Assuming a discount rate of 10% and a perpetual growth rate of 3%, the terminal value at the end of Year 5 can be calculated as:

$$TV = \frac{FCF_6}{r-g} = \frac{180 \cdot (1+0.03)}{0.10-0.03} \approx 2640 \text{ million}$$

The present value of each free cash flow and the terminal value are:

$$PV_1 = \frac{100}{(1+0.10)^1} \approx 90.91 \text{ million}$$
$$PV_2 = \frac{120}{(1+0.10)^2} \approx 99.17 \text{ million}$$
$$PV_3 = \frac{140}{(1+0.10)^3} \approx 105.05 \text{ million}$$
$$PV_4 = \frac{160}{(1+0.10)^4} \approx 109.36 \text{ million}$$
$$PV_5 = \frac{180}{(1+0.10)^5} \approx 111.37 \text{ million}$$
$$PV_{TV} = \frac{2640}{(1+0.10)^5} \approx 1638.62 \text{ million}$$

Summing up the present values:

$$V_0 = 90.91+99.17+105.05+109.36+111.37+1638.62 \approx 2154.48 \text{ million}$$

This calculation gives an intrinsic value of approximately \$2.154 billion for the company.

Readers, whether novices or seasoned investors, should grasp the significance of each step in the DCF analysis. Critical evaluation of assumptions and sensitivity analysis by varying discount rates and growth rates can substantially enhance the robustness and reliability of the DCF model.

3.8 Valuation of Bonds and Fixed-Income Securities

The valuation of bonds and fixed-income securities forms the backbone of any comprehensive investment strategy. Proper understanding of these instruments' intrinsic value allows investors to make informed decisions about portfolio allocation and risk management. This section will methodically cover the essential concepts and practical approaches to valuing these instruments.

At the heart of bond valuation is the concept of present value (PV). A bond is essentially a structured series of cash flows, consisting of periodic coupon payments and the eventual repayment of the principal at maturity. The fair value of a bond is the sum of the present values of all expected future cash flows, discounted at an appropriate rate. The discount rate typically reflects the bond's yield to maturity (YTM), which is the internal rate of return (IRR) a bondholder can expect if the bond is held until it matures.

The fundamental formula for bond valuation can be expressed as follows:

$$P = \sum_{t=1}^{T} \frac{C}{(1+r)^t} + \frac{F}{(1+r)^T}$$

where:

- P is the present price of the bond.
- C is the periodic coupon payment.
- r is the discount rate or yield to maturity.
- F is the face value of the bond.
- T is the total number of periods until maturity.

This formula illustrates that each coupon payment and the principal repayment are discountable cash flows. Accurate estimation of the discount rate r is critical, as it encapsulates the bond's risk characteristics, including interest rate risk, credit risk, and liquidity risk.

Bonds can broadly categorize into two types: zero-coupon bonds and coupon-bearing bonds. Zero-coupon bonds do not make periodic interest payments; instead, they are sold at a discount to their face value. The valuation of zero-coupon bonds simplifies to a single present value calculation:

$$P = \frac{F}{(1+r)^T}$$

Conversely, coupon-bearing bonds necessitate the evaluation of multiple discounting cash flows. Let's demonstrate this with an example. Suppose we have a bond with a face value of $1,000, a 5% annual coupon rate, and 10 years to maturity. Assuming the yield to maturity is also 5%, the bond's price can be calculated as follows:

$$P = \sum_{t=1}^{10} \frac{50}{(1+0.05)^t} + \frac{1000}{(1+0.05)^{10}}$$

Calculations show that each coupon payment of $50 is discounted to its present value, and the face value repayment of $1,000 is similarly discounted.

Next, let's delve into the concept of the Yield Curve, which is crucial for evaluating bonds with different maturities. The yield curve graphically represents yields across various maturities, typically showing an upward slope under normal market conditions, implying higher yields for longer-term investments. The shapes of yield curves—normal, inverted, and flat—provide insights into market expectations for future interest rates and economic activity.

When valuing corporate bonds, it is vital to incorporate credit spreads, which reflect the additional yield over a risk-free rate to compensate for default risk. The formula adjusts to:

$$r = r_f + \text{credit spread}$$

where r_f is the yield on a comparable-duration risk-free bond, such as a U.S. Treasury bond.

Advanced valuation methods like the binomial tree model or the Monte Carlo simulation address bonds with embedded options or other complex features. These methods factor scenarios for interest rate paths, allowing for a more nuanced valuation.

In practical portfolio management, bond investors must regularly assess portfolio duration—the weighted average time to receive the bond's cash flows—which measures sensitivity to interest rate changes. Adjustments in bond holdings can effectively manage and hedge interest rate risk, ensuring that the portfolio's risk-return profile aligns with the investor's objectives.

By grasping these principles, investors can skillfully navigate the bond market, identifying mispriced opportunities and executing strategies that enhance returns while managing associated risks.

3.9 Valuation of Equity Instruments

Valuing equity instruments is a fundamental task for any investor aiming to make informed decisions in the stock market. Equities, commonly known as stocks or shares, represent ownership in a company and entitle shareholders to a portion of the profits, typically distributed in the form of dividends. The valuation of equity instruments can be approached through various methodologies, each providing unique insights and serving different investment strategies.

The two primary approaches to equity valuation are intrinsic valuation and relative valuation. Intrinsic valuation attempts to determine the 'true' value of an equity based on fundamental analysis, while relative valuation assesses the value based on the pricing of comparable companies.

Intrinsic Valuation: Discounted Cash Flow (DCF) Analysis

One of the most robust methods for intrinsic valuation is the Discounted Cash Flow (DCF) analysis. This method involves projecting the future cash flows of a company and then discounting those cash flows to their present value using an appropriate discount rate. The steps involved in executing a DCF analysis are as follows:

1. **Forecasting Free Cash Flows (FCFs)**: The first step is to estimate the company's future free cash flows. Free cash flow is the cash generated by the company after accounting for capital expenditures needed to maintain or expand the asset base. The formula for free cash flow can be expressed as:

$$\text{FCF} = \text{EBIT}(1 - \text{Tax Rate}) + \text{Depreciation} - \text{CAPEX} - \Delta\text{Working Capital}$$

where EBIT is Earnings Before Interest and Taxes, Tax Rate is the corporate tax rate, Depreciation is the non-cash charge, CAPEX stands for capital expenditures, and ΔWorking Capital is the change in working capital.

2. **Determining the Discount Rate**: The discount rate applied to future cash flows should reflect the riskiness of those cash flows. Typically, the Weighted Average Cost of Capital (WACC) is used as the discount rate. WACC is calculated based on the company's cost of equity and cost of debt, weighted by their respective proportions in the company's capital structure:

$$\text{WACC} = \left(\frac{E}{E+D}\right) \text{Cost of Equity} + \left(\frac{D}{E+D}\right) \text{Cost of Debt}(1 - \text{Tax Rate})$$

where E is the market value of equity, D is the market value of debt, and the Cost of Equity is commonly estimated using the Capital Asset Pricing Model (CAPM):

$$\text{Cost of Equity} = R_f + \beta(R_m - R_f)$$

with R_f being the risk-free rate, β the equity beta, and R_m the expected market return.

3. **Calculating the Present Value of Future Cash Flows**: Each of the projected free cash flows is discounted back to the present value using the discount rate (WACC). The formula for the present value of an individual cash flow is:

$$\text{PV} = \frac{\text{FCF}}{(1 + \text{WACC})^t}$$

where t is the time period. Summing the present values of all projected cash flows provides the total intrinsic value of the firm.

4. **Terminal Value Calculation**: Since it is impractical to project cash flows indefinitely, a terminal value is calculated at the end of a forecast period. The terminal value represents the present value of all subsequent cash flows beyond the forecast horizon, often estimated using a perpetuity growth model:

$$\text{Terminal Value} = \frac{\text{FCF}_{n+1}}{(\text{WACC} - g)}$$

where FCF_{n+1} is the free cash flow in the first year after the forecast period, and g is the perpetual growth rate.

Adding the present value of the projected free cash flows and the terminal value gives the enterprise value of the company. To obtain the equity value, subtract the net debt (total debt minus cash and equivalents) from the enterprise value.

Relative Valuation: Price Multiples

Relative valuation involves comparing a company's value metrics with those of similar companies. This method hinges on the law of one price, which asserts that in an efficient market, similar assets should sell for similar prices. Commonly used price multiples in relative valuation include:

- **Price-to-Earnings (P/E) Ratio**: This ratio compares the current share price to the earnings per share (EPS):

  $$\text{P/E Ratio} = \frac{\text{Share Price}}{\text{EPS}}$$

  A high P/E ratio could indicate that the stock is overvalued, or it may reflect high growth expectations. Conversely, a low P/E ratio might suggest undervaluation or underlying issues with the company.

- **Price-to-Book (P/B) Ratio**: This ratio compares the market value of a company's equity to its book value:

  $$\text{P/B Ratio} = \frac{\text{Market Value of Equity}}{\text{Book Value of Equity}}$$

  The P/B ratio is particularly useful for valuing companies with significant tangible assets. A P/B ratio below 1 might indicate undervaluation, assuming no significant issues with the company's fundamentals.

- **Price-to-Sales (P/S) Ratio**: This ratio compares a company's market capitalization to its total sales:

  $$\text{P/S Ratio} = \frac{\text{Market Capitalization}}{\text{Total Sales}}$$

  The P/S ratio can be valuable for valuation in industries where earnings might be more volatile or companies that are not yet profitable.

- **Enterprise Value-to-EBITDA (EV/EBITDA) Ratio**: This ratio provides a measure of a company's value relative to its earnings before interest, taxes, depreciation, and amortization:

$$\text{EV/EBITDA} = \frac{\text{Enterprise Value}}{\text{EBITDA}}$$

  The EV/EBITDA ratio is often used for valuing firms with high levels of fixed assets or varying capital structures, offering a more holistic measure than the P/E ratio.

Investors often use these multiples to compare a company's valuation against its peers or industry norms. Such comparison helps to identify potentially undervalued or overvalued stocks based on market trends and economic cycles.

In analyzing equities, it's crucial to blend both intrinsic and relative valuation methods. Each has its strengths and weaknesses, and integrating them can offer a more comprehensive view of a stock's value. Skilled investors not only rely on quantitative measures but also incorporate qualitative factors such as management quality, competitive landscape, and macroeconomic conditions to make well-rounded investment decisions.

3.10 Valuation of Derivatives

Understanding the valuation of derivatives is crucial for any sophisticated trader or investor. Derivatives, which include options, futures, and swaps, derive their value from underlying assets such as stocks, bonds, commodities, or market indices. The valuation of these financial instruments demands a thorough grasp of complex mathematical models and market behavior.

The most notable models for option pricing include the Black-Scholes-Merton (BSM) model and the Binomial Tree model. Each provides a framework for assessing the theoretical value of options under certain conditions.

Black-Scholes-Merton (BSM) Model

The BSM model is a seminal approach for pricing European options. It is predicated on several key assumptions: the markets are frictionless, there are no arbitrage opportunities, and the underlying asset follows a geometric Brownian motion with constant volatility and interest rates. The BSM formula for a European call option is:

$$C = S_0\Phi(d_1) - Ke^{-rT}\Phi(d_2)$$

where:

$$d_1 = \frac{\ln(S_0/K) + (r + \sigma^2/2)T}{\sigma\sqrt{T}}$$

$$d_2 = d_1 - \sigma\sqrt{T}$$

In this formula, C is the call option price, S_0 is the current stock price, K is the option strike price, r is the risk-free interest rate, σ is the volatility of the stock, T is the time to maturity, and Φ is the cumulative distribution function of the standard normal distribution.

The put option price P can be derived from the call option price using the put-call parity:

$$P = C - S_0 + Ke^{-rT}$$

Binomial Tree Model

The Binomial Tree model offers a flexible and intuitive approach to option pricing by discretizing the time to maturity into several steps or intervals. This model represents possible future movements in the price of the underlying asset at each step as an "up" or "down" movement, forming a recombining tree. The value of the option is then computed by backward induction through the tree.

Consider a single-period binomial model with the following parameters:

- S_0: Initial stock price
- u: Factor by which the price increases in an up state
- d: Factor by which the price decreases in a down state
- p: Risk-neutral probability of an up state
- $1-p$: Risk-neutral probability of a down state

The value of the underlying asset in the up and down states after one period is $S_u = S_0 \cdot u$ and $S_d = S_0 \cdot d$, respectively. The risk-neutral probability p is given by:

$$p = \frac{e^{r\Delta t} - d}{u - d}$$

where r is the continuously compounded risk-free interest rate, and Δt is the length of the period.

To price a one-period European call option, we first determine the possible payoff at maturity:

$$C_u = \max(0, S_u - K)$$
$$C_d = \max(0, S_d - K)$$

Then, the present value of the option price is computed by discounting the expected payoff at the risk-free rate:

$$C = e^{-r\Delta t}[p \cdot C_u + (1 - p) \cdot C_d]$$

Extending this approach to multiple periods involves iterating through the binomial tree to compute the payoff at each node and discounting back to the present value.

Futures and Forward Contracts

Valuing futures and forward contracts involves determining the fair price at which these contracts should be traded to prevent arbitrage opportunities. The classical no-arbitrage pricing for a forward contract is derived from the cost-of-carry model:

$$F_0 = S_0 e^{(r-q)T}$$

where F_0 is the forward price, S_0 is the spot price of the underlying asset, r is the risk-free interest rate, q is the continuous dividend yield, and T is the time to maturity.

Futures contracts, being similar to forward contracts but traded on exchanges with daily settlement, follow a similar valuation principle. The price of a futures contract can be approximated by the forward price, assuming no significant differences in mark-to-market and margining processes.

Swaps

Swaps involve the exchange of cash flows between two parties. The most common type, the interest rate swap, entails exchanges of fixed interest rate payments for floating-rate payments. The valuation of a plain vanilla interest rate swap involves calculating the present value of both legs of the swap and netting them.

For a fixed-for-floating interest rate swap:

$$\text{Value of Swap} = V_{\text{fixed}} - V_{\text{floating}}$$

where V_{fixed} is the present value of the fixed leg, and V_{floating} is the present value of the floating leg. The fixed leg is valued as the sum of the present values of all fixed payments, whereas the floating leg is typically valued as the notional principal, since the floating rate resets frequently to match market rates.

By mastering these sophisticated valuation techniques and their underlying assumptions and calculations, traders and investors can enhance their ability to evaluate and manage derivative positions effectively.

Chapter 4

Time Series Analysis

Time series analysis is essential for understanding patterns and making forecasts in financial markets, characterized by data points collected at regular intervals. This chapter covers the types of time series data, the importance of stationarity, and various modeling techniques such as autoregressive (AR) models, moving average (MA) models, and their combinations (ARIMA). It also explores seasonal models, volatility modeling with GARCH and ARCH models, and the methods for forecasting and evaluating time series models to enhance predictive accuracy and decision-making.

4.1 Introduction to Time Series Analysis

Time series analysis is foundational in the realm of quantitative finance, providing the tools necessary to decipher patterns and make informed forecasts based on past data. Financial markets are inherently complex, and understanding their behavior over time is crucial for formulating effective trading strategies, risk management, and portfolio optimization.

At its core, time series analysis involves examining data points collected at successive intervals, such as daily stock prices, monthly unemployment rates, or yearly GDP growth figures. This chapter aims to guide you through the essential concepts and techniques of time series analysis, ensuring you build a robust framework for analyzing historical data and predicting future trends.

A time series $\{y_t\}$ can be formally defined as a sequence of observations $(y_1, y_2, \ldots, y_T)$ indexed in time. Unlike cross-sectional data, time series data points are not independent of each other; each observation is potentially influenced by preceding values. Recognizing and modeling these dependencies is a critical step toward understanding the underlying process that generates the data.

One fundamental concept in time series analysis is stationarity. A time series is stationary if its statistical properties, such as mean, variance, and autocorrelation, remain constant over time. This trait simplifies the modeling process as it implies that the series does not exhibit trends or seasonality. However, real-world financial data often display non-stationary behavior, necessitating techniques to transform them into stationary series.

Another key aspect of time series analysis is distinguishing between different types of time series data. A primary classification includes:

- **Trend:** Long-term progression or movement in the series, which can be upward, downward, or flat. Trend analysis helps identify the general direction of the data over extended periods.
- **Seasonality:** Regular, periodic fluctuations that occur within shorter, consistent intervals, such as quarterly earnings cycles.
- **Cyclic Patterns:** Irregular, non-periodic fluctuations associated with economic cycles rather than seasonal events.
- **Noise:** Random variations that do not follow any discernible pattern and are considered as residual or error terms after accounting for trend, seasonality, and cyclic patterns.

To model these elements, time series analysis leverages a variety of techniques like Autoregressive (AR) models, Moving Average (MA) models, and their integrated forms, known as ARIMA (Autoregressive Integrated Moving Average) models. Each approach has its strengths and applications, and understanding their nuances is critical for accurate modeling.

For instance, an AR model expresses the current value of the series as a linear function of its past values plus a random shock. Mathematically, an ARp model is represented as:

$$y_t = \phi_0 + \phi_1 y_{t-1} + \phi_2 y_{t-2} + \ldots + \phi_p y_{t-p} + \epsilon_t,$$

where ϕ_i represents the parameters, and ϵ_t denotes the white noise error term.

Similarly, MA models depict the current value as a function of past error terms, represented as:

$$y_t = \mu + \epsilon_t + \theta_1 \epsilon_{t-1} + \theta_2 \epsilon_{t-2} + \ldots + \theta_q \epsilon_{t-q},$$

where θ_i are the parameters, and μ is the mean of the series.

Combining these, the ARMA (Autoregressive Moving Average) model caters to both aspects of autocorrelation and error term influences, which evolves into ARIMA when differencing is applied to ensure stationarity.

Volatility modeling, another significant component, deals with the variability of time series data, capturing clustering effects through models like ARCH (Autoregressive Conditional Heteroskedasticity) and GARCH (Generalized ARCH). These models are vital for understanding risk and potential price swings, adding another layer of sophistication to time series analysis.

To effectively utilize these models, the process begins with rigorous data exploration and visualization. Plotting the time series, identifying trends, seasonality, and testing for stationarity (using augmented Dickey-Fuller tests, for example) are preliminary steps. Once the model is fitted, forecasting and evaluation through diagnostic checks ensure reliability and accuracy, enabling actionable insights.

This chapter will deepen your grasp on these concepts, guiding you from fundamental principles to advanced modeling techniques. By mastering time series analysis, you can enhance your predictive models, contributing to more robust and profitable trading strategies.

4.2 Types of Time Series Data

Time series data in financial markets are essentially a sequence of data points indexed in time order, typically occurring at consecutive and equally spaced periods. Understanding the different types of time series data is crucial for selecting the appropriate modeling and forecasting techniques. The nature of the data informs how it should be treated and analyzed.

Regular Time Series: This type encompasses data points collected at consistent, uniform time intervals. These intervals could be days, weeks, months, or even seconds in high-frequency trading scenarios. For instance, daily closing prices of a stock constitute a regular time series. Regular time series data are often more straightforward to analyze because they maintain consistent periodicity, which allows for standard techniques such as Autoregressive Moving Average (ARMA) models to be readily applied.

$$Price_t = \theta_0 + \theta_1 Price_{t-1} + \epsilon_t$$

Irregular Time Series: Unlike regular time series, irregular time series data points are not spaced at uniform intervals. Such datasets are common in the analysis of market events, where the occurrence of data is event-driven, such as the timestamps of trades executed during a day. Addressing irregular time series often requires interpolation techniques or transforming the data into a regular format for standard analysis methods to be applicable.

Univariate Time Series: This involves a single variable tracked over time, such as the closing price of a stock. The analysis of univariate time series focuses on modeling this single data stream to forecast future values. Techniques like Simple Moving Average (SMA) and Exponential Smoothing (ES) are often used in this context.

$$SMA_t = \frac{1}{n} \sum_{i=0}^{n-1} Price_{t-i}$$

Multivariate Time Series: In this type, multiple variables are tracked simultaneously. For example, analyzing the closing prices of multiple related stocks or a stock and its trading volume together represents a multivariate time series. The interdependencies between these variables can provide richer insights and more robust forecasting models, employing techniques such as Vector Autoregression (VAR):

$$\begin{aligned} Price_{1,t} &= \theta_{10} + \theta_{11} Price_{1,t-1} + \theta_{12} Volume_{t-1} + \epsilon_{1,t} \\ Volume_t &= \theta_{20} + \theta_{21} Price_{1,t-1} + \theta_{22} Volume_{t-1} + \epsilon_{2,t} \end{aligned}$$

Seasonal Time Series: These data show regular patterns that repeat at known, fixed intervals, such as daily, weekly, monthly, or annually. Seasonality in financial data might reflect phenomena like increased consumer spending during holidays or variations in trading volumes during different times of the year. Identifying and modeling the seasonal component can significantly enhance forecast accuracy. Seasonal decomposition of time series (STL) is a commonly used technique for this purpose:

$$Y_t = T_t + S_t + E_t$$

where Y_t is the observed value, T_t represents the trend component, S_t the seasonal component, and E_t the residual (error) component.

Non-Seasonal Time Series: These lack any apparent seasonal pattern and typically are modeled by focusing on trends and random variations. The absence of seasonality simplifies the analysis as one can focus on trend extraction and noise filtering without accounting for regular periodic fluctuations.

High-Frequency Time Series: Characterized by data collected at millisecond or second intervals, common in algorithmic and high-frequency trading scenarios. These series present unique challenges such as handling large datasets and noise. Techniques specific to high-frequency data include microstructure models and time series aggregation to reduce computational complexity and highlight the underlying market trends.

Recognizing and distinguishing between these types ensures that the most suitable analytical methods are applied, facilitating more accurate modeling and more insightful interpretation. In financial trading and investing, this nuanced understanding can make the difference between a strategy that merely performs and one that excels.

4.3 Stationarity and Non-Stationarity

In time series analysis, the concept of stationarity is of paramount importance. A stationary time series has statistical properties, such as mean, variance, and autocorrelation structure, that are constant over time. This constancy implies that the same model can be applied across different segments of the time series without significant changes in the parameters. Recognizing whether a time series is stationary or non-stationary is a critical initial step in choosing the appropriate modeling techniques and ensuring reliable forecasts.

Stationarity can broadly be categorized into three types: strict (or strong) stationarity, weak (or second-order) stationarity, and trend stationarity. A time series $\{X_t\}$ is strictly stationary if the joint distribution of any subset of X_t remains unchanged over time. Formally, for any integer k and time points $t_1, t_2, \ldots, t_k$, the joint distribution of $(X_{t_1}, X_{t_2}, \ldots, X_{t_k})$ is the same as that of $(X_{t_1+h}, X_{t_2+h}, \ldots, X_{t_k+h})$ for all h.

Weak stationarity, which is the most commonly used form, requires that the first two moments of the time series are constant over time. Specifically, a time series is weakly stationary if:

- The mean $E[X_t]$ is constant over time, i.e., $E[X_t] = \mu$.
- The variance $Var(X_t)$ is constant over time, i.e., $Var(X_t) = \sigma^2$.
- The covariance between X_t and X_{t+h} depends only on the lag h, not on time t, i.e., $Cov(X_t, X_{t+h}) = \gamma(h)$.

Trend stationarity differs in that it allows for the presence of a deterministic trend in the data. Such a time series can be rendered stationary by removing the trend component.

Understanding non-stationarity is equally essential, as most financial time series exhibit non-stationarity due to trends, seasonal effects, or variability over time. Non-stationary data poses challenges for model estimation and inference, often leading to unreliable and spurious results. Non-stationarity can manifest in several forms, including unit roots, structural breaks, and changing variances.

One common method for determining stationarity is through visual inspection of the time series plot. Stationary time series typically have a constant mean around which they fluctuate, while non-stationary series exhibit noticeable trends or changing variances over time. Formal statistical tests provide a more rigorous approach for detecting non-stationarity. Key tests include:

Dickey-Fuller Test: The Augmented Dickey-Fuller (ADF) test is used to test the null hypothesis that a unit root is present in an autoregressive model of the time series. The test involves estimating the following regression:

$$\Delta X_t = \alpha + \beta t + \gamma X_{t-1} + \delta_1 \Delta X_{t-1} + \delta_2 \Delta X_{t-2} + \ldots + \delta_p \Delta X_{t-p} + \epsilon_t$$

Where $\Delta X_t = X_t - X_{t-1}$. The presence of a unit root implies non-stationarity, and a significant test statistic γ rejects the null hypothesis.

KPSS Test: The Kwiatkowski-Phillips-Schmidt-Shin (KPSS) test evaluates the null hypothesis that the time series is stationary around a deterministic trend (trend-stationary) against the alternative of a unit root. Unlike the ADF test, here the null hypothesis is stationarity.

If a time series is found to be non-stationary, several transformation techniques can be applied to achieve stationarity:

- **Differencing:** Taking the difference of successive observations, $\Delta X_t = X_t - X_{t-1}$, is often effective. This process can be repeated to achieve the desired level of stationarity.
- **Log Transformation:** Applying a logarithmic transformation can stabilize the variance.
- **Detrending:** Removing a deterministic trend through regression techniques can render the series stationary.
- **Seasonal Differencing:** For series with seasonal effects, subtracting the value from the same season in the previous cycle, $X_t - X_{t-s}$, can be useful.

Ensuring stationarity before adopting time series models is crucial because many statistical methods, including ARIMA, depend on the assumption of stationarity. Identifying and transforming a non-stationary time series into a stationary one is an integral part of the modeling process, laying a reliable foundation for accurate and meaningful forecasts.

4.4 Autoregressive (AR) Models

Autoregressive (AR) models are foundational tools in time series analysis, characterized by the principle that current values in a series can be expressed as a linear function of previous values and a stochastic (random) term. These models are valuable for their simplicity and effectiveness in capturing temporal dependencies within data.

An AR model of order p, denoted as AR(p), includes p lagged observations. The general form of an AR(p) model is given by:

$$X_t = \phi_1 X_{t-1} + \phi_2 X_{t-2} + \cdots + \phi_p X_{t-p} + \epsilon_t$$

where:

- X_t is the value of the time series at time t,
- $\phi_1, \phi_2, \ldots, \phi_p$ are the coefficients of the model,
- ϵ_t is a white noise error term with mean zero and constant variance, $\epsilon_t \sim N(0, \sigma^2)$.

The coefficients ϕ_i represent the weights of the lagged values, providing insight into how past values influence the current value. The selection of the order p is critical and can be determined using various model selection criteria such as the Akaike Information Criterion (AIC), the Bayesian Information Criterion (BIC), or through autocorrelation and partial autocorrelation functions.

Fitting an AR Model:

The process of fitting an AR model involves estimating the coefficients ϕ_i. This can be achieved using methods such as the Yule-Walker equations, least squares regression, or maximum likelihood estimation. Consider the following steps to fit an AR model:

1. **Model Identification:**

    - Compute the autocorrelation function (ACF) and the partial autocorrelation function (PACF) of the time series.
    - Identify the order p using the PACF, where partial correlations are significant up to lag p.

2. **Parameter Estimation:**

    - Use Yule-Walker equations to estimate the ϕ_i coefficients.
    - Alternatively, use least squares regression by minimizing the residual sum of squares.
    - Evaluate the model's goodness-of-fit using AIC, BIC, or adjusted R-squared.

3. **Diagnostics:**

- Check the residuals of the fitted model to ensure they resemble white noise.
- Use diagnostic plots such as the histogram of residuals, the ACF of residuals, and the Q-Q plot to confirm normality and independence.

Example: Fitting an AR(2) Model

Consider a time series $\{X_t\}$. The PACF suggests that $p = 2$. The AR(2) model is therefore:

$$X_t = \phi_1 X_{t-1} + \phi_2 X_{t-2} + \epsilon_t$$

Assume we estimate ϕ_1 and ϕ_2 using the Yule-Walker equations:

$$\begin{cases} \gamma(0) = \phi_1\gamma(1) + \phi_2\gamma(2) + \sigma^2 \\ \gamma(1) = \phi_1\gamma(0) + \phi_2\gamma(1) \\ \gamma(2) = \phi_1\gamma(1) + \phi_2\gamma(0) \end{cases}$$

where $\gamma(k)$ is the autocovariance function at lag k. Solving these equations yields the coefficients ϕ_1 and ϕ_2.

Using a Python code snippet with libraries such as Statsmodels simplifies the fitting process:

```
import statsmodels.api as sm

# Example time series data
ts_data = [constructed time series data]

# Fit an AR(2) model
model = sm.tsa.ARIMA(ts_data, order=(2, 0, 0))
result = model.fit()

# Output the coefficients
print(result.params)
```

This code will estimate the parameters ϕ_1 and ϕ_2 and provide diagnostics to assess the fit.

Understanding AR models equips investors and traders with tools to model and anticipate future market movements effectively. They can capture and use the temporal structure inherently present in financial data to make more informed decisions. As a practical tool, AR models offer simplicity and a clear interpretation, making them a powerful addition to any financial analyst's toolkit. The key to their successful application lies in careful model selection, accurate parameter estimation, and thorough diagnostic checking to ensure robustness and reliability in predictions.

4.5 Moving Average (MA) Models

The Moving Average (MA) model is a fundamental component of time series analysis, crucial for understanding the stochastic behavior of financial data. An MA model expresses the output of a time series as a linear combination of past error terms. This approach allows for capturing the noise structure in the data, providing valuable insights for forecasting.

An MA model of order q, denoted as MA(q), is represented mathematically as:

$$X_t = \mu + \epsilon_t + \theta_1 \epsilon_{t-1} + \theta_2 \epsilon_{t-2} + \cdots + \theta_q \epsilon_{t-q}$$

Here:

- X_t is the observed value at time t.
- μ is the mean of the series.
- $\epsilon_t, \epsilon_{t-1}, \ldots, \epsilon_{t-q}$ are white noise error terms, often assumed to be independently and identically distributed (i.i.d) with zero mean and constant variance σ^2.
- $\theta_1, \theta_2, \ldots, \theta_q$ are the parameters of the model.

Understanding the MA Model Structure

The Moving Average model is intuitive since it suggests that each value of the time series is influenced not only by a current random shock but also by a series of preceding shocks. These shocks or "errors" are essentially the part of X_t that cannot be predicted by past values. The finite sum of these errors gives the model its term "moving average."

An insightful way to perceive the MA model is through its impulse response function, which delineates how a shock at time t propagates through future values $X_{t+1}, X_{t+2}, \ldots$. The parameters θ_i determine the magnitude and direction of this propagation.

Estimation of MA Models

Estimating the parameters θ_i in an MA model typically involves methods such as Maximum Likelihood Estimation (MLE). This method maximizes the likelihood function, which is the probability of observing the given data as a function of the parameters.

$$L(\theta_1, \theta_2, \ldots, \theta_q, \sigma^2) = \prod_{t=1}^{N} f(X_t|\theta_1, \theta_2, \ldots, \theta_q, \sigma^2)$$

Where $f(X_t|\theta_1, \theta_2, \ldots, \theta_q, \sigma^2)$ is the probability density function of X_t conditional on the parameters.

Diagnostic Checking

Once the MA model parameters are estimated, it is crucial to perform diagnostic checks to ensure the model's adequacy. One common diagnostic tool is the examination of residuals:

$$\hat{\epsilon}_t = X_t - \hat{X}_t$$

Where $\hat{X}_t$ is the fitted value from the model, and $\hat{\epsilon}_t$ are the residuals. The residuals should resemble white noise if the model is appropriate. This can be evaluated using the autocorrelation function (ACF) of the residuals. Ideally, the ACF of residuals should be close to zero for all lags.

Practical Application: Rolling Window Analysis

Rollingly combining several MA models over a moving window can enhance forecasting accuracy, especially in a volatile financial market. This method recalculates the model parameters for every new data point by "rolling" the window, ensuring that the model continuously adapts to changing market conditions.

Example Code Snippet

For practical implementation, consider the following Python code snippet using the Statsmodels library:

```
import numpy as np
import pandas as pd
import statsmodels.api as sm

# Example time series data
data = sm.datasets.macrodata.load_pandas().data['realgdp']
data = np.log(data).diff().dropna()

# Fit an MA model
ma_model = sm.tsa.ARMA(data, order=(0, 1)).fit()
print(ma_model.summary())
```

Forecasting with MA Models

The MA models' forecasting capability relies on the persistence and structure of past errors. Forecasts can be generated using the estimated parameters and observed residuals:

$$\hat{X}_{T+h|T} = \mu + \sum_{i=1}^{\min(q,h-1)} \theta_i \hat{\epsilon}_{T+i-h}$$

This equation shows that future values (h steps ahead) are forecasts as combinations of past shocks.

Incorporating MA models into a broader trading and investing strategy allows traders to better manage risks by recognizing and adapting to the underlying noise in financial returns. Continuous evaluation and iteration of the model through new data ensure that it remains relevant and accurate in different market conditions, providing a robust foundation for predictive trading and investment decisions.

4.6 Autoregressive Integrated Moving Average (ARIMA) Models

Autoregressive Integrated Moving Average (ARIMA) models are a powerful class of forecasting models designed for analyzing and predicting time series data. They combine three key components: autoregression (AR), integration (I), and moving average (MA). This blend makes ARIMA models versatile and effective in capturing various patterns within financial time series data.

To start, consider the basic structure of ARIMA models, represented as ARIMA(p,d,q). Each parameter has a specific role:

- **p** (autoregressive order): The number of lagged observations incorporated into the model.
- **d** (differencing order): The number of times the data must be differenced to induce stationarity.
- **q** (moving average order): The number of lagged forecast errors in the prediction equation.

The ARIMA model can be formally expressed with the following equation:

$$y_t = c + \phi_1 y_{t-1} + \phi_2 y_{t-2} + \cdots + \phi_p y_{t-p} + \theta_1 \epsilon_{t-1} + \theta_2 \epsilon_{t-2} + \cdots + \theta_q \epsilon_{t-q} + \epsilon_t, \tag{4.1}$$

where:

- y_t is the actual value at time t.
- c is a constant term.
- ϕ_i are the coefficients for the autoregressive terms.
- ϵ_t is the white noise error term at time t.
- θ_j are the coefficients for the moving average terms.

Step-by-Step Modeling:

To construct an ARIMA model, follow these steps:

- **1. Identification:** This involves determining the values of p, d, and q.

  Firstly, assess stationarity. If the time series exhibits trends or varying variance, differencing is required. The number of differences taken to render the series stationary determines d. The augmented Dickey-Fuller (ADF) test is commonly used to test for stationarity.
- **2. Parameter Estimation:** Once stationarity is achieved, identify the potential values of p and q. The autocorrelation function (ACF) and partial autocorrelation function (PACF) plots aid in selecting these parameters. Significant spikes in PACF indicate the autoregressive terms p, and significant spikes in ACF suggest the moving average terms q.
- **3. Model Fitting:** Utilize statistical software to estimate the parameters of the ARIMA model. Packages such as statsmodels in Python, or forecast in R, efficiently handle ARIMA modeling.
- **4. Model Diagnostics:** Validate the model by diagnosing residuals. Residuals should mimic white noise—i.e., they should have a mean of zero, constant variance, and no autocorrelation. The Ljung-Box test can verify the absence of autocorrelation in residuals.

Differencing for Stationarity:

Differencing helps to achieve stationarity by subtracting consecutive observations. The equation for first differencing is:

$$y'_t = y_t - y_{t-1}. \tag{4.2}$$

If first differencing is insufficient, second differencing may be applied:

$$y''_t = y'_t - y'_{t-1} = (y_t - y_{t-1}) - (y_{t-1} - y_{t-2}) = y_t - 2y_{t-1} + y_{t-2}. \tag{4.3}$$

Forecasting with ARIMA:

Once the ARIMA model is fitted, it can be used for forecasting future values. Here's an example calculation:

Assume an ARIMA(2,1,1) model fitted to a stock price series, where:

$$y_t = 10 + 0.5y_{t-1} - 0.3y_{t-2} + 0.4\epsilon_{t-1} + \epsilon_t. \tag{4.4}$$

Using the most recent observations y_{t-1} and y_{t-2} along with forecast error ϵ_{t-1}, a one-step ahead forecast $\hat{y}_{t+1}$ can be calculated. Accurate model fitting and parameter estimation are critical for reliable predictions.

Practical Application:

ARIMA models are essential in financial markets for tasks such as predicting stock prices, exchange rates, and economic indicators. For instance, a trader might use an ARIMA model to forecast the future price of a security, adjusting their portfolio accordingly to maximize returns or minimize risk.

Understanding and applying ARIMA models involve extensive practice and a solid grasp of time series concepts. Mastery of these models can significantly enhance decision-making and forecasting accuracy in the realm of quantitative finance.

4.7 Seasonal Models and SARIMA

Seasonal patterns in financial data often represent some of the most predictable and recurring components. Recognizing and modeling these patterns can substantially improve forecasting accuracy. A Seasonal Autoregressive Integrated Moving Average (SARIMA) model extends the ARIMA model by directly integrating seasonality into the model framework.

When dealing with time series data, seasonality refers to regular patterns or cycles that repeat over a specific period, such as daily, monthly, or quarterly intervals. An example might be the quarterly earnings reports of a company, which exhibit significant influence on stock prices with noticeable patterns every fiscal quarter.

The SARIMA model incorporates seasonality by including seasonal terms in the autoregressive (AR), integrated (I), and moving average (MA) components of the ARIMA model. It achieves this by adjusting these components to account for seasonal differences. The seasonal part of the SARIMA model is characterized by the seasonal autoregressive order (P), the seasonal differencing order (D), the seasonal moving average order (Q), and the length of the seasonal cycle (s).

The general form of a SARIMA model can be expressed as:

$$\text{SARIMA}(p, d, q)(P, D, Q)_s$$

where (p, d, q) are the non-seasonal orders and $(P, D, Q)_s$ are the seasonal orders. These parameters are defined as:

- *Non-seasonal AR order* p: the number of lag observations included in the model.
- *Non-seasonal differencing order* d: the number of times that raw observations are differenced to induce stationarity.
- *Non-seasonal MA order* q: the size of the moving average window.
- *Seasonal AR order* P: the number of seasonal autoregressive terms.
- *Seasonal differencing order* D: the number of seasonal differences required for stationarity.
- *Seasonal MA order* Q: the number of seasonal moving average terms.
- *Seasonal period* s: the number of observations per seasonal cycle.

A practical example of a SARIMA model might look like SARIMA(1,1,1)(1,1,1)$_{12}$ for monthly data, indicating that both the non-seasonal and seasonal orders are included at lag 1 for AR and MA components, with one differencing operation and a seasonal period of 12 months.

Seasonal Differencing Seasonal differencing aims to remove seasonal components from the series. Given a series Y_t, seasonal differencing is performed by subtracting the observation from the same season in the previous cycle:

$$Y_t - Y_{t-s}$$

This differencing can help to stabilize the mean of the time series by removing seasonal changes, which is necessary for the stationarity assumption in SARIMA modeling.

Model Identification and Estimation Identifying the correct SARIMA model involves determining the appropriate values of (p, d, q) and $(P, D, Q)_s$. This can be a complex process involving several steps:

- **Plotting the Autocorrelation Function (ACF) and Partial Autocorrelation Function (PACF):** These plots help to identify the presence of seasonal lags.
- **Seasonal Differencing:** Apply seasonal differencing and plot the differenced series to check for stationarity.
- **Check ACF and PACF of Differenced Series:** Look for significant lags that indicate the order of seasonal components.
- **Parameter Estimation:** Use maximum likelihood or other estimation techniques to determine the parameters. This is often performed using statistical software packages.
- **Model Diagnostics:** Ensure the residuals of the fitted model behave like white noise, with no remaining significant autocorrelation.

Step-by-step Example of SARIMA Model Let's consider an example involving monthly sales data. Suppose the data exhibits seasonality with a period of 12 months. The identified SARIMA model is SARIMA(1,1,1)(1,1,1)$_{12}$. Here, we briefly outline the steps:

- **Seasonal Differencing:** First, to achieve stationarity, apply seasonal differencing to the data:

$$Y_t = X_t - X_{t-12}$$

- **Fit the Model:** Using statistical software, estimate the SARIMA parameters for the differenced series.
- **Analyze Residuals:** Check the residuals of the fitted model by plotting the ACF and PACF of residuals to confirm there is no significant autocorrelation remaining.

Practical Applications of SARIMA Models SARIMA models excel in various fields where data exhibit strong seasonal patterns. Some common applications include:

- **Retail Sales Forecasting:** For predicting monthly or quarterly sales.
- **Economic Indicators:** Such as GDP with seasonal fluctuations.
- **Weather and Climate Data:** Forecasting temperature or precipitation patterns.
- **Energy Consumption:** Predicting electricity usage driven by seasonal demand.

SARIMA models are powerful tools for understanding and forecasting time series data where seasonality plays a critical role. By accurately capturing these seasonal patterns, investors and analysts can make more informed decisions, improving the robustness of their trading strategies and portfolio management practices.

4.8 GARCH and ARCH Models

Modeling and forecasting the volatility of financial time series is crucial for risk management, derivative pricing, and portfolio allocation. Autoregressive Conditional Heteroskedasticity (ARCH) and Generalized Autoregressive Conditional Heteroskedasticity (GARCH) models are powerful tools developed to address the dynamic variability in the volatility of time series data over time.

The foundation of these models lies in recognizing that financial time series often exhibit periods of volatility clustering, where large changes in prices are followed by more large changes, and small changes tend to be followed by small changes. This phenomenon violates the assumption of constant variance, hence necessitating models that can accommodate changing variances.

The ARCH model, proposed by Robert Engle in 1982, captures this heteroskedasticity by modeling the current variance as a function of past squared observations. If ϵ_t denotes the residuals or returns at time t, and σ_t^2 represents the conditional variance, the ARCH(q) model can be represented as:

$$\sigma_t^2 = \alpha_0 + \alpha_1 \epsilon_{t-1}^2 + \alpha_2 \epsilon_{t-2}^2 + \cdots + \alpha_q \epsilon_{t-q}^2,$$

where $\alpha_0 > 0$ and $\alpha_i \geq 0$ for $i = 1, 2, \ldots, q$.

While the ARCH model successfully incorporates changing variance, it requires a high order q to effectively model volatility, often resulting in significant parameter estimation challenges. To address this, Tim Bollerslev extended the ARCH model to the GARCH model in 1986, which models the variance with both past squared returns and past variances.

The standard form of the GARCH(p, q) model is given by:

$$\sigma_t^2 = \alpha_0 + \alpha_1 \epsilon_{t-1}^2 + \cdots + \alpha_q \epsilon_{t-q}^2 + \beta_1 \sigma_{t-1}^2 + \cdots + \beta_p \sigma_{t-p}^2,$$

where $\alpha_0 > 0$, $\alpha_i \geq 0$ for $i = 1, 2, \ldots, q$, and $\beta_j \geq 0$ for $j = 1, 2, \ldots, p$.

The GARCH model strikes a balance by capturing long-term and short-term volatility components efficiently. This mixed approach allows it to model financial time series with greater flexibility and fewer parameters compared to pure ARCH models.

To estimate these models, Maximum Likelihood Estimation (MLE) is commonly employed. Given the time series data $\{\epsilon_t\}$, the likelihood function for the GARCH model can be expressed as:

$$L(\theta) = \prod_{t=1}^{T} \frac{1}{\sqrt{2\pi\sigma_t^2}} \exp\left(-\frac{\epsilon_t^2}{2\sigma_t^2}\right),$$

where θ represents all the parameters in the GARCH model. Optimization techniques are then used to find the parameter values that maximize the likelihood function.

One important aspect of fitting these models is ensuring stationarity and positive variance. The stationarity condition for GARCH(1,1) requires $\alpha_1 + \beta_1 < 1$. For higher-order models, analogous conditions must be met to ensure the process will return to a constant mean and variance over time.

GARCH models have been expanded into numerous variants to capture different features of financial data. For example, the EGARCH (Exponential GARCH) model allows for asymmetric effects of positive and negative returns on volatility, which is particularly important in financial markets where, often, bad news increases volatility more than good news of the same magnitude. The EGARCH(1,1) model can be expressed as:

$$\log(\sigma_t^2) = \alpha_0 + \alpha_1 \frac{\epsilon_{t-1}}{\sigma_{t-1}} + \gamma \left[\left| \frac{\epsilon_{t-1}}{\sigma_{t-1}} \right| - E\left(\left| \frac{\epsilon_{t-1}}{\sigma_{t-1}} \right| \right) \right] + \beta_1 \log(\sigma_{t-1}^2),$$

where γ captures the asymmetric effect.

Another extension is the GJR-GARCH model, which incorporates a leverage effect, allowing different impacts of positive and negative shocks on volatility.

$$\sigma_t^2 = \alpha_0 + \alpha_1 \epsilon_{t-1}^2 + \gamma \epsilon_{t-1}^2 I_{\{\epsilon_{t-1}<0\}} + \beta_1 \sigma_{t-1}^2,$$

where $I_{\{\epsilon_{t-1}<0\}}$ is an indicator function that equals 1 if $\epsilon_{t-1} < 0$ and 0 otherwise.

By understanding the dynamics of volatility through these models, investors and analysts can better manage and forecast the risk associated with financial portfolios. When selecting an appropriate model, it is critical to consider the nature of the data, the economic context, and the specific requirements of the analysis being undertaken.

4.9 Forecasting with Time Series Models

Forecasting is a fundamental objective in time series analysis, aiming to predict future values based on previously observed data. Accurate forecasts are crucial for traders and investors to make informed decisions, manage risks, and optimize their portfolios. This section delves into the key methods and considerations for effective forecasting using time series models, particularly ARIMA and its variations, while integrating practical examples and guidelines.

The forecasting process begins by selecting an appropriate model, which typically hinges on the nature of the time series data and the desired forecasting horizon. ARIMA (AutoRegressive Integrated Moving Average) models are among the most popular for general-purpose time series forecasting due to their flexibility in handling various types of data patterns.

$$\text{ARIMA}(p,d,q) = AR(p) \text{ Integrated of order } d \text{ MA}(q)$$

Here, p represents the order of the autoregressive part, d the degree of differencing needed to make the series stationary, and q the order of the moving average part. The general form of an ARIMA model is:

$$(1-\phi_1 B-\phi_2 B^2-\ldots-\phi_p B^p)(1-B)^d y_t = (1+\theta_1 B+\theta_2 B^2+\ldots+\theta_q B^q)\epsilon_t$$

where B is the backshift operator, y_t represents the time series data, and ϵ_t symbolizes white noise.

Model Selection and Validation

Model selection involves iteratively fitting different ARIMA models and selecting the one with the best performance based on criteria such as the Akaike Information Criterion (AIC) or Bayesian Information Criterion (BIC).

To validate the selected model, it is essential to:

- **Split the Data:** Divide the time series into training and test sets. The training set is used to fit the model, while the test set evaluates the forecast accuracy.
- **Check Diagnostic Plots:** Examine residual plots to ensure they behave like white noise, confirming no significant patterns remain

in the residuals. Autocorrelation function (ACF) and partial autocorrelation function (PACF) plots of the residuals are helpful diagnostic tools.

- **Evaluate Metrics:** Use metrics like Mean Absolute Error (MAE), Mean Squared Error (MSE), or Root Mean Squared Error (RMSE) to quantify forecast accuracy.

Generating Forecasts

Once an ARIMA model is suitably validated, generating forecasts involves using the model's estimated parameters to predict future values. For illustration, consider a simple ARIMA(1,1,1) model applied to a financial time series y_t:

$$(1 - \phi_1 B)(1 - B)y_t = (1 + \theta_1 B)\epsilon_t$$

The forecasts can be computed iteratively starting from the end of the observed data. Let $\hat{y}_{t+h|t}$ denote the forecast of y at time $t + h$ based on data up to time t:

$$\hat{y}_{t+1|t} = y_t + \phi_1(y_t - y_{t-1}) + \theta_1\epsilon_t$$

More complex models, such as ARIMA with seasonal components (SARIMA), can be used when the data exhibit seasonal patterns. SARIMA models extend ARIMA by incorporating seasonality through additional seasonal differencing and seasonal AR and MA terms.

Using External Regressors

Sometimes, external regressors (exogenous variables) can improve forecast accuracy. These models are referred to as ARIMAX models. The general form of an ARIMAX model with an exogenous variable x_t is:

$$y_t = \beta x_t + \text{ARIMA}(p, d, q)$$

Integrating x_t captures additional exogenous information that might influence the time series, such as macroeconomic indicators, interest rates, or other relevant variables.

Practical Example

To illustrate, let's apply an ARIMA(1,1,1) model to forecast stock prices:

- **Data Preparation:** Collect the historical stock price data and perform differencing to make the series stationary.

- **Model Fitting:** Fit ARIMA(1,1,1) to the differenced data using the training set.

- **Diagnostics:** Examine residuals for randomness using ACF and PACF plots.

- **Forecasting:** Generate forecasts for the test set period and compare them against actual values.

The practical steps involve the following R or Python code snippet for fitting an ARIMA model and generating forecasts:

```
# R code example
library(forecast)
fit <- auto.arima(stock_prices)
forecasted_values <- forecast(fit, h=10)
plot(forecasted_values)
```

```
# Python code example
from statsmodels.tsa.arima.model import ARIMA
model = ARIMA(stock_prices, order=(1, 1, 1))
fit = model.fit()
forecasted_values = fit.forecast(steps=10)
plt.plot(forecasted_values)
```

Successful forecasting with time series models relies on a thorough understanding of the underlying data characteristics, rigorous model validation, and careful consideration of exogenous factors when relevant. These steps equip traders and investors with powerful tools for anticipating market movements and optimizing their strategies.

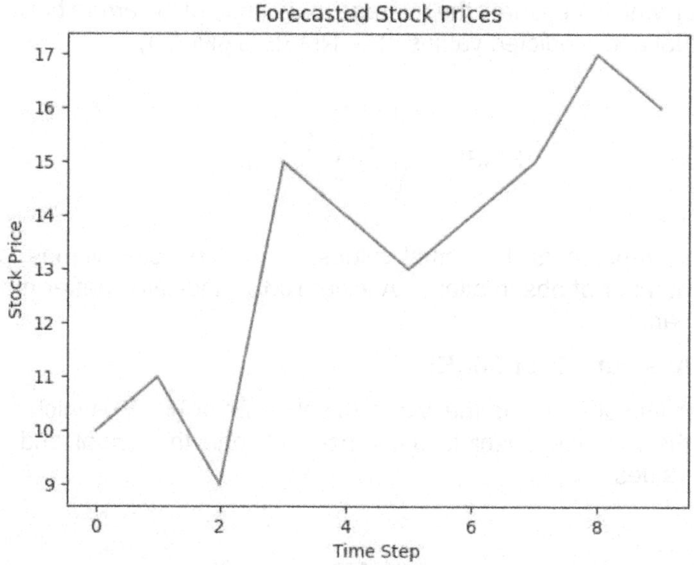

4.10 Model Evaluation and Diagnostics

Model evaluation and diagnostics are critical steps in the time series modeling process, ensuring that the chosen model adequately captures the underlying data structure and provides reliable forecasts. Without thoroughly evaluating and diagnosing our models, we risk deploying strategies based on flawed or suboptimal models, leading to potential financial losses and misinformed decisions.

Evaluating a time series model involves several key metrics and diagnostic checks. Let's delve into these tools and methods to ascertain the adequacy and performance of our models.

1. In-Sample and Out-of-Sample Performance

The performance of a time series model is typically evaluated using both in-sample and out-of-sample data. In-sample data consists of the data points used to build and estimate the model parameters, while out-of-sample data refers to a separate set of data points used to test the model's forecasting ability.

Root Mean Square Error (RMSE)

One of the most commonly used metrics is the Root Mean Square Error (RMSE), which measures the average magnitude of the errors between the actual and predicted values. The RMSE is given by:

$$\text{RMSE} = \sqrt{\frac{1}{N}\sum_{t=1}^{N}(y_t - \hat{y}_t)^2}$$

where y_t represents the actual values, $\hat{y}_t$ the predicted values, and N the number of observations. A lower RMSE indicates better model performance.

Mean Absolute Error (MAE)

Another useful metric is the Mean Absolute Error (MAE), which measures the average absolute difference between the actual and predicted values:

$$\text{MAE} = \frac{1}{N}\sum_{t=1}^{N}|y_t - \hat{y}_t|$$

The MAE, like the RMSE, provides insight into the model's prediction accuracy but is less sensitive to large errors.

2. Residual Analysis

The residuals, defined as the difference between the actual and predicted values ($e_t = y_t - \hat{y}_t$), are central to model diagnostics. Analyzing the residuals helps ensure that the model assumptions are not violated.

Autocorrelation Function (ACF) of Residuals

The residuals should ideally be white noise, meaning they should have a mean of zero, constant variance, and no autocorrelation. Plotting the autocorrelation function (ACF) of the residuals helps identify if any autocorrelations are present. Significant spikes in the ACF plot indicate that the residuals are not random and suggest that the model has not captured all the information in the data.

Ljung-Box Test

The Ljung-Box test provides a statistical test for the presence of autocorrelation in the residuals. The null hypothesis of the Ljung-Box test states that the residuals are independently distributed. The test statistic is given by:

$$Q = N(N+2)\sum_{k=1}^{h}\frac{\hat{\rho}_k^2}{N-k}$$

where $\hat{\rho}_k$ is the sample autocorrelation at lag k, N is the number of observations, and h is the number of lags being tested. A significant p-value (typically less than 0.05) indicates that the residuals are not independently distributed.

3. Normality of Residuals

Assuming normality in the residuals is important for predictive intervals and hypothesis testing. Assessing the normality can be done using visual methods such as Q-Q plots, where the sample quantiles of residuals are plotted against theoretical quantiles from a normal distribution. Additionally, statistical tests like the Shapiro-Wilk test can be applied:

$$W = \frac{\left(\sum_{i=1}^{n} a_i r_{(i)}\right)^2}{\sum_{i=1}^{n}(y_i - \bar{y})^2}$$

where a_i are constants derived from the sample size, $r_{(i)}$ are ordered residuals, y_i are residuals, and $\bar{y}$ is the mean of residuals. A significant p-value here also suggests deviation from normality.

4. Parameter Stability

The stability of parameter estimates over time is another crucial aspect. Methods like the CUSUM (Cumulative Sum) test can help identify parameter shifts. The CUSUM test plots the cumulative sum of residuals and detects changes in the mean level:

$$S_i = \sum_{j=1}^{i}(e_j - \bar{e})$$

where S_i is the cumulative sum at time i and $\bar{e}$ is the average residual. Significant deviations from zero indicate parameter instability.

5. Forecasting Accuracy

Finally, evaluating the model's forecasting accuracy is essential. Metrics like the out-of-sample RMSE and the Mean Absolute Percentage Error (MAPE) provide insight into the model's ability to generalize to unseen data:

$$\text{MAPE} = \frac{1}{N}\sum_{t=1}^{N}\left|\frac{y_t - \hat{y}_t}{y_t}\right| \times 100$$

Lower values of MAPE indicate more accurate forecasts.

By thoroughly applying these evaluation and diagnostic techniques, we can ensure our time series models are well-suited for predictive tasks, thereby enhancing our decision-making process and boosting confidence in our trading and investment strategies.

Chapter 5

Stochastic Processes in Finance

Stochastic processes are fundamental to modeling the random behavior of financial markets. This chapter introduces key concepts such as Brownian motion, stochastic differential equations, and geometric Brownian motion, which are crucial for option pricing and risk management. It covers martingales, Ito's Lemma, and stochastic calculus, offering insights into their applications in finance. The chapter also delves into mean-reverting processes and jump processes, providing a comprehensive understanding of complex financial phenomena and their practical implications.

5.1 Introduction to Stochastic Processes

In quantitative finance, stochastic processes form the backbone of many models used to describe and predict the behavior of financial markets. A stochastic process is essentially a collection of random variables indexed by time, which provides a mathematical framework for modeling the seemingly unpredictable movements observed in financial markets. These processes allow for the incorporation of randomness and uncertainty into models, enabling more realistic representations of asset prices, interest rates, and other financial variables.

To ground our discussion, let us consider a simple example. Suppose we observe the price of a stock at different times $t_1, t_2, \ldots, t_n$. The sequence of prices $\{S(t_1), S(t_2), \ldots, S(t_n)\}$ can be thought of as a realization of a stochastic process. Here, $S(t)$ denotes the price of the stock at time t. The key characteristic of a stochastic process is that $S(t)$ exhibits random behavior, influenced by a variety of factors ranging from macroeconomic indicators to company-specific news.

A formal definition of a stochastic process can be expressed as follows. Let $(\Omega, \mathcal{F}, \mathbb{P})$ be a probability space, where Ω is the sample space, $\mathcal{F}$ is the sigma-algebra representing the set of all possible events, and $\mathbb{P}$ is the probability measure. A stochastic process $\{X_t\}_{t \in T}$ is a family of random variables defined on this probability space, indexed by time $t \in T$. For simplicity, we often consider the index set T to be either the non-negative integers $\mathbb{N}_0$ or the non-negative reals $\mathbb{R}_+$, corresponding to discrete-time and continuous-time processes, respectively.

There are several types of stochastic processes, each with distinct characteristics and applications. Some of the most commonly encountered in finance include:

- **Brownian Motion:** Also known as Wiener process, Brownian motion is a continuous-time stochastic process that serves as a fundamental building block for many financial models. It is characterized by having continuous paths and stationary, independent increments.
- **Poisson Process:** This process is used to model the occurrence of discrete events over time, such as the arrival of orders or the occurrence of jumps in asset prices. The Poisson process has independent increments and the number of events occurring in a given interval follows a Poisson distribution.
- **Mean-Reverting Processes:** These processes, such as the Ornstein-Uhlenbeck process, are used to model variables that tend to revert to a long-term mean over time. They are particularly useful for modeling interest rates and volatility.
- **Geometric Brownian Motion:** Widely used in option pricing models, this process is a modification of Brownian motion that ensures the modeled variable, such as an asset price, remains non-negative.

To illustrate the concept of a stochastic process, consider the Brownian motion $W(t)$, which satisfies the following properties:

1. *Initial Condition:* $W(0) = 0$ with probability 1.
2. *Independent Increments:* For any $0 \leq t_1 < t_2 < \cdots < t_n$, the increments $W(t_2) - W(t_1)$, $W(t_3) - W(t_2)$, ..., $W(t_n) - W(t_{n-1})$ are independent.
3. *Stationary Increments:* The distribution of $W(t+s) - W(t)$ depends only on the length of the interval s.
4. *Normal Increments:* The increment $W(t+s) - W(t)$ is normally distributed with mean 0 and variance s, i.e., $W(t+s) - W(t) \sim \mathcal{N}(0, s)$.
5. *Continuous Paths:* $W(t)$ has continuous sample paths with probability 1.

This process plays a central role in financial models due to its simplicity and tractability. It underpins the Black-Scholes model for option pricing, among others.

A stochastic process can be described through its transition dynamics. For example, for a discrete-time process $\{X_t\}_{t \in \mathbb{N}_0}$, the transition probability $P(X_{t+1} \leq x \mid X_t = y)$ quantifies the probability that the process transitions from state y at time t to a state less than or equal to x at time $t+1$. For continuous-time processes, the transition probability density function $p(x, t+s \mid y, t)$ serves an analogous role.

In the study of stochastic processes, certain mathematical tools and results become indispensable. These include concepts such as:

- *Martingales:* A class of stochastic processes that generalize the notion of a fair game. For a process $\{M_t\}_{t \in T}$ to be a martingale with respect to a filtration $\{\mathcal{F}_t\}_{t \in T}$, it must satisfy the condition $\mathbb{E}[M_{t+s} \mid \mathcal{F}_t] = M_t$ for all $t, s \geq 0$.
- *Ito's Lemma:* A fundamental result in stochastic calculus that provides the differential of a function of a stochastic process. If $f(t, X(t))$ is a function of time t and a stochastic process $X(t)$ governed by the stochastic differential equation (SDE) $dX(t) = \mu(X(t), t)dt + \sigma(X(t), t)dW(t)$, then Ito's Lemma states:

$$df(t, X(t)) = \left(\frac{\partial f}{\partial t} + \mu(X(t), t)\frac{\partial f}{\partial X} + \frac{1}{2}\sigma^2(X(t), t)\frac{\partial^2 f}{\partial X^2} \right) dt + \sigma(X(t), t)\frac{\partial f}{\partial X} dW(t).$$

- *Stochastic Integrals:* Integration with respect to stochastic processes, primarily Brownian motion, leading to results central to financial modeling and derivative pricing.

By understanding and leveraging stochastic processes, traders and financial analysts can develop more sophisticated models that more accurately reflect the dynamics of financial markets. This foundational knowledge enables the calculation of probabilities, the pricing of complex derivatives, and the effective management of financial risks.

Continuing from this introductory understanding, the next sections will delve deeper into specific types of stochastic processes and their applications in finance, building a robust framework for mastering mathematical models crucial for market success.

5.2 Brownian Motion and Wiener Processes

The concept of Brownian motion, also known as a Wiener process, is paramount in the landscape of financial modeling. This stochastic process models the random movement of particles suspended in a fluid, historically observed by the botanist Robert Brown in 1827. In finance, Brownian motion is extensively employed to describe the unpredictable paths of asset prices, making it a cornerstone of modern quantitative finance.

A Wiener process, $W(t)$, is a type of Brownian motion that satisfies specific mathematical properties, making it exceptionally suitable for financial applications. The essential characteristics of a Wiener process are:

- **Initial Value:** $W(0) = 0$.
- **Independent Increments:** For any $0 \leq t_1 < t_2 < \ldots < t_n$, the increments $W(t_{i+1}) - W(t_i)$ are independent random variables.
- **Normality of Increments:** For any $s < t$, the increment $W(t) - W(s) \sim \mathcal{N}(0, t - s)$, meaning it follows a normal distribution with mean 0 and variance $t - s$.
- **Continuous Paths:** The function $t \mapsto W(t)$ is almost surely continuous.

These properties are foundational in formulating the behavior of stock prices and other financial variables in a stochastic setting. Next, we delve into the mathematical formulation and interpretation of these characteristics.

Mathematical Formulation:

Brownian motion $B(t)$, or Wiener process $W(t)$, can be formally defined using stochastic calculus. The differential form is expressed as:

$$dW(t) = \epsilon\sqrt{dt},$$

where $\epsilon \sim \mathcal{N}(0,1)$ is a standard normal random variable. This representation highlights that the change in $W(t)$ over an infinitesimal time interval dt is normally distributed with mean 0 and variance dt.

Connection to Financial Modeling:

In financial markets, asset prices do not follow simple deterministic trajectories; they exhibit random fluctuations driven by a myriad of unpredictable factors. The Wiener process is instrumental in modeling these random fluctuations. When we describe the price of a stock $S(t)$ under the influence of Brownian motion, we often see the process illustrated as:

$$S(t) = S(0)\exp\left(\left(\mu - \frac{\sigma^2}{2}\right)t + \sigma W(t)\right),$$

where μ represents the drift rate (expected return), and σ denotes the volatility of the stock (standard deviation of returns).

Practical Implementation:

To simulate a Wiener process in practice, one can use a discrete-time approximation. Consider a time interval $[0,T]$ divided into n small increments of length $\Delta t = \frac{T}{n}$. The Wiener process can be discretely approximated by:

$$W_{t_{i+1}} = W_{t_i} + \epsilon_i\sqrt{\Delta t}, \quad i = 0, 1, \ldots, n-1,$$

where ϵ_i are independent standard normal random variables. This series of steps can be visualized and computed efficiently using numerical methods or computing software.

Geometric Interpretation:

Brownian motion charts the path of continuous, irregular motion, encapsulating the erratic behavior of asset prices over time. This intrinsic property is pivotal for traders and portfolio managers in understanding risk and formulating strategies.

Applications in Financial Instruments:

One prominent application of Wiener processes is in the Black-Scholes option pricing model, which defines the dynamics of asset prices using geometric Brownian motion. This model underpins the pricing of derivatives and risk management strategies.

Another critical use is in the construction of Monte Carlo simulations for pricing complex financial derivatives and managing risk. Here, the random paths generated by Wiener processes provide insight into the probable future values of financial instruments, allowing traders to make data-driven decisions.

Understanding Brownian motion and Wiener processes equips investors with a powerful framework for predicting market behavior, assessing risk, and implementing robust financial strategies. With their profound implications across various financial domains, mastery of these stochastic processes is indispensable for sophisticated traders and investors.

5.3 Stochastic Differential Equations (SDEs)

Stochastic Differential Equations (SDEs) are a pivotal tool in financial modeling, offering a robust mathematical framework to describe the evolution of variables subjected to random influences. These equations extend ordinary differential equations (ODEs) by incorporating stochastic terms, typically represented by Brownian motion or other stochastic processes.

To understand the essence of SDEs, let us first consider a general form of the equation:

$$dX_t = \mu(X_t, t)dt + \sigma(X_t, t)dW_t,$$

where X_t represents the stochastic process of interest, $\mu(X_t, t)$ is the drift term indicating the deterministic trend, $\sigma(X_t, t)$ is the diffusion term capturing the random fluctuations, and W_t denotes a standard Brownian motion.

- **Drift and Diffusion Terms**

  The drift term $\mu(X_t, t)$ can be interpreted as the expected rate of change of the process over an infinitesimally small time interval dt. It dictates the systematic part of the process's movement.

  The diffusion term $\sigma(X_t, t)$ scales the random shocks introduced by dW_t, where dW_t is the increment of the standard Brownian motion representing the stochastic component. This Brownian increment has properties $\mathbb{E}[dW_t] = 0$ and Var$(dW_t) = dt$.

- **Solving SDEs**

  To solve an SDE analytically or numerically, an initial condition X_0 is necessary. In many financial applications, explicit solutions are challenging, and therefore numerical methods such as Euler-Maruyama or Milstein schemes are employed. Below is an illustration of the Euler-Maruyama method for approximating solutions to SDEs:

  $$X_{t+\Delta t} \approx X_t + \mu(X_t, t)\Delta t + \sigma(X_t, t)\Delta W_t,$$

  where Δt is a discrete time step, and $\Delta W_t \sim \mathcal{N}(0, \Delta t)$.

- **Example: The Black-Scholes Model**

  A classic example of an SDE in finance is the Black-Scholes model, which underpins option pricing theory. It describes the price dynamics S_t of a stock as follows:

  $$dS_t = \mu S_t dt + \sigma S_t dW_t,$$

  where μ is the drift coefficient, σ is the volatility of the stock, and W_t is a standard Brownian motion. By applying Ito's Lemma and solving the resulting SDE, the Black-Scholes formula for pricing European call and put options is derived.

- **Multidimensional SDEs**

  In practice, financial models often involve multiple interrelated variables, necessitating the use of multidimensional SDEs. A system of SDEs can be written as:

  $$d\boldsymbol{X}_t = \boldsymbol{\mu}(\boldsymbol{X}_t, t)dt + \boldsymbol{\Sigma}(\boldsymbol{X}_t, t)d\boldsymbol{W}_t,$$

  where $\boldsymbol{X}_t$ is a vector of processes, $\boldsymbol{\mu}$ is a vector of drift terms, $\boldsymbol{\Sigma}$ is a matrix of diffusion terms, and $\boldsymbol{W}_t$ is a vector of correlated Brownian motions.

- **Practical Applications**

SDEs are profoundly beneficial for modeling various financial phenomena, such as interest rates via the Vasicek or CIR models, exchange rates, and commodities prices. The Vasicek model, as an example, describes the evolution of interest rates with mean reversion characteristics:

$$dr_t = \theta(\mu - r_t)dt + \sigma dW_t,$$

where r_t is the interest rate, θ is the speed of mean reversion, μ is the long-term mean level, and σ is the volatility.

By defining the dynamics of financial variables through SDEs, we gain a powerful means to simulate future states and assess the risk and return profiles, which are indispensable for making informed investment decisions. Incorporating stochastic elements into differential equations reflects a more realistic outlook on financial markets, where uncertainty and volatility are pervasive.

5.4 Geometric Brownian Motion

Geometric Brownian Motion (GBM) is a fundamental model in quantitative finance used to describe the stochastic process underlying the price evolution of financial assets such as stocks. This model is pivotal due to its ability to capture the continuous and multiplicative nature of returns, as well as its analytical tractability. A deep understanding of GBM is essential for implementing various financial models, particularly in the realm of option pricing.

At its core, the GBM assumes that the logarithm of the price of a financial asset follows a Brownian motion with drift. Mathematically, the evolution of the asset price S_t under GBM can be expressed as a stochastic differential equation (SDE):

$$dS_t = \mu S_t \, dt + \sigma S_t \, dW_t$$

Here:

- S_t denotes the asset price at time t.
- μ is the drift coefficient, representing the expected rate of return of the asset.

- σ is the volatility coefficient, capturing the standard deviation of the asset's returns.
- W_t represents a standard Wiener process or Brownian motion.

The SDE characterizes the instantaneous change in the asset price dS_t as the sum of two components:

- $\mu S_t\,dt$, the deterministic part representing the growth rate of the asset price.
- $\sigma S_t\,dW_t$, the stochastic part capturing the uncertainty due to market volatility.

To gain deeper insights, we can solve the above SDE using Ito's calculus. Applying Ito's Lemma, the solution to this SDE is given by:

$$S_t = S_0 \exp\left(\left(\mu - \frac{\sigma^2}{2}\right)t + \sigma W_t\right)$$

This solution reveals several important characteristics of GBM:

- The term $\left(\mu - \frac{\sigma^2}{2}\right)$ represents the adjusted drift, accounting for the volatility.
- σW_t captures the stochastic shocks to the asset price.

One of the key motivations for using GBM in financial modeling is its adherence to the properties of real financial markets:

- **Non-negativity**: S_t remains positive since it is an exponential function, aligning with the reality that asset prices cannot be negative.
- **Log-normal distribution**: The asset price S_t follows a log-normal distribution, meaning that $\log(S_t)$ is normally distributed. This property is consistent with empirical observations of asset returns.

In practical applications, the GBM provides the foundation for the Black-Scholes-Merton model for option pricing. By assuming that the underlying asset follows a GBM, the Black-Scholes formula offers a closed-form solution for pricing European options, thereby facilitating efficient market operations.

Consider an example where we price a European call option using the Black-Scholes formula. Let:

- S_0 be the current stock price.
- K be the strike price.
- T be the time to maturity.
- r be the risk-free interest rate.
- σ be the volatility of the stock.

The price C of the European call option is given by:

$$C = S_0 N(d_1) - K e^{-rT} N(d_2)$$

where:

$$d_1 = \frac{\log\left(\frac{S_0}{K}\right) + \left(r + \frac{\sigma^2}{2}\right) T}{\sigma\sqrt{T}}$$

$$d_2 = d_1 - \sigma\sqrt{T}$$

and $N(\cdot)$ represents the cumulative distribution function of the standard normal distribution.

This example underscores the practical significance of GBM in financial modeling, particularly for derivatives pricing.

Understanding GBM and its applications extends beyond theoretical knowledge. It equips traders and analysts with robust tools to model price movements, assess risk, and devise hedging strategies. The continuous-time modeling capability of GBM suits various complex financial instruments, making it indispensable in the modern finance toolkit.

5.5 Martingales in Finance

A martingale is a powerful concept in the probability theory applied extensively in financial modeling. In the context of finance, a martingale is a stochastic process where the conditional expectation of the next value, given all prior values, is equal to the present value. This property makes martingales central to the study of fair games and efficient markets, where the future price movements are theoretically unpredictable based on current information.

Initially, let's denote a stochastic process $\{X_t\}_{t\geq 0}$ adapted to a filtration $\{\mathcal{F}_t\}_{t\geq 0}$, signifying that X_t is measurable with respect to the information available up to time t. The process $\{X_t\}$ is a martingale if for all $t \geq 0$,

$$\mathbb{E}[X_{t+s} \mid \mathcal{F}_t] = X_t \quad \text{for all } s \geq 0.$$

This equation implies that the best estimate of the future value X_{t+s}, given the present information $\mathcal{F}_t$, is simply X_t, underscoring no systematic tendency to rise or fall.

In financial applications, martingales are instrumental in the modeling of asset prices under the assumption of no arbitrage. The Martingale Representation Theorem plays a crucial role here, stating that any martingale can be represented as an integral with respect to a Brownian motion, given certain technical conditions.

Consider the pricing of financial derivatives. Suppose an asset price process S_t follows the dynamics described by a geometric Brownian motion in a risk-neutral world. The risk-neutral valuation allows us to express the discounted price process as a martingale. Assume that S_t evolves according to the stochastic differential equation (SDE):

$$dS_t = S_t(rdt + \sigma dW_t),$$

where r is the risk-free rate, σ is the volatility, and W_t represents a standard Brownian motion. In this framework, the discounted asset price $\tilde{S}_t = e^{-rt}S_t$ should exhibit martingale properties. To show this, we apply Ito's Lemma to $\tilde{S}_t$:

$$d\tilde{S}_t = \frac{\partial \tilde{S}_t}{\partial S_t} dS_t + \frac{\partial \tilde{S}_t}{\partial t} dt + \frac{1}{2} \frac{\partial^2 \tilde{S}_t}{\partial S_t^2} dS_t^2.$$

Since $\tilde{S}_t = e^{-rt}S_t$, partial derivatives yield:

$$\frac{\partial \tilde{S}_t}{\partial S_t} = e^{-rt}, \quad \frac{\partial \tilde{S}_t}{\partial t} = -re^{-rt}S_t, \quad \text{and} \quad dS_t^2 = \sigma^2 S_t^2 dt.$$

Substituting these into Ito's lemma:

$$d\tilde{S}_t = e^{-rt}dS_t - re^{-rt}S_tdt + \frac{1}{2}\sigma^2 S_t^2 e^{-rt}dt.$$

Replacing dS_t with its SDE,

$$d\tilde{S}_t = e^{-rt}S_t(rdt + \sigma dW_t) - re^{-rt}S_tdt + \frac{1}{2}\sigma^2 S_t^2 e^{-rt}dt.$$

This simplifies to:

$$d\tilde{S}_t = e^{-rt}S_t\sigma dW_t,$$

which is a martingale because its expectation, conditional on existing information, remains its current value.

Martingales are not only theoretical constructs but also practical tools in trading strategies. For instance, in the design of hedging strategies, the martingale property ensures that the value of the portfolio — constructed dynamically through trading — remains fair, neither over- nor under-priced given current market conditions.

In option pricing models such as the Black-Scholes framework, the concept of a martingale under the risk-neutral measure is foundational. Here, the price of an option is the expected present value of its payoff, discounted at the risk-free rate under the risk-neutral measure. Let $C(S_t, t)$ denote the price of a European call option, where S_t is the underlying asset price and t represents time. The payoff at maturity T is $\max(S_T - K, 0)$, where K is the strike price. The risk-neutral valuation formula is given by:

$$C(S_t, t) = e^{-r(T-t)}\mathbb{E}^Q[\max(S_T - K, 0) \mid \mathcal{F}_t],$$

where $\mathbb{E}^Q$ denotes expectation under the risk-neutral measure Q.

Martingales also underpin more advanced financial models, such as exotic options pricing and the construction of interest rate models. The Heath-Jarrow-Morton (HJM) framework for modeling forward interest rates utilizes martingales to ensure no arbitrage, applying them to evolve the entire forward rate curve consistently over time.

Understanding martingales' theoretical aspects lays a robust foundation for comprehensively grasping their practical implications in financial markets. By leveraging the martingale property, one ensures that pricing models are aligned with the principle of no arbitrage, thus maintaining model consistency and integrity in predicting future market dynamics.

5.6 Ito's Lemma and Its Applications

In stochastic processes, Ito's Lemma stands as a cornerstone for the application of calculus to random functions, particularly those driven by Brownian motion. This powerful tool facilitates the transformation of stochastic differential equations (SDEs) and underpins many crucial models in quantitative finance.

To comprehend Ito's Lemma, consider a function $f(t, X_t)$ where X_t is a stochastic process. Suppose X_t follows the SDE:

$$dX_t = \mu(X_t, t)dt + \sigma(X_t, t)dW_t$$

where W_t denotes the Wiener process (standard Brownian motion), μ is the drift term, and σ is the diffusion term.

Ito's Lemma provides the differential of $f(t, X_t)$ as:

$$df(t, X_t) = \left(\frac{\partial f}{\partial t} + \frac{\partial f}{\partial X_t}\mu + \frac{1}{2}\frac{\partial^2 f}{\partial X_t^2}\sigma^2\right) dt + \frac{\partial f}{\partial X_t}\sigma dW_t$$

The lemma essentially extends the classic chain rule to stochastic calculus, accommodating the presence of the stochastic component dW_t. The additional term $\frac{1}{2}\frac{\partial^2 f}{\partial X_t^2}\sigma^2 dt$ captures the variance introduced by the underlying Brownian motion.

To illustrate Ito's Lemma, let us apply it to the geometric Brownian motion, X_t, given by the SDE:

$$dX_t = \mu X_t dt + \sigma X_t dW_t$$

Consider the function $f(X_t) = \ln(X_t)$. According to Ito's Lemma:

$$df(X_t) = \left(\frac{\partial f}{\partial X_t}\mu X_t + \frac{1}{2}\frac{\partial^2 f}{\partial X_t^2}\sigma^2 X_t^2\right) dt + \frac{\partial f}{\partial X_t}\sigma X_t dW_t$$

First, compute the required partial derivatives:

$$\frac{\partial f}{\partial X_t} = \frac{1}{X_t}, \quad \text{and} \quad \frac{\partial^2 f}{\partial X_t^2} = -\frac{1}{X_t^2}$$

Thus, substituting back in gives:

$$d(\ln(X_t)) = \left(\frac{1}{X_t}(\mu X_t) + \frac{1}{2}\left(-\frac{1}{X_t^2}\right)\sigma^2 X_t^2\right) dt + \frac{1}{X_t}(\sigma X_t) dW_t$$

$$= \left(\mu - \frac{\sigma^2}{2}\right) dt + \sigma dW_t$$

This result is an expression of the differential of the logarithm of the process X_t, illustrating how volatility impacts the drift term through Ito's correction term $-\frac{\sigma^2}{2}$.

The applications of Ito's Lemma are vast and profoundly impactful in quantitative finance. One paramount application is in deriving the Black-Scholes equation for option pricing. Assuming a stock price S_t following the geometric Brownian motion:

$$dS_t = \mu S_t dt + \sigma S_t dW_t$$

For a European call option with payoff $\max(S_T - K, 0)$, the option price $C(t, S_t)$ depends on both t and S_t. Applying Ito's Lemma to $C(t, S_t)$:

$$dC = \left(\frac{\partial C}{\partial t} + \mu S_t \frac{\partial C}{\partial S_t} + \frac{1}{2}\sigma^2 S_t^2 \frac{\partial^2 C}{\partial S_t^2}\right) dt + \sigma S_t \frac{\partial C}{\partial S_t} dW_t$$

By constructing a risk-neutral portfolio and following the no-arbitrage argument, it leads to the famous Black-Scholes partial differential equation (PDE):

$$\frac{\partial C}{\partial t} + r S_t \frac{\partial C}{\partial S_t} + \frac{1}{2}\sigma^2 S_t^2 \frac{\partial^2 C}{\partial S_t^2} = rC$$

where r is the risk-free rate.

Ito's Lemma is similarly employed in evaluating other financial derivatives, calculating sensitivities (the 'Greeks'), and constructing hedging strategies. It also extends to exotic options and real options analysis, solidifying its status as an indispensable asset in the toolkit of financial engineers.

Understanding and applying Ito's Lemma equips traders and investors with sophisticated methods to model and analyze financial instruments subjected to stochastic behaviors, ultimately fostering more informed and strategic decision-making in the dynamic landscape of quantitative finance.

5.7 Stochastic Calculus

Stochastic calculus forms the backbone of modern quantitative finance, providing the mathematical framework necessary for modeling the randomness inherent in financial markets. Unlike deterministic calculus, stochastic calculus handles functions that evolve over time with inherent randomness. This section delves into the essential elements of stochastic calculus, such as Itô integrals and Itô's Lemma, which are integral to the modeling of financial derivatives and risk management.

The foundation of stochastic calculus lies in the Itô integral. For a given stochastic process X_t and a standard Brownian motion W_t, the Itô integral $\int_0^t X_s\,dW_s$ represents the integral of X with respect to W over the interval $[0,t]$. The key property of the Itô integral is its non-deterministic nature, fundamentally distinguishing it from the classic Riemann-Stieltjes integral.
To illustrate, consider a simple Itô integral:

$$\int_0^t X_s\,dW_s.$$

Here, X_s is an adapted process, meaning its value at any time s depends only on information available up to that point. The integral above accumulates increments that depend critically on the path taken by the Brownian motion W_t, thus embedding uncertainty into the integral's outcome.

A pivotal result in stochastic calculus is Itô's Lemma, which serves as the stochastic calculus counterpart to the chain rule in deterministic calculus. Itô's Lemma allows us to express the differential of a function $f(X_t,t)$, where X_t is a stochastic process. If X_t follows a stochastic differential equation (SDE) of the form:

$$dX_t = \mu(X_t,t)\,dt + \sigma(X_t,t)\,dW_t,$$

then Itô's Lemma states that:

$$df(X_t, t) = \frac{\partial f}{\partial t}\,dt + \frac{\partial f}{\partial X}\,dX_t + \frac{1}{2}\frac{\partial^2 f}{\partial X^2}\sigma^2(X_t, t)\,dt.$$

By applying this lemma, we can derive the dynamics of complex functions of stochastic processes, which is critical in option pricing and other financial applications.

As an applied example, consider the Black-Scholes model, a cornerstone in financial derivatives pricing. In this model, the price of a stock S_t is assumed to follow a geometric Brownian motion:

$$dS_t = \mu S_t\,dt + \sigma S_t\,dW_t,$$

where μ is the drift rate and σ is the volatility. Applying Itô's Lemma to the function $f(S_t, t) = \ln(S_t)$, we get:

$$df(S_t, t) = \frac{\partial \ln(S_t)}{\partial t}\,dt + \frac{\partial \ln(S_t)}{\partial S_t}\,dS_t + \frac{1}{2}\frac{\partial^2 \ln(S_t)}{\partial S_t^2}\sigma^2 S_t^2\,dt.$$

Simplifying the partial derivatives and substituting the SDE yields:

$$d\ln(S_t) = \left(\mu - \frac{\sigma^2}{2}\right)dt + \sigma dW_t.$$

This result exemplifies how stochastic calculus facilitates the transformation of financial models, translating them into forms that are mathematically tractable and practically applicable.

A more complex yet essential application involves deriving pricing formulas for financial derivatives such as options. The celebrated Black-Scholes formula for a European call option price is a consequence of solving the Black-Scholes partial differential equation (PDE) derived through Itô's Lemma.

To sum up, stochastic calculus is indispensable for quantitative finance. Itô integrals and Itô's Lemma enable precise manipulation and modeling of stochastic processes, making them invaluable tools for pricing derivatives, managing risk, and formulating trading strategies.

5.8 Applications of Stochastic Processes in Option Pricing

Stochastic processes play a pivotal role in the pricing of options, as they provide a framework to model the random behavior of underlying financial assets. Options are financial derivatives whose value is contingent on the price of an underlying asset, such as stocks, commodities, or indices. The valuation of these derivatives requires a robust mathematical model to capture the inherent uncertainty and risk of financial markets. In this section, we delve into several applications of stochastic processes in option pricing, demystifying complex theories and presenting practical strategies.

Black-Scholes-Merton Model The cornerstone of modern option pricing is the Black-Scholes-Merton (BSM) model, which leverages a specific type of stochastic process known as geometric Brownian motion (GBM). The BSM model was a pioneering approach, formulated by Fischer Black, Myron Scholes, and Robert Merton, to determine the price of European-style options.

The underlying asset price S_t is assumed to follow a GBM, characterized by the stochastic differential equation (SDE):

$$dS_t = \mu S_t \, dt + \sigma S_t \, dW_t \tag{5.1}$$

where μ represents the drift rate, σ the volatility, and W_t is a standard Wiener process (Brownian motion).

Using the principles of stochastic calculus, the BSM model derives the pricing formula for a European call option as:

$$C = S_0 \Phi(d_1) - K e^{-rT} \Phi(d_2) \tag{5.2}$$

with

$$d_1 = \frac{\ln(S_0/K) + (r + \sigma^2/2)T}{\sigma\sqrt{T}} \quad \text{and} \quad d_2 = d_1 - \sigma\sqrt{T} \tag{5.3}$$

Here, S_0 is the current price of the underlying asset, K the strike price, T the time to maturity, r the risk-free interest rate, and Φ the cumulative distribution function of the standard normal distribution. This model elegantly captures the nuances of option pricing under the assumption of log-normally distributed asset prices and continuous trading.

Risk-Neutral Valuation A crucial concept in option pricing is the risk-neutral measure, which simplifies the valuation by transforming the actual probability measure to a risk-neutral one. Under the risk-neutral measure $\mathbb{Q}$, the expected return of the underlying asset equals the risk-free rate, eliminating the need to estimate the risk premium. The asset price S_t under the risk-neutral measure follows:

$$dS_t = rS_t\,dt + \sigma S_t\,dW_t^{\mathbb{Q}} \tag{5.4}$$

The risk-neutral valuation principle asserts that the present value of the option is the discounted expected payoff under $\mathbb{Q}$:

$$C = e^{-rT}\mathbb{E}^{\mathbb{Q}}[\text{Payoff}] \tag{5.5}$$

For a European call option, the payoff at maturity T is $\max(S_T - K, 0)$. Therefore, the option price is:

$$C = e^{-rT}\mathbb{E}^{\mathbb{Q}}[\max(S_T - K, 0)] \tag{5.6}$$

By leveraging stochastic processes, we can evaluate this expectation, leading to the well-known BSM formula.

Alternative Stochastic Models While the BSM model is foundational, it relies on the assumption of constant volatility, which is often refuted by market observations exhibiting volatility clustering and jumps. Hence, several alternative models have been proposed to address these limitations.

One such model is the Heston model, which incorporates stochastic volatility by allowing the variance of the underlying asset to follow its own mean-reverting stochastic process:

$$dS_t = \mu S_t\,dt + \sqrt{v_t}S_t\,dW_t^S \tag{5.7}$$

$$dv_t = \kappa(\theta - v_t)\,dt + \xi\sqrt{v_t}\,dW_t^v \tag{5.8}$$

where v_t represents the stochastic variance, κ the rate of mean reversion, θ the long-term variance, ξ the volatility of variance, and W_t^S and W_t^v are correlated Wiener processes with correlation coefficient ρ.

This model better captures the empirical characteristics of financial markets, such as the volatility smile. Numerical techniques, like Monte Carlo simulations or Fourier transform methods, are typically employed to price options under stochastic volatility models due to their analytical complexity.

Jump-Diffusion Models Another significant extension involves incorporating jumps into the asset price dynamics, envisioning abrupt jumps in asset prices alongside the continuous diffusion process. The Merton jump-diffusion model is formulated as:

$$dS_t = (\mu - \lambda k)S_t\,dt + \sigma S_t\,dW_t + S_t(J-1)dN_t \tag{5.9}$$

where J represents the random jump size, N_t a Poisson process with intensity λ, and $k = \mathbb{E}[J-1]$ the average relative jump size. The term λk adjusts for the jump risk.

In jump-diffusion models, the option pricing problem entails evaluating expectations under a compound Poisson process, often utilizing Fourier-transform techniques or characteristic functions.

The richness of stochastic processes and their ability to model the intricate behavior of financial markets make them indispensable tools in modern option pricing. By tailoring these models to capture various market phenomena, investors and financial engineers can more precisely determine the value of complex derivatives, enhancing their risk management and trading strategies.

5.9 Mean-Reverting Processes

Mean-reverting processes are essential stochastic models used in finance, particularly in the context of interest rates, foreign exchange rates, and commodity prices. A mean-reverting process describes a system where the variable tends to move towards its historical average or long-term mean over time. This characteristic can be crucial for modeling assets that do not necessarily follow a purely random walk, providing a more realistic approach to certain financial instruments.

A commonly used mean-reverting process is the Ornstein-Uhlenbeck (OU) process. The OU process is defined by the following stochastic differential equation (SDE):

$$dX_t = \theta(\mu - X_t)\,dt + \sigma\,dW_t,$$

where:

- X_t is the state variable at time t,
- θ is the rate of reversion to the mean,
- μ is the long-term mean or equilibrium level,
- σ is the volatility of the process, and
- W_t is a standard Wiener process (or Brownian motion).

The term $\theta(\mu - X_t)$ in the equation represents the drift component of the process, which drives the variable X_t towards the mean μ. The strength of this drift increases as the distance from the mean μ becomes larger. The second term $\sigma\, dW_t$ captures the random fluctuations around the mean due to the inherent market volatility.

To understand the implications and applications of mean-reverting processes, let's explore some practical examples and conduct a deeper analysis.

Long-Term Stability: The Concept of Mean Reversion

The essence of mean reversion lies in its property of long-term stability. Unlike geometric Brownian motion, which assumes that the price of an asset undergoes a continuous exponential growth process, mean-reverting processes are designed for scenarios where the prices oscillate around a historical mean. This property makes them suitable for modeling interest rates with the Vasicek model, given by:

$$dr_t = a(b - r_t)dt + \sigma\, dW_t,$$

where:

- r_t is the short-term interest rate at time t,
- a is the speed of mean reversion,
- b is the long-term mean rate,
- σ is the volatility of interest rates, and
- W_t is a standard Wiener process.

The Vasicek model captures the mean-reverting nature of interest rates by bringing rates back toward the mean level b with a speed a.

Calibration and Estimation in Practice

To apply a mean-reverting model like the OU process, it is essential to calibrate the parameters θ, μ, and σ through historical data. This involves statistical techniques, such as Maximum Likelihood Estimation (MLE) or Generalized Method of Moments (GMM). The calibration process ensures that the model accurately reflects the empirical behavior of the financial time series being studied.

Consider a data set of daily commodity prices. The first step is to estimate the long-term mean μ from the historical price series. Next, the rate of mean reversion θ and volatility σ can be estimated by fitting the SDE to the observed price changes. This process involves solving the likelihood function derived from the stochastic differential equation.

Practical Application: Trading Strategies

Mean-reverting properties can be leveraged to develop profitable trading strategies. One common approach is statistical arbitrage, where the mean reversion characteristic is exploited by buying undervalued securities and selling overvalued ones, expecting their prices to revert to the mean. Pairs trading is a popular form of statistical arbitrage where two historically correlated assets are traded together. When the price ratio of the pair diverges significantly from its historical mean, a trading signal is generated.

For instance, if two stocks, A and B, historically maintain a mean-reverting price spread, an observed significant deviation might suggest an opportunity: sell the outperforming stock and buy the underperforming one. When the spread narrows, positions are closed for a profit.

Limitations and Considerations

While mean-reverting processes provide a structured way to model certain financial phenomena, their applicability has limitations. Not all financial time series exhibit mean-reverting behavior; some may follow trends or experience regime shifts. It is critical to perform thorough data analysis and hypothesis testing to confirm the mean-reverting characteristics of a particular series before employing these models.

Mean-reverting models also assume continuous adjustment toward the mean, which might not hold in markets with abrupt shifts or jumps. In such cases, models incorporating jump processes or regime-switching might be more appropriate.

By understanding the dynamics and practical applications of mean-reverting processes, traders and investors can better model and predict the behavior of financial instruments, enhancing their strategy formulation and risk management techniques.

5.10 Jump Processes and Poisson Processes

In financial modeling, jump processes play a crucial role in capturing sudden and significant movements in asset prices that cannot be explained by continuous models alone. Unlike the smooth paths of Brownian motion, jump processes contain discontinuities that align more closely with real market behaviors such as stock prices leaping due to unexpected news or economic events. Among the various types of jump processes, Poisson processes provide a foundational framework for understanding and modeling these jumps.

The Poisson process is a stochastic process that counts the number of events that occur in a fixed interval of time. These events are assumed to happen independently of one another, and the process has increments that are both stationary and independent. For a Poisson process $\{N(t) : t \geq 0\}$ with rate $\lambda > 0$, the number of jumps in any interval of length t follows a Poisson distribution with parameter λt.

The probability mass function (PMF) for a Poisson random variable $N(t)$, which denotes the number of jumps in the interval $[0, t]$, is given by:

$$P(N(t) = k) = \frac{(\lambda t)^k e^{-\lambda t}}{k!}, \quad k = 0, 1, 2, \ldots$$

where λ is the rate parameter, representing the average number of jumps per unit time.

The memoryless property of the Poisson process is particularly useful in financial contexts, indicating that the waiting time until the next jump is exponentially distributed and independent of when the last jump occurred. If the waiting time until the first jump is denoted by a random variable T_1, it follows that:

$$P(T_1 > t) = e^{-\lambda t}, \quad t \geq 0$$

The exponential distribution of waiting times simplifies the analytical treatment of jump processes.

When modeling financial assets, a common approach is to incorporate jumps into the classic Geometric Brownian Motion (GBM) model, resulting in a Jump-Diffusion model. The Jump-Diffusion model, proposed by Merton, describes the price dynamics of an asset $S(t)$ by combining both continuous diffusion and discrete jumps:

$$dS(t) = \mu S(t)dt + \sigma S(t)dW(t) + S(t^-)(e^{J_i} - 1)dN(t)$$

where:

- μ is the drift rate of the continuous part.
- σ is the volatility of the continuous part.
- $W(t)$ is a standard Brownian motion.
- $N(t)$ is a Poisson process with rate λ.
- J_i are i.i.d random variables representing the percentage jump sizes, typically assumed to be normally distributed, i.e., $J_i \sim N(\mu_J, \sigma_J^2)$.
- $S(t^-)$ denotes the asset price just before the jump at time t.

The term $S(t^-)(e^{J_i} - 1)dN(t)$ captures the magnitude and effect of the jumps: when a jump occurs, the asset price jumps instantly by a factor of $e^{J_i} - 1$.

To solve and simulate such models, consider a time discretization approach. Over a small time increment Δt, we can approximate the changes in the asset price as:

$$\Delta S \approx \mu S(t)\Delta t + \sigma S(t)\Delta W(t) + S(t)[(e^J - 1)\Delta N(t)]$$

where $\Delta W(t)$ is the increment in a standard Brownian motion (typically drawn from a normal distribution $N(0, \Delta t)$) and $\Delta N(t)$ is the increment in the Poisson process (typically drawn from a Poisson distribution $Pois(\lambda\Delta t)$). If $\Delta N(t) = 1$, a jump occurs during the interval Δt; otherwise, $\Delta N(t) = 0$ signifies no jump.

Jump processes extend beyond Poisson processes. Another frequently used jump process is the compound Poisson process, where the jump sizes are randomized, typically modeled by another stochastic process. This compound nature allows flexibility in modeling various distributions of jump sizes, accommodating more complex real-world phenomena.

By integrating jump components into financial models, traders and investors can capture a more realistic picture of market behaviors and better manage risks associated with sudden price changes. Such models are particularly invaluable for pricing exotic options and managing portfolios sensitive to jump risks.

Jump processes and Poisson processes offer a powerful toolkit to enrich the predictive accuracy and robustness of quantitative models in finance, thus aligning theoretical models more closely with empirical observations. In practice, blending continuous and jump components generates a nuanced and comprehensive understanding of market dynamics, aiding investors in devising more resilient trading strategies.

Chapter 6

Risk Management and Measurement

Effective risk management and measurement are crucial for ensuring financial stability and maximizing returns. This chapter explores the various types of financial risks, including market, credit, operational, and liquidity risks, and introduces key risk metrics like Value at Risk (VaR) and Expected Shortfall (ES). Techniques such as stress testing, scenario analysis, and the use of credit derivatives are discussed. Additionally, the chapter examines risk management frameworks and regulations that guide the industry's best practices and compliance standards.

6.1 Introduction to Risk Management

Risk management is the cornerstone of sustainable investing and trading. It plays a vital role in safeguarding assets and ensuring long-term profitability amidst market uncertainties. This section delves into the essence of risk management, introducing fundamental concepts and highlighting their importance in financial decision-making.

At its core, risk management involves identifying, assessing, and prioritizing risks followed by coordinated efforts to minimize, monitor, and control the probability or impact of unfortunate events. The ultimate goal is to manage risk exposures in a way that balances the potential for both rewards and losses.

In the financial markets, risks are omnipresent and assume various forms. Proper risk management strategies enable traders and investors to protect their portfolios from market volatility, sudden economic shifts, and unexpected financial shocks. By understanding and implementing robust risk management practices, investors can make informed decisions that enhance portfolio stability and performance.

The process of risk management can be broadly categorized into four key stages: risk identification, risk assessment, risk mitigation, and continuous monitoring. Each of these stages is crucial for developing a comprehensive risk management framework.

Risk Identification involves recognizing the different types of risks that an investment or trading strategy may face. These risks could stem from various sources, such as fluctuating market conditions, issuer defaults, operational failures, or liquidity constraints. Identifying these risks early on is critical to addressing them effectively.

In the **Risk Assessment** stage, the identified risks are analyzed to understand their potential impact on the portfolio. This involves quantifying the risks using various metrics and models. Popular risk metrics include Value at Risk (VaR) and Expected Shortfall (ES), which provide insights into the potential losses under normal and extreme market conditions.

Risk Mitigation centers on developing strategies to manage and reduce the identified risks. This can involve diversification, where investments are spread across different asset classes to reduce exposure to any single risk. Hedging strategies, using instruments like options, futures, or credit derivatives, are also employed to protect against adverse price movements or credit events.

Continuous Monitoring is the ongoing process of overseeing the portfolio's risk exposure and adjusting the risk management strategies as necessary. This stage ensures that the risk management framework remains effective over time and adapts to changing market conditions.

Effective risk management is not a one-time task but a continuous process that evolves with the market landscape. For instance, during periods of high market volatility, stress testing and scenario analysis become particularly valuable. These techniques simulate extreme market conditions to evaluate the portfolio's resilience and prepare for potential adverse scenarios.

Stress testing involves applying hypothetical adverse conditions to financial models to predict the potential impact on asset values and overall portfolio performance. Scenario analysis, on the other hand, explores specific events or changes in underlying factors to assess their effects on the portfolio. This helps investors and traders understand how different variables can affect their investments and allows them to implement preemptive measures.

Risk management also entails adherence to regulatory frameworks and industry standards designed to promote stability and transparency in the financial markets. Regulatory guidelines provide a structured approach to managing risks and ensuring compliance with legal requirements. This includes maintaining adequate capital reserves, implementing robust internal controls, and conducting regular audits and assessments.

An integral part of risk management is also understanding behavioral biases that may influence decision-making. Cognitive biases such as overconfidence, herd behavior, and loss aversion can affect how risks are perceived and managed. Awareness of these biases is crucial for maintaining objectivity and making rational investment choices.

Overall, the practice of risk management is an essential skill for traders and investors aiming for long-term success. By systematically identifying, assessing, and mitigating risks, one can navigate the complexities of the financial markets with greater confidence and resilience. This proactive approach not only safeguards assets but also positions investors to capitalize on opportunities while minimizing potential losses.

6.2 Types of Financial Risks

Understanding the diverse spectrum of financial risks is pivotal for developing robust risk management strategies. Each type of risk has unique characteristics and implications, requiring tailored approaches for effective mitigation. We explore the principal categories: market risk, credit risk, operational risk, and liquidity risk, providing clarity on their sources, impacts, and management techniques.

Market risk arises from fluctuations in market prices, such as equity prices, interest rates, foreign exchange rates, and commodity prices. It is the potential loss due to adverse market movements and is commonly subdivided into equity risk, interest rate risk, currency risk, and commodity risk. Quantitative models are often deployed to estimate market risk, utilizing metrics like Value at Risk (VaR) and Expected Shortfall (ES) to quantify potential losses under normal and stress conditions.

$$\text{VaR} = \text{the maximum loss not exceeded with a given probability over a specified}$$

Equity risk pertains to the volatility in stock prices, impacting portfolios holding shares or equity derivatives. Interest rate risk affects fixed-income securities and is of particular concern to banks and financial institutions whose assets and liabilities may not be perfectly matched. Currency risk, or exchange rate risk, involves the potential for loss from fluctuations in foreign exchange rates, critical for multi-national companies and investors with cross-border investments. Commodity risk involves potential losses from changes in commodity prices, relevant to sectors reliant on raw materials such as oil, metals, and agricultural products.

Credit risk is the possibility of a loss arising from a borrower's failure to repay a loan or meet contractual obligations. It is typically encapsulated in two primary types: default risk and credit spread risk. Default risk is the potential loss due to a borrower's insolvency, leading to the inability to make required payments. Credit spread risk is tied to fluctuations in the difference between yields on debt instruments with differing credit qualities. The wider the spread, the higher the perceived risk of the issuer. Credit derivatives like Credit Default Swaps (CDS) are often employed as hedging tools, transferring credit risk from one party to another.

Operational risk encompasses losses stemming from inadequate or failed internal processes, systems, people, or external events. It is an expansive category that includes fraud, human error, system failures, and natural disasters. A critical element of operational risk management is the establishment of robust internal controls, comprehensive disaster recovery plans, and a culture of risk awareness across the organization. Unlike market or credit risks, operational risk is often unique to the specific circumstances and infrastructure of each institution.

Liquidity risk involves the potential inability to meet short-term financial obligations due to an inability to convert assets into cash without significant loss in value. This can be further divided into funding liquidity risk and market liquidity risk. Funding liquidity risk refers to the inability to secure funds to meet cash flow needs, whereas market liquidity risk pertains to the difficulty in selling assets quickly at their fair market value. A classic example of liquidity risk manifested during the 2007-2008 financial crisis when even highly rated instruments could not find buyers, leading to severe market dislocations.

Effective risk management requires a nuanced understanding of these risk types, their interdependencies, and the sophisticated models used to quantify and mitigate their impacts. By establishing a strong risk management framework, incorporating quantitative techniques and regulatory compliance, financial institutions can navigate the complexities of the financial landscape with greater confidence and stability.

6.3 Value at Risk (VaR)

Value at Risk (VaR) represents a critical metric within financial risk management, widely adopted to quantify the potential loss in the value of a portfolio over a given time period for a specified confidence interval. By offering a probabilistic estimate of potential losses, VaR functions as an essential tool for both financial institutions and investors to manage and mitigate risks effectively.

VaR is expressed in three key dimensions:

- The *time horizon* over which the risk is assessed (e.g., 1 day, 10 days).
- The *confidence level*, which indicates the probability that the value will not exceed the estimated loss (commonly 95% or 99%).
- The *loss amount* or *loss percentage* that is at risk, typically expressed in the portfolio's base currency.

A VaR calculation may state, for example, that there is a 1% chance of the portfolio losing 5% or more of its value over a given day.

Given its widespread use, multiple methods can be employed to compute VaR, each with its advantages and limitations. We will delve into three primary methods: Historical Simulation, the Variance-Covariance approach (including its parametric variations), and the Monte Carlo Simulation.

Historical Simulation

Historical simulation is a non-parametric approach that leverages historical market data to simulate potential future outcomes. The primary steps involve:

1. Gather past market data for the portfolio assets over a chosen time horizon.

2. Compute the corresponding returns for each time period.

3. Rank the historical returns from worst to best.

4. Identify the VaR threshold based on the desired confidence level.

For instance, with a confidence level of 99% using historical data from the past 1000 days, the VaR would correspond to the 10th-worst return.

While simple to implement, historical simulation relies heavily on the assumption that past market behavior is indicative of future performance, which may not always hold true, especially in periods of structural change or unprecedented market conditions.

Variance-Covariance Method

The Variance-Covariance method, also known as the parametric method, assumes that asset returns are normally distributed and utilizes the mean and standard deviation of those returns to estimate VaR. The formula for VaR in this approach is:

$$\text{VaR}_\alpha = \mu + Z_\alpha \sigma$$

where:

- μ is the mean return of the portfolio.

- σ is the standard deviation of returns (i.e., volatility).

- Z_α is the z-score corresponding to the desired confidence level (e.g., -2.33 for 99% confidence assuming a one-tail normal distribution).

For a portfolio, the mean μ can be calculated as:

$$\mu = \sum_{i=1}^{n} w_i \mu_i$$

where w_i are the weights and μ_i the means of individual assets. The portfolio variance σ^2 can be derived using the covariance matrix Σ:

$$\sigma^2 = \boldsymbol{w}^T \Sigma \boldsymbol{w}$$

Here, w is the weight vector of portfolio allocations. This approach simplifies computation but presumes normality of returns, which may not account for fat tails and skewness observed in real-world financial returns.

Monte Carlo Simulation

Monte Carlo Simulation offers a more sophisticated and flexible means of estimating VaR by generating numerous random samples from specified probability distributions to model future price paths. The procedure typically involves:

1. Specify the statistical properties (distribution, mean, volatility) of each asset's returns.
2. Generate a large number of random scenarios (trial runs) to simulate potential future returns.
3. Calculate the portfolio's return for each scenario.
4. Derive the VaR from the distribution of simulated portfolio returns.

Monte Carlo methods can accommodate non-normal distributions and complex dependencies, making them more versatile, though computationally intensive. They offer deeper insights into the tail risk and allow stress testing under extreme conditions, thus providing a comprehensive risk assessment.

The selection of the appropriate VaR methodology depends on the specific needs of the portfolio, availability of data, and computational resources. Regardless of the chosen method, VaR serves as a cornerstone risk metric, pivotal for making informed decisions and safeguarding against potential adverse market movements.

By systematically integrating VaR into the broader risk management framework, organizations can enhance their financial stability, align their risk appetite with their strategic objectives, and foster a proactive approach in navigating the volatile landscapes of financial markets.

6.4 Expected Shortfall (ES)

Expected Shortfall (ES), also known as Conditional Value at Risk (CVaR), is a risk measure that quantifies the expected return on a portfolio in the worst-case scenario of losses beyond a specified Value at

Risk (VaR) threshold. Unlike VaR, which only provides the maximum loss expected within a certain confidence level, ES adds value by estimating the average of those losses that exceed VaR, offering a more comprehensive picture of tail risk.

Mathematically, the Expected Shortfall at a confidence level α is defined as the expected return in the worst α percent of cases. Formally, if L is the loss random variable and VaR_α represents the α-quantile of the loss distribution, then the Expected Shortfall at level α is given by:

$$\text{ES}_\alpha = \mathbb{E}[L \mid L \geq VaR_\alpha]$$

This definition signifies that ES considers the tail of the loss distribution, providing a more conservative and arguably more accurate measure of potential portfolio losses during extreme market conditions.

To illustrate the application of Expected Shortfall, consider a simple example. Suppose we have a portfolio with a loss distribution that follows a normal distribution with mean $\mu = 0$ and standard deviation $\sigma = 1$. To calculate the ES at the 95% confidence level:

- Determine the 95% VaR. For a standard normal distribution, the 95th percentile is 1.645. Therefore, $VaR_{0.95} = 1.645\sigma = 1.645$.
- Compute ES using the properties of the normal distribution. For a normal distribution, ES at confidence level α can be approximated by:

$$\text{ES}_\alpha = \mu + \frac{\sigma\phi(\Phi^{-1}(\alpha))}{1-\alpha}$$

where ϕ is the probability density function (PDF) and Φ^{-1} is the inverse cumulative distribution function (CDF) of the standard normal distribution. For $\alpha = 0.95$, $\Phi^{-1}(0.95) = 1.645$ and $\phi(1.645)$ is approximately 0.103:

$$\text{ES}_{0.95} = 0 + \frac{1 \cdot 0.103}{1 - 0.95} \approx 2.06$$

Thus, the ES at the 95% confidence level for our portfolio is estimated to be 2.06, indicating an average of the worst 5% losses.

Moving beyond theoretical computation, consider how Expected Shortfall integrates into broader risk management practices:

- **Stress Testing and Scenario Analysis**: ES is often employed in conjunction with stress testing and scenario analysis to simulate and analyze potential losses under extreme yet plausible market conditions. By assessing the expected losses in these scenarios, risk managers can better prepare for and mitigate the impact of adverse events.
- **Regulatory Compliance**: Regulatory bodies are increasingly advocating for the use of ES over VaR due to its ability to capture tail risk. For example, the Basel III framework encourages financial institutions to consider ES when calculating minimum capital requirements.
- **Comparing Risk Across Portfolios**: Since ES measures tail risk, it allows for more effective comparison of the risk profiles of different portfolios. Investment managers can use ES to assess and compare how portfolios might perform under extreme market conditions, guiding strategic decisions.
- **Portfolio Optimization**: Incorporating ES into the portfolio optimization process helps in constructing portfolios that are not only expected to perform well under normal conditions but also robust enough to withstand market shocks. Optimization models may include ES as a constraint or objective to achieve an optimal balance between return and tail risk.
- **Credit Risk Management**: In credit portfolios, ES is particularly useful for pricing and managing the risk of credit derivatives. By estimating the average loss given extreme defaults, financial institutions can price credit default swaps (CDSs) and other credit derivatives more accurately.

Implementing ES as part of your risk management strategy enhances your ability to anticipate and respond to extreme losses, providing a more cautious and comprehensive approach to safeguarding your investment portfolio. The mathematical rigor and statistical grounding of ES make it a crucial tool for sophisticated traders and investors aiming to navigate volatile markets effectively.

6.5 Stress Testing and Scenario Analysis

Stress testing and scenario analysis are indispensable tools in the arsenal of any sophisticated risk management strategy. These methodologies allow investors and risk managers to evaluate how extreme but plausible adverse conditions could impact the financial health of portfolios and institutions. By examining the potential effects of outlier events, market disruptions, and economic downturns, one can enhance the robustness and resilience of their investment strategies.

Stress testing, defined as a dynamic process of assessing the financial system's vulnerability to adverse market conditions, often employs historical events or hypothetical constructs to simulate extreme market reactions. Central to stress testing is the identification of factors that could lead to significant financial losses and the examination of their potential ramifications. This process involves creating and applying stress scenarios to test the limits of portfolios and develop mitigation strategies.

Scenario analysis, on the other hand, focuses on assessing the impact of specific events that may not necessarily be extreme but are of particular concern due to their plausibility. This can include regulatory changes, geopolitical events, or the introduction of new market variables that could alter the investment landscape. By developing a range of scenarios based on different assumptions, investors can better understand the potential outcomes and adjust their strategies accordingly.

A crucial aspect of both stress testing and scenario analysis is the development of plausible scenarios. These scenarios should be relevant, capturing the specific risk factors that could affect the portfolio or institution. They must also be severe enough to test the limits without being excessively improbable. Historical examples, such as the 2008 financial crisis, provide valuable insights and serve as a foundation for constructing effective stress tests.

For illustrative purposes, consider a portfolio heavily weighted in equities. A relevant stress test may involve a sudden market crash, similar to the Black Monday event of 1987. By applying this historical data to the current portfolio, we can evaluate potential drawdowns and identify vulnerabilities. The mathematical representation of such a stress test could be illustrated as follows:

$$\Delta P = \sum_{i=1}^{n} (w_i \cdot \Delta S_i)$$

where ΔP represents the change in portfolio value, w_i is the weight of the i-th asset in the portfolio, and ΔS_i represents the change in the value of the i-th asset under the stressed conditions.

Scenario analysis might look at a geopolitical risk, such as a potential conflict that could raise oil prices significantly. By modeling this scenario, an investor can assess how such an event would impact their holdings, particularly in sectors vulnerable to energy price fluctuations. For example, if the current price of oil is P_0 and in the scenario it rises by 20

$$P_1 = P_0 \cdot (1 + 0.20)$$

Investors can then re-calculate the expected returns of their portfolio under this scenario, using adjusted prices for energy-dependent assets and potential cross-sector impacts.

A more sophisticated implementation involves Monte Carlo simulations, where thousands of scenarios with varying parameters are generated and analyzed. This approach captures a wide range of possibilities and provides a distribution of potential outcomes, offering deeper insights into the risks.

$$E[P] = \int_{-\infty}^{\infty} P(x)f(x)\,dx$$

Here, $E[P]$ is the expected value of the portfolio under various simulated scenarios, $P(x)$ is the portfolio value as a function of the scenario parameters x, and $f(x)$ is the probability density function of those parameters.

The efficacy of stress testing and scenario analysis also depends on continuous reassessment and adaptation. As markets evolve, previously improbable events may become more likely, and new risks may emerge. Regular updates to stress scenarios ensure that risk management strategies remain relevant and proactive.

In practice, institutions often complement these methodologies with stress test results to inform their capital allocation and liquidity management decisions. Regulatory bodies, including the Federal Reserve and the European Central Bank, mandate regular stress tests to ensure systemic stability and resilience.

By integrating stress testing and scenario analysis into the broader risk management framework, traders and investors are better equipped to anticipate and navigate financial turbulence. This strategic foresight not only safeguards assets but also enhances the potential for capitalizing on market opportunities amidst adversity.

6.6 Credit Risk and Credit Derivatives

Credit risk, also known as default risk, stems from the possibility that a borrower will fail to meet its obligations, leading to financial losses for the lender or investor. Accurate measurement and management of credit risk are pivotal for financial stability and optimal portfolio performance. This section delves into the nature of credit risk, introduces essential metrics and models for its evaluation, and explores the role and mechanics of credit derivatives in hedging and transferring credit risk.

Understanding Credit Risk

Credit risk arises in various financial transactions, including loans, bonds, and derivatives. Its impact can be profound, extending beyond individual defaults to systemic financial disruptions. To effectively manage credit risk, it is crucial to distinguish between two primary sources: *idiosyncratic risk*, which pertains to individual borrowers, and *systemic risk*, influenced by macroeconomic conditions and market correlations.

Credit Risk Metrics

To evaluate credit risk, financial experts deploy various quantitative metrics. The most common include:

- **Probability of Default (PD):** The likelihood that a borrower will default over a specific time horizon, typically one year.
- **Loss Given Default (LGD):** The proportion of the exposure that will be lost if the borrower defaults, after accounting for recoveries.
- **Exposure at Default (EAD):** The total value exposed to default risk at the time of default.

These metrics combine to estimate the *Expected Loss (EL)* using the formula:

$$\mathrm{EL} = \mathrm{PD} \times \mathrm{LGD} \times \mathrm{EAD}$$

Advanced models, such as the *CreditMetrics* framework and the *Merton model*, offer comprehensive approaches to assessing credit risk by incorporating various borrower-specific and macroeconomic factors.

Credit Derivatives

Credit derivatives are financial instruments designed to transfer or hedge credit risk. The most prevalent types of credit derivatives include Credit Default Swaps (CDS), Collateralized Debt Obligations (CDOs), and Total Return Swaps (TRS).

Credit Default Swaps (CDS)

A CDS is a bilateral contract where the buyer pays periodic premiums to the seller in exchange for protection against the default of a reference entity. If a default occurs, the seller compensates the buyer, typically by paying the par value of the defaulted asset. This transfer of risk allows investors to manage credit exposure without altering their core holdings. The pricing of CDS contracts relies heavily on the perceived creditworthiness of the reference entity and market conditions.

The annual premium, or *CDS spread*, reflects the cost of protection and serves as an implied measure of credit risk. The spread can be calculated using the following formula:

$$\text{CDS Spread} = \frac{\text{Expected Loss}}{\text{Notional Amount}}$$

where the expected loss is a function of the PD, LGD, and EAD metrics described earlier.

Collateralized Debt Obligations (CDOs)

CDOs pool together a diversified portfolio of debt instruments, such as bonds or loans, and issue tranches with varying degrees of credit risk. Each tranche receives different priority in claims, offering a spectrum of risk and return profiles. The senior tranches typically have lower yields but greater credit protection, while junior tranches offer higher yields with increased risk exposure. This stratification allows investors to select tranches that align with their risk tolerance and return objectives.

The pricing and risk assessment of CDOs require complex modeling techniques, including Monte Carlo simulations and copula functions, to capture the correlations between the underlying assets.

Total Return Swaps (TRS)

In a TRS, one party (the total return payer) agrees to pay the total return of a reference asset, including interest and capital gains, to the counterparty (the total return receiver), while receiving fixed or floating payments in return. This structure allows the payer to offload the credit risk of the reference asset, while the receiver gains exposure to the asset's performance without the need for direct ownership. TRS contracts are particularly useful for entities seeking synthetic exposure to credit markets or aiming to manage asset-liability mismatches.

Applications and Strategic Use of Credit Derivatives

Credit derivatives play a pivotal role in modern risk management strategies. They provide mechanisms for hedging credit risk, enhancing portfolio diversification, and exploiting arbitrage opportunities. Banks and financial institutions use CDS to protect against loan defaults, while asset managers employ CDOs and TRS to tailor credit exposure to investment goals. Moreover, credit derivatives facilitate regulatory capital management by enabling institutions to achieve more efficient risk-weighted asset profiles.

Understanding the nuances and applications of credit derivatives can empower sophisticated traders to navigate complex credit markets effectively. By leveraging these instruments within a comprehensive risk management framework, investors can enhance portfolio resilience and achieve superior risk-adjusted returns.

6.7 Market Risk

Market risk, also known as systematic risk, represents the potential financial loss due to unfavorable movements in market prices. This type of risk affects a broad range of assets and is driven by macroeconomic factors such as interest rates, inflation, currency exchange rates, and geopolitical events. Unlike specific risks associated with individual investments, market risk is inherent to the entire market or market segments. Therefore, it cannot be eliminated through diversification but can be managed and mitigated using various strategies and financial instruments.

A critical component in understanding market risk is recognizing its different forms:

- **Equity Risk:** This pertains to the volatility in stock prices. Investment values can fluctuate due to changes in market perceptions, company performance, and broader economic conditions.
- **Interest Rate Risk:** Variations in interest rates can significantly impact the value of bonds and other fixed-income securities. As

interest rates rise, bond prices typically fall, and vice versa.

- **Currency Risk:** Also known as exchange rate risk, this is the potential loss from adverse movements in currency exchange rates, impacting investments in foreign assets.
- **Commodity Risk:** Price changes in commodities such as oil, gold, and agricultural products can affect portfolios that include these assets or derivatives based on them.

To manage market risk, investors and financial institutions use several sophisticated tools and strategies. A fundamental approach involves measuring market risk accurately through quantitative metrics such as Value at Risk (VaR) and Expected Shortfall (ES). These metrics provide insights into the potential losses in a portfolio over a specified period and confidence level.

Value at Risk (VaR) is a widely-used risk measure that estimates the maximum loss expected (with a given confidence level) over a specified time horizon. For example, a daily VaR at a 95% confidence level might indicate that there is only a 5% chance that the portfolio will lose more than a certain dollar amount in one day. The formula for VaR in a simple portfolio might be expressed as:

$$\text{VaR} = Z_\alpha \times \sigma_P \times \sqrt{T}$$

where Z_α is the critical value from the standard normal distribution corresponding to the desired confidence level, σ_P is the portfolio standard deviation, and T is the time horizon.

Expected Shortfall (ES), also known as Conditional Value at Risk (CVaR), takes the analysis a step further by estimating the average loss in scenarios where the VaR threshold is exceeded. This provides a more comprehensive view of potential tail risks. The formulation of ES, assuming a normal distribution, is given by:

$$\text{ES} = \frac{1}{1-\alpha}\int_\alpha^1 \text{VaR}(p)\,dp$$

where α is the confidence level, and VaR(p) is the VaR at probability p.

In addition to these quantitative techniques, qualitative analysis plays a crucial role in managing market risk. Monitoring economic indicators, political developments, and market sentiments can provide early warnings and allow for proactive risk mitigation actions. For instance, during periods of economic uncertainty, traders might choose to reduce exposure to highly volatile assets or increase positions in safer, less-correlated instruments.

Another effective strategy involves the use of **hedging instruments**. Derivatives such as futures, options, and swaps can be employed to offset potential losses from adverse price movements. For example, an investor holding a portfolio of stocks might purchase put options on a market index to hedge against a potential market downturn.

- **Futures Contracts:** Agreements to buy or sell an asset at a predetermined price at a specified future date. They are often used to hedge against price fluctuations.

- **Options Contracts:** Provide the right, but not the obligation, to buy (call option) or sell (put option) an asset at a predetermined price before a specified date.

- **Swaps:** Financial agreements to exchange cash flows or other financial instruments. Interest rate swaps and currency swaps are common types.

Diversification remains a foundational principle in market risk management. By constructing a portfolio with assets that have low or negative correlations, the overall risk can be reduced. While diversification cannot eliminate market risk entirely, it can smooth out the impact of adverse price movements in any single asset class.

Advanced techniques such as **dynamic hedging** and **portfolio insurance** are used to adjust hedging strategies continuously in response to market conditions. These techniques often involve sophisticated algorithmic trading models that can rapidly respond to changes in risk exposure.

Understanding and managing market risk is imperative for both individual investors and institutional portfolio managers. By leveraging a combination of quantitative metrics, economic analysis, hedging strategies, and diversification, it is possible to safeguard investments and enhance potential returns despite the inevitable fluctuations in market conditions. Each approach and instrument has its advantages and limitations, making it essential to tailor risk management strategies to align with specific investment goals and risk tolerance levels.

6.8 Operational Risk

Operational risk is an essential component of comprehensive risk management, pertaining to the potential for loss resulting from inadequacies or failures in internal processes, people, systems, or from external events. This category of risk is often underestimated but can have profound implications for the financial stability of an institution.

At its core, operational risk covers a broad array of scenarios, ranging from human errors, system failures, and fraud, to the impact of unforeseen external events like natural disasters or regulatory changes. Effective management of operational risk requires a multifaceted approach, including robust internal controls, diligent oversight, and continuous monitoring.

To elucidate, let us consider key areas within operational risk:

- **Internal Processes:** Procedural errors and process inefficiencies can significantly impact an organization's operations. For instance, a failure in the settlement process of financial transactions due to outdated procedures can result in financial loss and reputational damage. Regular audits and updates to workflows, coupled with automation, can mitigate these risks.
- **People:** Personnel-related risks encompass errors due to lack of training, fraud, or even insufficient personnel to handle critical tasks. Implementing comprehensive training programs, fostering a culture of accountability, and establishing stringent hiring practices can reduce these risks. For example, establishing a clear segregation of duties can prevent fraud and ensure critical checks and balances are maintained.
- **Systems:** Technology is pivotal in modern financial operations, but it also introduces risks. System failures, cybersecurity breaches, and data integrity issues are primary concerns. Regular system updates, rigorous testing protocols, and robust cybersecurity measures are essential. Utilizing redundancy and backup systems can also ensure continuity in the face of hardware failures or cyber-attacks.
- **External Events:** Natural disasters, regulatory shifts, and geopolitical events can disrupt operations. Developing contingency plans, maintaining adequate insurance coverage, and staying

abreast of regulatory developments are critical strategies for mitigating these risks. For illustration, consider a scenario where a regulatory change mandates new reporting requirements; having flexible and adaptive reporting systems in place can ensure compliance without operational disruptions.

Quantifying operational risk can be challenging due to its qualitative nature, but several quantitative and qualitative approaches can aid in assessment. One widely used method is the *Loss Distribution Approach (LDA)*.

LDA involves:

1. *Data Collection*: Gathering historical loss data related to operational risk events.

2. *Statistical Analysis*: Fitting statistical distributions to model the frequency and severity of losses. This typically involves using distributions such as the Poisson distribution for frequency and the log-normal or gamma distribution for severity.

3. *Risk Metrics Calculation*: Combining these distributions to estimate risk metrics such as VaR for operational risk. For example, if the annual loss frequency follows a Poisson distribution with parameter λ and the loss severity follows a log-normal distribution with parameters μ and σ^2, the aggregate annual loss can be modeled and used to calculate the operational VaR.

To exemplify, suppose an institution identifies that the mean annual loss frequency λ for a particular operational risk is 5 incidents per year, and the loss severity follows a log-normal distribution with parameters $\mu = 2$ and $\sigma = 0.5$. The total annual loss distribution can then be simulated or analytically derived to forecast potential losses at a specified confidence level.

Stress testing and scenario analysis also play a vital role in managing operational risk. By constructing hypothetical scenarios—such as a major IT failure or a critical regulatory change—and assessing their impact, institutions can better prepare for and mitigate potential operational disruptions. For example, a financial institution may perform a scenario analysis to understand the repercussions of a cyber-attack that compromises client data, allowing them to bolster their defenses and response strategies accordingly.

Lastly, a robust operational risk management framework is crucial for embedding risk management practices into the institution's culture and operations. This framework typically incorporates the following elements:

- **Governance**: Well-defined roles and responsibilities, clear reporting lines, and active oversight from senior management and the board of directors.
- **Risk Identification and Assessment**: Regular identification and comprehensive assessment of potential operational risks through audits, risk assessments, and monitoring activities.
- **Control Activities**: Implementation of preventive and detective controls to mitigate identified risks. These may include access controls, transaction validation processes, and regular reconciliations.
- **Monitoring and Reporting**: Ongoing monitoring of risk indicators and effective reporting mechanisms to ensure timely detection and response to operational risks.
- **Culture and Training**: Cultivating a risk-aware culture through continuous training and awareness programs, ensuring that all employees understand their roles in mitigating operational risk.

Through meticulous management of operational risk, institutions can safeguard their operations, ensure compliance with regulatory requirements, and maintain their reputation in an increasingly complex financial landscape. The integration of sophisticated risk management frameworks alongside advanced analytical tools enables institutions to navigate and mitigate this multifaceted risk efficiently.

6.9 Liquidity Risk

Liquidity risk refers to the potential difficulty of an entity to meet its short-term financial obligations due to the inability to convert assets into cash without significant loss. It poses a threat to both individual investors and financial institutions, impacting market positions and financial stability.

Liquidity risk can be bifurcated into two primary categories: market liquidity risk and funding liquidity risk. While market liquidity risk pertains to the capability of trading a particular asset without causing a significant impact on its price, funding liquidity risk involves an entity's ability to secure the necessary funding to meet liabilities. Addressing these risks is essential for maintaining healthy market operations and financial soundness.

Market Liquidity Risk

Market liquidity risk arises when an investor or institution cannot promptly execute a large transaction without affecting asset prices. This is primarily due to insufficient market depth or the widening of bid-ask spreads. During volatile market conditions, liquidity can vanish rapidly, making it difficult to close or adjust positions without incurring considerable costs.

Measuring Market Liquidity

One common measure of market liquidity is the bid-ask spread, defined as the difference between the highest price a buyer is willing to pay (bid) and the lowest price a seller is willing to accept (ask). Smaller spreads indicate higher liquidity.

$$\text{Bid-Ask Spread} = \text{Ask Price} - \text{Bid Price}$$

Additionally, liquidity can be evaluated using metrics such as market depth, which refers to the volume of buy and sell orders at various price levels. Greater depth typically equates to higher liquidity, as larger transactions can be executed without substantially moving the market price.

Funding Liquidity Risk

Funding liquidity risk entails the danger of an entity's inability to meet its short-term cash flow needs. It can manifest when financial obligations cannot be fulfilled because liquid assets cannot be sold or funding cannot be arranged at reasonable rates. This type of risk is critical for financial institutions relying heavily on short-term borrowing to finance long-term assets.

Managing Funding Liquidity Risk

To manage funding liquidity risk, institutions often maintain liquidity buffers, usually in the form of highly liquid assets such as Treasury bonds that can be quickly sold with minimal loss. Additionally, maintaining diverse funding sources, such as short-term loans, lines of credit, and long-term debt, helps mitigate the risk of relying solely on a single funding mechanism.

$$\text{Liquidity Coverage Ratio (LCR)} = \frac{\text{High-Quality Liquid Assets}}{\text{Total Net Cash Outflows over 30 days}}$$

The Liquidity Coverage Ratio (LCR) is a regulatory measure aimed at ensuring financial institutions have adequate liquid assets to cover net cash outflows for a 30-day stress period. A minimum LCR of 100% indicates sufficient liquidity on hand to withstand short-term financial stress.

Stress testing and scenario analysis are essential tools for assessing liquidity risk. These processes involve simulating extreme but plausible scenarios to gauge the potential impact on an institution's liquidity position. Stress tests can help identify vulnerabilities and ensure preparedness for adverse conditions.

Impacts and Implications

The implications of liquidity risk are far-reaching. A liquidity shortfall can lead to fire sales, where assets are sold rapidly at depreciated prices, thereby exacerbating market instability. In extreme cases, a liquidity crisis can trigger broader financial turmoil, as witnessed during the 2008 financial crisis when the interbank lending market seized up, causing widespread panic and asset devaluation.

Understanding and managing liquidity risk is vital for safeguarding financial health. Both market participants and regulators play crucial roles in ensuring robust liquidity management practices are in place. By maintaining adequate liquidity reserves, employing rigorous stress tests, and diversifying funding sources, institutions can better navigate the complexities of liquidity risk and contribute to overall market stability.

6.10 Risk Management Frameworks and Regulations

Understanding risk management frameworks and regulations is paramount for any financial institution striving for stability and compliance in an increasingly complex financial landscape. The goal of risk management frameworks is to establish a structured approach to identifying, measuring, managing, and monitoring risks. Regulatory bodies, meanwhile, set forth guidelines and standards to ensure the sound operation of financial markets and protect stakeholders.

A robust risk management framework typically consists of several core components: risk identification, risk assessment, risk mitigation, risk monitoring, and risk reporting. Many organizations adopt globally recognized frameworks such as the International Organization for Standardization (ISO) 31000, the Committee of Sponsoring Organizations of the Treadway Commission (COSO) ERM framework, and the Basel Committee on Banking Supervision guidelines.

The ISO 31000 standard provides principles and generic guidelines on risk management. It is a widely adopted framework that helps organizations increase the likelihood of achieving objectives, improve the identification of opportunities and threats, and effectively allocate and use resources for risk treatment. The standard emphasizes the need for risk management to be integrated into an organization's overall governance and strategic direction.

COSO's Enterprise Risk Management (ERM) framework is another influential model. It outlines a holistic approach to risk management, linking it to an organization's strategy, operations, reporting, and compliance. COSO ERM insists on the embedding of risk management practices within the organization's culture and operational activities. This integration helps ensure that risk considerations are factored into decision-making at all levels of the organization.

The Basel Committee on Banking Supervision has established international benchmarks for banking regulation known as the Basel Accords. These accords—Basel I, Basel II, Basel III, and the recent amendments in Basel IV—set forth requirements for capital adequacy, stress testing, and liquidity standards. Their primary aim is to strengthen the regulation, supervision, and risk management of banks globally.

Basel III, introduced in response to the 2008 financial crisis, expanded the scope of regulatory oversight to include new regulatory requirements for bank liquidity and systemic risk. It focuses on enhancing the bank capital requirements through stricter rules on what constitutes capital. Moreover, it introduced two key liquidity ratios: the Liquidity Coverage Ratio (LCR) and the Net Stable Funding Ratio (NSFR). These ratios aim to ensure that financial institutions have sufficient high-quality liquid assets to withstand a 30-day stressed funding scenario and maintain stable funding over a longer-term horizon, respectively.

In practice, the implementation of a risk management framework necessitates thorough risk assessments. Organizations need to conduct qualitative and quantitative analyses, employing tools like Value at Risk (VaR), stress testing, and scenario analysis. Regular risk assessments allow firms to understand potential impacts, probabilistic occurrences, and interconnectedness of risks.

Furthermore, comprehensive risk mitigation strategies are vital. Mitigation efforts may include diversification of investment portfolios, hedging strategies using derivatives, implementing strong internal controls, and establishing contingency plans. These measures help in reducing exposure to identified risks and mitigating potential adverse outcomes.

Risk monitoring is an ongoing process, necessitated by the constantly evolving nature of financial markets and external environments. Organizations should use Key Risk Indicators (KRIs) and other monitoring tools to keep track of their risk profiles and triggers for adverse trends. Effective risk monitoring allows for timely adjustments in strategies and helps maintain compliance with regulatory requirements.

Finally, transparent risk reporting ensures that stakeholders are kept informed of the risk exposures and management efforts. Regular and clear communication between the risk management team, senior management, and the board of directors helps in ensuring that risk management is aligned with the organization's objectives and regulatory obligations.

Regulatory bodies such as the Securities and Exchange Commission (SEC) in the United States, the Financial Conduct Authority (FCA) in the United Kingdom, and the European Securities and Markets Authority (ESMA) in the European Union, among others, play an essential role in maintaining market integrity. They set forth rules and conduct supervision activities to enforce compliance with legal and regulatory standards.

Regulations such as the Dodd-Frank Act in the United States and the Markets in Financial Instruments Directive (MiFID II) in the European Union are examples of comprehensive regulatory frameworks designed to enhance market transparency, protect investors, and reduce systemic risk. These regulations require extensive reporting, the implementation of robust risk management practices, and the adherence to strict compliance standards.

Navigating the labyrinth of risk management frameworks and regulations can be challenging but is crucial for any financial professional.

Staying informed about the latest regulatory changes and continuously refining the risk management processes can help organizations not only to comply with regulations but also to achieve sustainable growth and stability. By fostering a culture of risk awareness and establishing strong risk management practices, firms can better anticipate and mitigate the impacts of adverse events, ultimately contributing to their long-term success.

Chapter 7

Portfolio Theory and Optimization

Portfolio theory and optimization are pivotal for constructing efficient investment portfolios. This chapter begins with Modern Portfolio Theory (MPT), emphasizing the trade-off between risk and return and the efficient frontier. It covers various optimization techniques, including mean-variance optimization and the Black-Litterman model, along with multi-factor models and risk parity approaches. The chapter also addresses practical aspects like diversification, performance measurement, and attribution, equipping readers with the tools to apply these concepts in real-world portfolio management.

7.1 Introduction to Portfolio Theory

The field of portfolio theory constitutes the cornerstone of modern investment strategy, providing a structured framework for selecting a collection of securities that collectively yield the highest expected return for a given level of risk. This section aims to elucidate the foundational principles of portfolio theory, setting the stage for more advanced topics covered in subsequent sections.

Portfolio theory begins with the understanding that investors are risk-averse, meaning they prefer a stable and predictable return over a volatile and unpredictable one. This fundamental assumption drives the need for diversification, which is the process of spreading investments across various securities to reduce exposure to any single asset's volatility. By combining assets that do not perfectly correlate, investors can minimize the overall risk of their portfolio without sacrificing potential returns.

Central to portfolio theory is the concept of the risk-return trade-off. In essence, every investment choice involves balancing the potential for higher returns against the possibility of greater risk. This trade-off is quantified using metrics such as expected return, which is the weighted average of possible returns, and standard deviation, which measures the investment's volatility.

To illustrate these concepts, consider a simple portfolio comprising two assets, A and B. Asset A has an expected return $E(R_A)$ and a standard deviation σ_A, while Asset B has an expected return $E(R_B)$ and a standard deviation σ_B. If ρ_{AB} represents the correlation coefficient between the returns of assets A and B, the expected return $E(R_P)$ of the portfolio P that consists of portions w_A and w_B of these two assets can be calculated as:

$$E(R_P) = w_A E(R_A) + w_B E(R_B)$$

Similarly, the portfolio's standard deviation σ_P, which represents the overall risk, is given by:

$$\sigma_P = \sqrt{w_A^2 \sigma_A^2 + w_B^2 \sigma_B^2 + 2 w_A w_B \sigma_A \sigma_B \rho_{AB}}$$

This formula encapsulates the essence of diversification. When the correlation ρ_{AB} between the assets is low (or negative), the portfolio's risk is reduced more significantly. Thus, combining different assets can lead to a portfolio with a lower risk than individual constituent assets.

The historical roots of portfolio theory can be traced back to the pioneering work of Harry Markowitz in the 1950s. His seminal paper, "Portfolio Selection," introduced the concept of mean-variance optimization, which involves choosing the portfolio with the best possible return for a given level of risk. This methodology later evolved into what is now known as Modern Portfolio Theory (MPT).

Central to MPT is the Efficient Frontier, a curve that plots the set of optimal portfolios delivering the highest expected return for a specified level of risk. Any portfolio that lies below this curve is suboptimal because it offers lower returns for a given risk compared to a portfolio on the efficient frontier. The Capital Market Line (CML) further extends this theory by incorporating the risk-free rate, enabling investors to find the optimal mix of risky and risk-free assets.

To further understand these principles, consider an investor who can invest in a risk-free asset with return R_f and a risky asset with return $E(R_M)$ and risk σ_M. The expected return $E(R_P)$ and standard deviation σ_P of a portfolio mix of these two assets can be described using the following equations:

$$E(R_P) = w_f R_f + w_R E(R_M)$$

$$\sigma_P = w_R \sigma_M$$

where w_f and w_R are the weights of the risk-free and the risky asset in the portfolio respectively. This linear relationship is represented by the CML in the risk-return space.

Understanding these foundational concepts prepares us to delve deeper into advanced techniques for portfolio optimization. By comprehensively grasping the principles of diversification, the risk-return trade-off, and the Efficient Frontier, investors can better navigate the complexities of financial markets and construct portfolios that align more closely with their investment goals.

Moreover, as we progress through the chapter, we will explore various optimization techniques beyond mean-variance optimization, considering different models like the Black-Litterman model, multi-factor models, and risk parity approaches, eventually empowering you to apply these concepts pragmatically in real-world portfolio management.

7.2 Modern Portfolio Theory (MPT)

Modern Portfolio Theory (MPT) represents a foundational framework in the field of finance, fundamentally changing how investors approach portfolio construction and risk management. Originating in the groundbreaking work of Harry Markowitz in 1952, MPT emphasizes the critical importance of diversification for optimizing the trade-off between risk and return. This theoretical approach provides investors with tools to construct portfolios that achieve maximum expected returns for a given level of risk, or alternatively, minimize risk for a given level of expected return.

At the core of MPT are several key concepts: expected return, risk (often measured as standard deviation), and the correlation between asset returns. By understanding and applying these concepts, investors can better manage their portfolios and make more informed investment decisions.

Expected Return is a measure of the mean or average return that an investment is expected to generate over a specified period. Mathematically, the expected return of a portfolio, $E(R_p)$, comprising n assets, each with an expected return $E(R_i)$ and a weight w_i in the portfolio, is given by:

$$E(R_p) = \sum_{i=1}^{n} w_i \cdot E(R_i)$$

Risk in MPT is quantified by the standard deviation (σ) of portfolio returns, which serves as a proxy for volatility. The standard deviation of a portfolio's return combines the variances of individual assets and their covariances. For a portfolio of n assets, the portfolio variance σ_p^2 is calculated as:

$$\sigma_p^2 = \sum_{i=1}^{n} \sum_{j=1}^{n} w_i w_j \sigma_{ij}$$

where σ_{ij} is the covariance between the returns of assets i and j. The corresponding portfolio standard deviation σ_p is:

$$\sigma_p = \sqrt{\sum_{i=1}^{n} \sum_{j=1}^{n} w_i w_j \sigma_{ij}}$$

Another fundamental concept in MPT is **Correlation**, which measures the degree to which two assets move in relation to each other. It is captured by the correlation coefficient ρ_{ij}, ranging from -1 to 1, where -1 indicates perfect negative correlation, 1 indicates perfect positive correlation, and 0 indicates no correlation. The covariance σ_{ij} between assets i and j is expressed in terms of their correlation coefficients:

$$\sigma_{ij} = \rho_{ij} \sigma_i \sigma_j$$

The primary innovation of MPT lies in the **Efficient Frontier**, a graphical representation of the set of optimal portfolios that offer the highest expected return for a defined level of risk. Portfolios that lie on the efficient frontier are considered efficient because they provide the best possible return for given risk levels. To construct the efficient frontier, investors select combinations of assets that maximize expected return for each possible level of portfolio risk, as defined by the above covariance structure.

An investor's decision-making process involves selecting a portfolio on the efficient frontier that aligns with their risk tolerance. This process is illustrated by solving the following quadratic programming problem:

$$\begin{aligned} \text{Maximize} \quad & E(R_p) = \sum_{i=1}^{n} w_i E(R_i) \\ \text{Subject to} \quad & \sigma_p = \sqrt{\sum_{i=1}^{n}\sum_{j=1}^{n} w_i w_j \sigma_{ij}} \\ & \sum_{i=1}^{n} w_i = 1 \\ & w_i \geq 0, \quad \text{for all } i \end{aligned}$$

where $\sum_{i=1}^{n} w_i = 1$ ensures that the allocated weights sum to 100%, and $w_i \geq 0$ asserts no short-selling of assets.

A significant extension of MPT is the **Capital Market Line (CML)**, which depicts the risk-return trade-off of portfolios that combine a risk-free asset with the market portfolio (the tangency portfolio on the efficient frontier). The slope of the CML represents the market price of risk (Sharpe ratio), providing investors a benchmark for evaluating the performance of their portfolios.

$$\text{CML: } E(R_p) = R_f + [E(R_m) - R_f]\frac{\sigma_p}{\sigma_m}$$

where R_f is the risk-free rate, $E(R_m)$ is the expected return of the market portfolio, and σ_m is the standard deviation of the market portfolio.

Understanding MPT empowers investors to strategically construct diversified portfolios that balance their unique risk preferences with return objectives. By diversifying across non-correlated assets and leveraging the principles of MPT, investors manage risk more effectively and potentially enhance their portfolios' risk-adjusted returns.

7.3 Efficient Frontier and Capital Market Line

Understanding the Efficient Frontier and Capital Market Line is essential for any investor aiming to optimize their portfolio. These concepts stem from Modern Portfolio Theory (MPT), which revolutionized the way we approach the trade-off between risk and return. The Efficient Frontier represents the set of portfolios that provide the highest expected return for a given level of risk. Constructing this frontier involves plotting expected returns against portfolio standard deviation, ultimately showcasing a boundary of optimal portfolios.

To construct and understand the Efficient Frontier, begin with the fundamental portfolio expected return and variance formulas. For a two-asset portfolio, the expected return $E(R_p)$ and standard deviation σ_p are determined as follows:

$$E(R_p) = w_1 E(R_1) + w_2 E(R_2)$$

$$\sigma_p^2 = w_1^2 \sigma_1^2 + w_2^2 \sigma_2^2 + 2 w_1 w_2 \sigma_{12}$$

where:

- $E(R_p)$ = expected return of the portfolio
- w_1, w_2 = weights of the assets in the portfolio
- $E(R_1), E(R_2)$ = expected returns of the individual assets
- σ_1, σ_2 = standard deviations of the individual assets
- σ_{12} = covariance between the two assets

In a multi-asset portfolio, these formulas extend to incorporate all assets, with covariance terms representing the relationships between each pair of assets. A matrix representation of these calculations facilitates computational efficiency, particularly in algorithmic trading where speed is critical.

Consider a portfolio comprised of n assets. Define the expected returns vector E, the covariance matrix Σ, and the weights vector w:

$$E(R_p) = \boldsymbol{w}^\top \boldsymbol{E}$$

$$\sigma_p^2 = \boldsymbol{w}^\top \boldsymbol{\Sigma} \boldsymbol{w}$$

Using modern optimization techniques, investors can identify portfolios that lie on the Efficient Frontier. Key among these techniques is Mean-Variance Optimization, which seeks to maximize expected return for a given level of risk or equivalently minimize risk for a given level of expected return. The outcome is a set of optimal portfolios forming the Efficient Frontier.

Next, the concept of the Capital Market Line (CML) builds on the Efficient Frontier to introduce the risk-free asset. The CML represents the line formed when an investor combines a risk-free asset with portfolios of risky assets. The risk-free rate R_f is a foundational component, often represented by the return on government bonds.

The equation governing the CML is given by:

$$E(R_p) = R_f + \frac{E(R_m) - R_f}{\sigma_m} \sigma_p$$

where:

- $E(R_p)$ = expected return of the portfolio on the CML
- R_f = risk-free rate
- $E(R_m)$ = expected return of the market portfolio
- σ_m = standard deviation of the market portfolio
- σ_p = standard deviation of the portfolio

Portfolios on the CML dominate those on the Efficient Frontier due to their higher Sharpe ratios, defined by:

$$S = \frac{E(R_p) - R_f}{\sigma_p}$$

The highest Sharpe ratio is achieved by the market portfolio, where only systematic risk, as opposed to unsystematic risk present in individual assets, remains after diversification.

Visualizing the Efficient Frontier and the CML aids comprehension. Consider the following figure demonstrating these concepts:

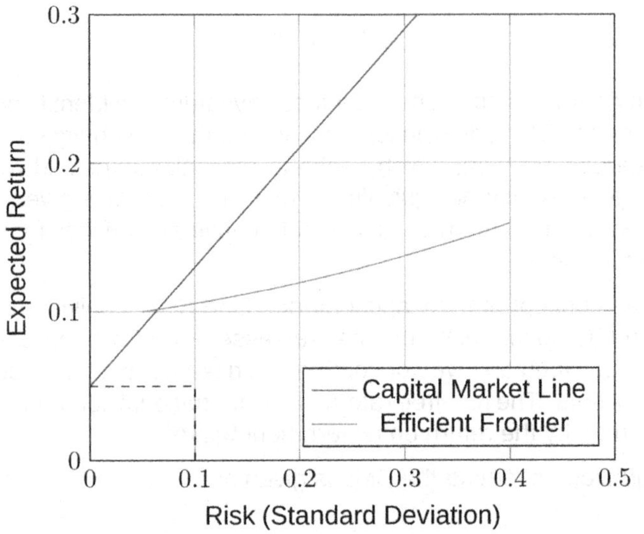

Figure 7.1: Efficient Frontier and Capital Market Line

Such graphical representations clarify how investors select portfolios, balancing expected returns against risk. Achieving clarity in these decisions enhances strategic investment planning and performance optimization.

By integrating Efficient Frontier theory and the CML, investors can refine their approach to constructing robust portfolios that meet their performance goals while managing risk effectively.

7.4 Portfolio Optimization Techniques

In this section, we delve into various portfolio optimization techniques that serve as the backbone of constructing and managing an investment portfolio. The primary objective of portfolio optimization is to balance risk and return according to the investor's preferences, ensuring that the portfolio aligns with their financial goals and risk tolerance.

One of the fundamental techniques in portfolio optimization is the mean-variance analysis introduced by Harry Markowitz. This approach involves constructing portfolios that are efficient, meaning they either achieve the maximum expected return for a given level of risk or minimize risk for a given level of expected return. The central tenets of mean-variance optimization (MVO) are rooted in the concepts of expected returns, variances, and covariances of asset returns.

To illustrate, consider a portfolio consisting of n assets. The expected return of the portfolio, $\boldsymbol{E}(R_p)$, is calculated as:

$$\boldsymbol{E}(R_p) = \sum_{i=1}^{n} w_i \boldsymbol{E}(R_i),$$

where w_i represents the weight of asset i in the portfolio, and $\boldsymbol{E}(R_i)$ denotes the expected return of asset i.

The portfolio's variance, which measures the risk, is given by:

$$\sigma_p^2 = \sum_{i=1}^{n} \sum_{j=1}^{n} w_i w_j \sigma_{ij},$$

where σ_{ij} is the covariance between the returns of asset i and asset j. The optimization problem can then be formulated as:

$$\begin{aligned} \text{minimize} \qquad & \sigma_p = \sqrt{\sum_{i=1}^{n} \sum_{j=1}^{n} w_i w_j \sigma_{ij}} \\ \text{subject to} \qquad & \boldsymbol{E}(R_p) = \sum_{i=1}^{n} w_i \boldsymbol{E}(R_i), \\ & \sum_{i=1}^{n} w_i = 1. \end{aligned}$$

This quadratic programming problem finds the weights w_i that minimize the portfolio's variance for a given expected return, outlining the efficient frontier.

While mean-variance optimization is elegant, it requires robust estimates of expected returns, volatilities, and correlations, which can be challenging to obtain accurately. To address some of these concerns, other methods have been developed. The Black-Litterman model is one such technique, which integrates investor views into the mean-variance framework to produce more reliable estimates.

The Black-Litterman model starts with a Bayesian approach to adjust the equilibrium market returns, typically derived from a global CAPM (Capital Asset Pricing Model). By introducing investor views, the model combines these with the equilibrium market returns to yield a new set of expected returns, incorporating both the market's perspective and investor's subjective insights.

Mathematically, the Black-Litterman model can be represented as:

$$\boldsymbol{E}(R_{BL}) = (\tau\boldsymbol{\Sigma})^{-1}(\tau\boldsymbol{\Pi} + \boldsymbol{P}^{\top}\boldsymbol{\Omega}^{-1}\boldsymbol{Q}),$$

where: - τ is a scalar representing the level of confidence in the prior equilibrium returns, - $\boldsymbol{\Sigma}$ is the covariance matrix of asset returns, - $\boldsymbol{\Pi}$ is the vector of equilibrium excess returns, - $\boldsymbol{P}$ is the matrix that identifies the assets involved in the views, - $\boldsymbol{\Omega}$ is the diagonal covariance matrix of the views, - $\boldsymbol{Q}$ is the vector of views.

By recalibrating the expected returns with this combined approach, the Black-Litterman model mitigates the sensitivity issues typical of traditional mean-variance optimization, potentially leading to more stable portfolio allocations.

Another significant method in portfolio optimization is the use of multi-factor models which expands upon single-factor models like the Capital Asset Pricing Model (CAPM). Multi-factor models, such as the Fama-French three-factor model, consider multiple sources of systematic risk, including market risk, size risk, and value risk. The general form of a multi-factor model is:

$$R_i = \alpha_i + \sum_{k=1}^{m} \beta_{ik} F_k + \epsilon_i,$$

where R_i is the return of asset i, α_i is the intercept, β_{ik} is the sensitivity of asset i to factor k, F_k is the return of factor k, and ϵ_i is the idiosyncratic error term.

Optimizing a portfolio with a multi-factor model involves determining the asset weights that achieve a desired combination of factor exposures, often through minimizing the tracking error or maximizing the expected return for a given risk profile.

Risk parity is another compelling strategy that focuses on distributing risk equally among the portfolio's components, rather than allocating capital based on perceived returns. The idea is to create a portfolio where each asset contributes equally to the overall portfolio risk, leading to potentially better-diversified exposures. Mathematically, this involves solving for weights w_i such that:

$$w_i \cdot \sigma_i = \frac{c}{\sigma_i},$$

where c is a constant ensuring that the sum of the weights is equal to 1.

Combining these advanced techniques, investors can construct and optimize portfolios that align closely with their risk tolerance and return expectations. By balancing mean-variance optimization with models like Black-Litterman, multi-factor analysis, and risk parity, an investor can create robust portfolios capable of navigating the complexities of financial markets.

7.5 Mean-Variance Optimization

Mean-variance optimization (MVO) is a cornerstone of Modern Portfolio Theory, introduced by Harry Markowitz in the 1950s. It forms the foundation for constructing portfolios that achieve the best possible return for a given level of risk. This approach hinges on quantifying both the expected returns and the risk (variance) of different assets, then combining them in a way that minimizes the portfolio's overall risk for a desired return. Understanding MVO requires comprehending a few key concepts: expected returns, variance, covariance, and the efficient frontier.

The expected return of a portfolio is a weighted sum of the expected returns of its individual assets. Mathematically, if a portfolio consists of n assets, the expected return $E(R_p)$ can be expressed as:

$$E(R_p) = \sum_{i=1}^{n} w_i E(R_i)$$

where w_i represents the weight of the i-th asset in the portfolio and $E(R_i)$ is the expected return of the i-th asset.

Risk (variance), on the other hand, considers the volatility of the portfolio's returns, calculated as the weighted sum of the covariances between all pairs of assets in the portfolio. For n assets, the portfolio variance σ_p^2 is given by:

$$\sigma_p^2 = \sum_{i=1}^{n} \sum_{j=1}^{n} w_i w_j \sigma_{ij}$$

where σ_{ij} is the covariance between the returns of asset i and asset j.

The objective of mean-variance optimization is to identify the set of portfolios that minimize risk for a given level of expected return or maximize return for a given level of risk. These portfolios form the efficient frontier, a graphical representation of the optimal trade-offs between risk and return.

To construct the efficient frontier, one typically employs the following steps:

- **Estimate Expected Returns and Covariance Matrix**: Collect historical return data for the assets in the portfolio. Use this data to compute the expected returns and the covariance matrix of these returns.

- **Optimization Problem Setup**: Formulate the problem as a quadratic optimization problem where the goal is to minimize the risk (variance) for a given level of return. The formal optimization problem can be stated as:

  $$\min_{\boldsymbol{w}} \boldsymbol{w}^T \Sigma \boldsymbol{w} \quad \text{subject to} \quad \boldsymbol{w}^T \boldsymbol{\mu} = \mu_p, \quad \boldsymbol{w}^T \mathbf{1} = 1, \quad \boldsymbol{w} \geq 0$$

  Here, $\boldsymbol{w}$ is the vector of asset weights, Σ is the covariance matrix, $\boldsymbol{\mu}$ is the vector of expected asset returns, and μ_p is the target portfolio return. The constraint $\boldsymbol{w}^T \mathbf{1} = 1$ ensures that the weights sum to 100%, and $\boldsymbol{w} \geq 0$ ensures no short selling if required.

- **Solve the Optimization Problem**: Use numerical optimization techniques to solve the quadratic programming problem. Many software tools and libraries, such as MATLAB, R, Python (using libraries like 'cvxopt' or 'scipy.optimize'), can be employed to find the optimal asset weights $\boldsymbol{w}$.

- **Construct Efficient Frontier**: Repeat the optimization for different levels of expected return μ_p to obtain the corresponding portfolio risk (variance σ_p^2). Plot these points to construct the efficient frontier.

To illustrate, consider a simple example with three assets: Stock A, Stock B, and Stock C. Suppose the expected returns are 8%, 10%, and 12%, respectively, with a covariance matrix Σ given by:

$$\Sigma = \begin{pmatrix} 0.04 & 0.006 & 0.008 \\ 0.006 & 0.09 & 0.01 \\ 0.008 & 0.01 & 0.16 \end{pmatrix}$$

By setting various targets for μ_p and solving the quadratic optimization problem, we can obtain the optimal weights for each target return. Plotting these optimal portfolios gives us the efficient frontier.

While MVO offers a systematic method to achieve risk-return optimization, it does come with limitations. Key assumptions, such as the normality of returns and the stability of the covariance matrix, might not always hold in real markets. Additionally, the need for accurate estimation of expected returns and covariances can be challenging, often leading to estimation errors impacting the optimization outcome.

By recognizing and addressing these limitations, sophisticated traders can utilize advanced techniques like shrinkage estimators for covariance matrices or consider alternative optimization models that incorporate different risk measures. Nevertheless, mean-variance optimization remains a fundamental tool in the quantitative finance toolkit, offering vital insights into the risk-return trade-offs that underpin effective portfolio management.

7.6 Black-Litterman Model

The Black-Litterman model, developed by Fischer Black and Robert Litterman, is an influential framework for portfolio construction that combines the principles of Modern Portfolio Theory (MPT) with subjective views on expected returns. It addresses some limitations of mean-variance optimization, particularly its sensitivity to input assumptions and the tendency to produce extreme portfolio weights. By incorporating an investor's views and ensuring more stable and intuitive outcomes, the Black-Litterman model enhances the optimization process.

At its core, the Black-Litterman model begins with the market equilibrium, represented by a global market portfolio. This portfolio's expected returns reflect the implied equilibrium returns, ensuring a starting point grounded in market consensus. The model then integrates the investor's specific views on certain assets, adjusting these implied returns accordingly.

The process can be outlined as follows:

- 1. **Derive Implied Market Equilibrium Returns (Π)**:

$$\Pi = \lambda \Sigma w_m$$

  Here, Π represents the implied equilibrium excess returns (over the risk-free rate), λ is the risk aversion coefficient, Σ signifies the covariance matrix of returns, and w_m denotes the market capitalization weights of the global market portfolio.

- 2. **Formulate Investor's Views**: Investor views are expressed in the form of expected returns for specific assets or a relative performance view between different assets. These views can be either absolute or relative. The views are incorporated in the following matrix form:

$$Q = P\mu + \epsilon$$

  where Q is a vector of the investor's view returns, P is a matrix indicating which assets the views pertain to, μ is the estimated return vector, and ϵ is the error term with a covariance matrix Ω.

- 3. **Blend Views with Market Equilibrium**: The combined estimation of the expected returns (μ_B) is achieved by adjusting the implied returns with the investor's views. This blending process is given by the formula:

$$\mu_B = [(\tau\Sigma)^{-1} + P^T\Omega^{-1}P]^{-1}[(\tau\Sigma)^{-1}\Pi + P^T\Omega^{-1}Q]$$

  In the above, τ is a scalar reflecting the uncertainty in the prior estimated returns. The matrix P drives which assets are affected by the views, and Ω accounts for the uncertainty in the views themselves.

- 4. **Optimize the Portfolio**: Using the blended expected returns μ_B and the covariance matrix Σ, the Black-Litterman model then applies standard mean-variance optimization. The optimized portfolio weights (w^*) are given by:

$$w^* = \frac{1}{\lambda}\Sigma^{-1}\mu_B$$

  These weights represent the optimal allocation of assets incorporating both market consensus and investor views.

The practical application of the Black-Litterman model can be better understood through an example. Suppose an investor believes that the technology sector (Asset A) will outperform the consumer goods sector (Asset B) by 5%. This opinion is integrated into the model as a relative view:

$$Q = \begin{bmatrix} 0.05 \end{bmatrix}, \quad P = \begin{bmatrix} 1 & -1 \end{bmatrix}$$

This view asserts a relative return expectation while the model intrinsically balances the overall portfolio to remain aligned with market equilibrium norms.

The Black-Litterman model elegantly unifies the theoretical underpinnings of market equilibrium with practical, subjective views, resulting in a more robust and well-behaved optimization process. This methodology mitigates the potential pitfalls of traditional mean-variance optimization, particularly when faced with estimation errors or excessively aggressive allocations.

The thoughtful calibration of inputs, including an accurate estimation of the covariance matrix Σ and precise formulation of Ω, is critical. Variability in these parameters can significantly influence the model's output and, consequently, the resulting portfolio allocations.

Ultimately, the Black-Litterman model equips portfolio managers with a sophisticated tool to merge objective market data with nuanced investment insights. This harmony allows for informed decision-making grounded in a blend of empirical evidence and strategic foresight.

7.7 Multi-Factor Models

In the evolving landscape of quantitative finance, Multi-Factor Models have emerged as powerful tools for understanding asset returns. These models aim to decompose the sources of risk and return in a portfolio by identifying multiple factors that influence asset prices. Unlike single-factor models such as the Capital Asset Pricing Model (CAPM), which only considers market risk, multi-factor models offer a more nuanced and comprehensive framework for portfolio management.

The foundation of multi-factor models is the Arbitrage Pricing Theory (APT), introduced by Stephen Ross in 1976. APT asserts that asset returns can be predicted through a linear relationship with various macroeconomic factors. These factors could range from interest rate changes, inflation rates, economic growth indicators, to sector-specific risks. The general form of a multi-factor model can be expressed as:

$$R_i = \alpha_i + \beta_{i1}F_1 + \beta_{i2}F_2 + \cdots + \beta_{in}F_n + \epsilon_i$$

where:

- R_i is the expected return of asset i,
- α_i is the asset-specific return component,
- $F_1, F_2, \ldots, F_n$ are the systematic factors,
- $\beta_{i1}, \beta_{i2}, \ldots, \beta_{in}$ are the factor sensitivities (betas) of asset i to each factor,
- ϵ_i is the idiosyncratic error term or unsystematic risk specific to asset i.

Each factor represents a specific source of systemic risk, and the factor sensitivities (β) quantify the sensitivity of the asset's returns to these factors. In practice, some of the widely recognized factors include:

- **Market Risk** (F_{mkt}): The overall market return, capturing the broad market movements.
- **Size (SMB)**: Small minus big, representing the size premium, where smaller companies tend to have higher returns.
- **Value (HML)**: High minus low, representing the value premium, where stocks with high book-to-market ratios tend to outperform.
- **Momentum**: The tendency of stocks that have performed well in the past to continue performing well in the short-term.
- **Liquidity**: The ease with which an asset can be bought or sold in the market without affecting its price.

These factors can be discovered through empirical research and financial theory. For instance, the Fama-French Three-Factor Model extends the CAPM by including size and value factors alongside market risk. Similarly, the Carhart Four-Factor Model introduces a momentum factor to capture the tendency of trending stocks.

Implementing a multi-factor model involves several steps:

1. **Identification of Factors**: Select relevant factors based on empirical evidence and theoretical underpinnings.

2. **Estimation of Factor Sensitivities**: Use regression analysis to estimate the factor loadings (β) for each asset. This involves historical return data and the identified factors.

3. **Construction of Factor Portfolios**: Create portfolios that are long on assets with high exposure to the factor and short on those with low exposure. These can serve to isolate and hedge specific risks.

4. **Performance Evaluation and Adjustment**: Regularly assess the model's performance and adjust the factors or factor loadings as necessary to account for changes in the market environment or emerging factor anomalies.

By adopting multi-factor models, investors can achieve several benefits. Enhanced risk management becomes feasible as portfolios can be tailored to hedge against specific types of risks. This approach also aids in uncovering additional sources of return that might be overlooked by simpler models. Additionally, the granularity provided by these models supports more effective performance attribution, helping to distinguish between skill and luck in investment performance.

Practical application of multi-factor models requires access to robust data and computational resources. Financial software, coupled with statistical tools, facilitates the estimation and continuous monitoring of factor exposures. In doing so, investors are equipped to build and manage portfolios that are both resilient to market fluctuations and positioned to take advantage of systematic risk factors.

Integrating multi-factor models into portfolio management workflows allows for a sophisticated and refined approach to investing. By acknowledging and leveraging the complexity inherent in financial markets, these models provide a robust framework for achieving superior risk-adjusted returns.

7.8 Risk Parity and Diversification

In the realms of portfolio construction and management, risk parity and diversification stand out as fundamental concepts that strive to balance and mitigate risk while aiming for optimal returns. This section expounds on risk parity strategies and the principles of diversification, elucidating their significance in crafting a balanced and resilient investment portfolio.

Risk parity is an investment strategy that allocates portfolio weights so that each asset contributes equally to the overall portfolio risk. Unlike traditional methods that may concentrate risk in a few high-volatility assets, risk parity focuses on creating a more balanced risk distribution across all assets. The essence of risk parity lies in its approach to dealing with the inherent uncertainty in financial markets, emphasizing stability and systematic risk dispersion.

Consider a portfolio with n assets. The risk contribution of the i-th asset to the total portfolio risk, denoted RC_i, is given by the formula:

$$RC_i = w_i \cdot \left(\frac{\partial \sigma_p}{\partial w_i}\right)$$

where w_i is the weight of asset i in the portfolio, and σ_p is the portfolio's overall standard deviation (risk). The goal in risk parity is to find a set of weights $\{w_i\}$ such that each RC_i is equal, meeting the condition:

$$w_i \cdot \left(\frac{\partial \sigma_p}{\partial w_i}\right) = w_j \cdot \left(\frac{\partial \sigma_p}{\partial w_j}\right) \quad \forall i, j$$

This equality ensures that no single asset disproportionately affects the total portfolio risk, achieving a state of risk parity.

To delve deeper, let's explore a practical example. Assume we construct a simple portfolio with two assets: Asset A and Asset B. Let their volatilities (standard deviations) be $\sigma_A = 10\%$ and $\sigma_B = 20\%$, and their correlation $\rho_{A,B} = 0.3$. The portfolio's overall risk σ_p can be calculated using the formula:

$$\sigma_p = \sqrt{w_A^2 \cdot \sigma_A^2 + w_B^2 \cdot \sigma_B^2 + 2 \cdot w_A \cdot w_B \cdot \sigma_A \cdot \sigma_B \cdot \rho_{A,B}}$$

The risk contributions from assets A and B are then:

$$RC_A = w_A \cdot \sigma_A \cdot \frac{\partial \sigma_p}{\partial w_A} \quad \text{and} \quad RC_B = w_B \cdot \sigma_B \cdot \frac{\partial \sigma_p}{\partial w_B}$$

By iterating and adjusting the weights w_A and w_B, we achieve equal risk contributions, ensuring a balanced risk structure.

While risk parity provides a sophisticated mechanism for risk distribution, its efficacy is further enhanced when combined with the foundational investment principle of diversification. Diversification aims to spread investments across various assets, sectors, or geographies to reduce unsystematic risk—risk specific to a particular asset or industry. The principle operates on the premise that a diverse array of investments will average out individual risks, safeguarding the portfolio against significant losses from any single asset or market segment.

To achieve diversification, investors generally adhere to the following strategies: - **Asset Allocation:** Distributing capital across different asset classes (e.g., equities, bonds, real estate, commodities). Each class responds differently to market conditions, decreasing the portfolio's overall volatility. - **Geographical Diversification:** Investing in markets across different countries and regions. This approach mitigates the risk of regional economic downturns affecting the entire portfolio. - **Sector Diversification:** Spreading investments within various industries (e.g., technology, healthcare, finance). Different sectors often react distinctively to economic cycles and market events, balancing potential negative impacts from sector-specific downturns. - **Instrument Diversification:** Incorporating various financial instruments (e.g., stocks, bonds, derivatives) to ensure the portfolio's robustness against diverse risk factors.

The combined implementation of risk parity and diversification leads to the construction of a more resilient portfolio, capable of weathering adverse market conditions while seeking consistent returns. By ensuring equal risk contribution and spreading investments across uncorrelated or low-correlation assets, investors can significantly reduce portfolio risk and enhance long-term performance.

This balanced approach is essential for contemporary portfolio management, representing both theoretical soundness and practical application. Leveraging these principles empowers investors to navigate the complexities of financial markets with greater confidence and security.

7.9 Performance Measurement and Attribution

Performance measurement and attribution are critical facets of portfolio management, providing insights into the efficacy of investment strategies and enabling investment managers to make informed decisions.

While performance measurement quantifies the returns achieved by the portfolio, performance attribution breaks down those returns to identify the sources of returns and areas for improvement.

To begin with performance measurement, one must first understand the basic metrics commonly used. The primary metric is the total return, calculated as:

$$\text{Total Return} = \frac{P_t - P_{t-1} + D_t}{P_{t-1}}$$

where P_t is the current portfolio value, P_{t-1} is the previous portfolio value, and D_t represents any dividends received during the period.

However, simple return metrics often do not account for risk. Thus, risk-adjusted measures such as the Sharpe Ratio, Sortino Ratio, and Jensen's Alpha are employed. The Sharpe Ratio is defined as:

$$\text{Sharpe Ratio} = \frac{R_p - R_f}{\sigma_p}$$

where R_p is the portfolio return, R_f is the risk-free rate, and σ_p is the standard deviation of the portfolio returns.

On the other hand, the Sortino Ratio, which addresses the limitation of the Sharpe Ratio by considering downside risk, is expressed as:

$$\text{Sortino Ratio} = \frac{R_p - R_f}{\sigma_d}$$

where σ_d is the standard deviation of the downside risk.

Jensen's Alpha assesses a portfolio's excess return over the predicted return by the Capital Asset Pricing Model (CAPM):

$$\alpha = R_p - [R_f + \beta(R_m - R_f)]$$

where β represents the portfolio's beta, and R_m is the market return. Positive alpha indicates outperformance relative to the expected return based on market risk.

Performance attribution, meanwhile, delves deeper into performance metrics by dissecting returns into contributing factors. This process includes analyzing asset allocation, market timing, and security selection effects. The Brinson-Fachler model is a prominent attribution method, decomposing active return into allocation and selection effects. The equations for these effects are:

$$\text{Allocation Effect} = \sum_{i=1}^{N} (w_{i,p} - w_{i,b})(R_{i,b} - R_b)$$

$$\text{Selection Effect} = \sum_{i=1}^{N} w_{i,b}(R_{i,p} - R_{i,b})$$

where $w_{i,p}$ and $w_{i,b}$ are the portfolio and benchmark weights for asset i, $R_{i,p}$ and $R_{i,b}$ are the portfolio and benchmark returns for asset i, and R_b is the total benchmark return.

Some models also consider the interaction effect, accounting for the combined impact of allocation and selection:

$$\text{Interaction Effect} = \sum_{i=1}^{N} (w_{i,p} - w_{i,b})(R_{i,p} - R_{i,b})$$

It's vital for portfolio managers to continuously evaluate these metrics to ensure their strategies align with investment goals and risk tolerance. By understanding the sources of returns and shortcomings within their portfolios, managers can adjust their strategies to optimize performance further. Effective use of performance measurement and attribution tools ensures that investment decisions are data-driven, enhancing transparency and accountability in the investing process.

7.10 Applying Optimization in Real Markets

For portfolio managers and individual investors alike, successfully applying optimization techniques in real markets is the ultimate test of practical financial acumen. Translating theoretical constructs into actionable investment strategies involves more than mathematical rigor; it necessitates an understanding of market dynamics, regulatory environments, and behavioral economics.

One of the primary challenges in implementing optimization is the estimation of inputs—namely, expected returns, risks (variances and covariances), and potential correlations among assets. Historical data is often the most accessible source, but it may not always predict future performance accurately. Thus, blending historical insights with forward-looking estimates, possibly through the incorporation of macroeconomic indicators and subjective judgments, can refine the optimization process.

Consider a hypothetical equity portfolio composed of five stocks: AAPL, MSFT, GOOGL, AMZN, and TSLA. The first step is calculating the expected returns and the covariance matrix. Using historical monthly returns data for the past five years, we begin by computing the arithmetic mean return for each stock:

$$\hat{R}_i = \frac{1}{T} \sum_{t=1}^{T} R_{i,t}$$

where $\hat{R}_i$ is the estimated return for asset i, and $R_{i,t}$ is the return of asset i at time t.

Next, the covariance matrix, Σ, is derived as follows:

$$\Sigma_{ij} = \frac{1}{T-1} \sum_{t=1}^{T} (R_{i,t} - \hat{R}_i)(R_{j,t} - \hat{R}_j)$$

where Σ_{ij} is the covariance between assets i and j.

The optimization process can then proceed by solving the mean-variance optimization problem. The objective function seeks to minimize portfolio variance for a given expected return:

$$\min_{\boldsymbol{w}} \boldsymbol{w}^T \Sigma \boldsymbol{w} \quad \text{subject to} \quad \boldsymbol{w}^T \mathbf{1} = 1 \quad \text{and} \quad \boldsymbol{w}^T \hat{\boldsymbol{R}} = R_p$$

where $\boldsymbol{w}$ is the vector of portfolio weights, $\mathbf{1}$ is a vector of ones, $\hat{\boldsymbol{R}}$ is the vector of expected returns, and R_p is the target expected return.

In practical scenarios, constraints are critical. Real-world portfolios often incorporate restrictions on maximum allocation to any single asset, sectors, or regions. For instance, a regulation might prevent a weight exceeding 10% for any single stock:

$$0 \leq w_i \leq 0.10 \quad \forall i$$

Advanced optimization incorporates risk management measures such as Conditional Value-at-Risk (CVaR). CVaR optimizes not just the expected return but minimizes the risk of extreme losses:

$$\min_{\boldsymbol{w}} \left\{ \alpha \cdot \boldsymbol{w}^T \Sigma \boldsymbol{w} + (1 - \alpha) \cdot \text{CVaR} \right\}$$

where $0 \leq \alpha \leq 1$ determines the weight between variance and CVaR considerations.

The Black-Litterman model addresses the difficulty of specifying precise expected returns. By blending a prior estimate of returns (often derived from a market equilibrium model such as the Capital Asset Pricing Model) with investor views, this model constructs a refined set of expected returns:

$$\hat{\boldsymbol{R}}_{BL} = \left(\tau \Sigma^{-1} + P^T \Omega^{-1} P \right)^{-1} \left(\tau \Sigma^{-1} \Pi + P^T \Omega^{-1} Q \right)$$

where τ is a scalar reflecting the uncertainty in the prior, Π represents equilibrium excess returns, P is a matrix identifying the investor's views, Ω is a diagonal covariance matrix of the error terms for the views, and Q is a vector of the returns attached to these views.

The implementation demands proficiency in systems such as R or Python. Here's a snippet illustrating the use of Python and the 'cvxpy' library to solve a mean-variance optimization problem:

```
import cvxpy as cp
import numpy as np

# Define input parameters
expected_returns = np.array([0.12, 0.10, 0.15, 0.13, 0.09])
cov_matrix = np.array([
    [0.04, 0.01, 0.02, 0.01, 0.03],
    [0.01, 0.05, 0.03, 0.01, 0.02],
    [0.02, 0.03, 0.06, 0.02, 0.01],
    [0.01, 0.01, 0.02, 0.04, 0.01],
    [0.03, 0.02, 0.01, 0.01, 0.05]
])
weights = cp.Variable(5)
risk = cp.quad_form(weights, cov_matrix)
ret = expected_returns @ weights

# Define constraints
constraints = [cp.sum(weights) == 1, weights >= 0, weights <= 0.10]

# Solve the optimization problem
prob = cp.Problem(cp.Minimize(risk), constraints)
prob.solve()

print("Optimal weights: ", weights.value)
```

This script estimates optimal weights for a predefined set of inputs, accommodating practical constraints such as non-negative weights and a cap on maximum individual asset exposure.

While algorithms and computational tools enable the execution of these strategies, human judgment remains indispensable. Market conditions evolve, and so must the optimization models. Regular rebalancing of portfolios ensures they remain aligned with the original investment objectives and risk tolerance.

Thus, applying optimization in real markets is a blend of scientific rigor and artful navigation through market intricacies. It encompasses continuous validation and adaptation of models to leverage mathematical constructs effectively while accommodating the fluid nature of financial markets.

Chapter 8

The Black-Scholes Model and Option Pricing

The Black-Scholes model is a cornerstone of modern option pricing theory. This chapter explains the model's derivation, underlying assumptions, and practical application in determining the fair value of options. It introduces the Black-Scholes formula, explores the Greeks for sensitivity analysis, and discusses the concept of implied volatility. Further, the chapter examines the model's limitations and potential extensions, providing a thorough understanding of both its theoretical foundations and real-world implications in financial markets.

8.1 Introduction to Options

Options are financial derivatives that provide investors with the right, but not the obligation, to buy or sell an underlying asset at a predetermined price, known as the strike price, before or at a specified expiration date. These instruments are versatile and widely used for various investment strategies, including hedging, speculation, and arbitrage. Understanding options forms the foundation for grasping the more complex facets of the Black-Scholes model.

An option contract typically comes in two forms: calls and puts. A call option grants the holder the right to buy the underlying asset, while a put option gives the holder the right to sell it. These rights create significant leverage, allowing investors to control larger positions with a relatively small amount of capital. However, this leverage also introduces potential risks, making it imperative for traders to fully understand option mechanics.

The value of an option is influenced by several factors known as the "option Greeks," such as delta, gamma, theta, vega, and rho. These sensitivity measures help quantify the risk and potential reward associated with holding an option under various market conditions.

Consider the basic payoff structures of call and put options to understand their potential outcomes. For a call option, the payoff at expiration can be expressed as:

$$\text{Payoff}_{\text{call}} = \max(S_T - K, 0)$$

where S_T is the underlying asset's price at expiration and K is the strike price. Conversely, the payoff for a put option is:

$$\text{Payoff}_{\text{put}} = \max(K - S_T, 0)$$

These payoff functions illustrate that call options are profitable when the underlying asset's price exceeds the strike price at expiration, while put options are beneficial when the asset's price falls below the strike price.

Besides intrinsic value, which is the immediate exercise value of the option, options also possess time value. The time value reflects the potential for future favorable movements in the underlying asset's price and decays as the expiration date approaches. Mathematically, the price of an option (C for calls and P for puts) can be decomposed into intrinsic value and time value as follows:

$$C = \max(S - K, 0) + \text{Time Value}$$

$$P = \max(K - S, 0) + \text{Time Value}$$

Investors engage in options trading for multiple strategic reasons. Hedging involves using options to reduce the risk of adverse price movements in an existing position. For instance, an investor holding a stock portfolio might purchase put options to protect against a potential decline in the portfolio's value. This strategy creates a safety net, ensuring that losses are limited even if the market moves unfavorably.

Speculation, on the other hand, involves taking positions in options based on expected future price movements of the underlying asset. A trader anticipating a significant rise in a stock's price might purchase call options to benefit from the anticipated increase. This speculative approach leverages options' inherent properties to maximize potential gains with comparatively lower capital outlay.

Arbitrage involves exploiting price discrepancies between different markets or instruments to secure risk-free profit. This strategy often requires sophisticated analytical tools and a deep understanding of market mechanics. For example, an investor might engage in put-call parity arbitrage by simultaneously buying and selling options and the underlying asset to capture price differentials.

The attractiveness of options as financial instruments lies in their adaptability and the diverse strategies they enable. From straightforward directional bets to complex multi-leg combinations, options provide unparalleled flexibility for constructing tailored investment strategies. Popular strategies include covered calls, protective puts, straddles, and strangles, each serving different market outlooks and risk tolerance levels.

One crucial aspect of options trading to comprehend is implied volatility. Implied volatility represents the market's expectation of the underlying asset's price volatility over the option's life. Unlike historical volatility, which looks back at past price movements, implied volatility is forward-looking and can significantly impact option pricing. High implied volatility typically leads to more expensive options, reflecting greater uncertainty about the future price movement of the underlying asset.

$$\text{Implied Volatility} = \sigma_{\text{impl}}$$

Given an options-pricing model like Black-Scholes, the implied volatility can be extracted by inputting the market price of the option into the model and solving for the volatility parameter. This volatility metric is a critical component for traders when assessing options' fair value and potential profitability.

Options, by their very nature, introduce significant complexities into trading and investing activities. Mastery of these instruments necessitates a solid grasp of their fundamental characteristics, pricing mechanisms, and the strategic avenues they unlock. Equipped with this knowledge, investors can proficiently navigate the dynamic landscape of options markets, leveraging these versatile tools to achieve robust financial outcomes.

8.2 Understanding the Black-Scholes Model

The Black-Scholes model, developed by Fischer Black, Myron Scholes, and Robert Merton, is one of the most significant advancements in financial economics. It provides a theoretical framework for determining the fair value of European-style options, making it an indispensable tool in derivatives trading. Understanding this model starts with grasping its fundamental principles, which combine concepts from stochastic processes, differential equations, and financial theory.

At its core, the Black-Scholes model is constructed around the concept of a continuously sampled and normally distributed stochastic process, commonly referred to as a geometric Brownian motion. This process models the price dynamics of the underlying asset, providing a realistic representation of its random walk. Mathematically, the price of the underlying asset $S(t)$ at time t is modeled by the stochastic differential equation (SDE):

$$dS(t) = \mu S(t)dt + \sigma S(t)dW(t)$$

Here, μ represents the drift coefficient (average rate of return), σ signifies the volatility (standard deviation of returns), and $W(t)$ denotes a Wiener process or standard Brownian motion. The presence of $dW(t)$ introduces the stochastic element, encapsulating the randomness inherent in asset price movements.

An integral part of the Black-Scholes model is the concept of no-arbitrage, which asserts that any pricing model should exclude arbitrage opportunities. Arbitrage, the act of exploiting price discrepancies across markets for risk-free profit, is a crucial consideration in both theoretical finance and practical trading. The Black-Scholes framework ensures that the price of an option is set in such a way that no arbitrage possibilities exist, thus providing a fair and equilibrium-consistent option valuation.

The Black-Scholes partial differential equation (PDE) is derived by constructing a riskless portfolio comprising a long position in the underlying asset and a short position in the option. This portfolio must yield the risk-free rate of return r, leading to the following PDE:

$$\frac{\partial f}{\partial t} + \frac{1}{2}\sigma^2 S^2 \frac{\partial^2 f}{\partial S^2} + rS\frac{\partial f}{\partial S} - rf = 0$$

In this equation, f represents the option price, t is the time, and S is the underlying asset's price. Solving this PDE with appropriate boundary conditions yields the Black-Scholes formula, which determines the price of a European call or put option.

One of the model's elegant features is its reliance on the assumption of continuous trading and the absence of transaction costs. Additionally, it presumes that the underlying asset's returns are log-normally distributed, meaning that while the asset prices themselves can vary widely, their logarithms follow a normal distribution. This log-normality assumption aligns well with observed financial market behavior over practical time horizons.

The Black-Scholes formula for the price C of a European call option is expressed as:

$$C = S_0 N(d_1) - Ke^{-rT} N(d_2)$$

Where:

$$d_1 = \frac{\ln(S_0/K) + (r + \sigma^2/2)T}{\sigma\sqrt{T}}$$

$$d_2 = d_1 - \sigma\sqrt{T}$$

In these equations:

- S_0 is the current price of the underlying asset.
- K denotes the option's strike price.
- T represents the time to maturity.
- r is the risk-free interest rate.
- σ signifies the volatility of the underlying asset.
- $N(\cdot)$ is the cumulative distribution function of the standard normal distribution.

The counterpart formula for a European put option P is derived analogously:

$$P = Ke^{-rT}N(-d_2) - S_0N(-d_1)$$

These closed-form solutions provide traders and investors with exact prices for European options, enabling efficient market operations and risk management.

Understanding the Black-Scholes model also requires recognizing its assumptions and limitations. While the model assumes no dividends, constant volatility, constant interest rates, and the possibility of continuously hedging, real markets seldom conform perfectly to these conditions. Consequently, applying the Black-Scholes model involves a blend of theoretical rigor and practical adjustments, helping market participants devise robust trading strategies while acknowledging the model's boundaries.

Such comprehension lays the groundwork for exploring the Greeks, implied volatility, and other advanced topics, ultimately enriching one's ability to navigate the complexities of financial markets with confidence and precision.

8.3 Derivation of the Black-Scholes Equation

The derivation of the Black-Scholes equation is both a remarkable and intricate achievement in financial mathematics. The model was developed by Fischer Black and Myron Scholes, and it provides a theoretical framework for pricing European options. The derivation employs stochastic calculus, particularly Itô's lemma, to model the dynamics of the underlying asset's price movement in a continuous time framework. Here, we will delineate this derivation step-by-step, ensuring clarity through each mathematical transformation and conceptual leap.

Consider an asset whose price at time t is denoted by $S(t)$. To model the evolution of $S(t)$, we assume it follows a geometric Brownian motion characterized by the stochastic differential equation:

$$dS(t) = \mu S(t)dt + \sigma S(t)dW(t)$$

where:

- μ is the drift rate of the asset.

- σ is the volatility of the asset price.
- $W(t)$ is a Wiener process or standard Brownian motion.

To proceed, consider a European call option on this asset with price $C(S,t)$ at time t when the asset price is S. Our objective is to determine a partial differential equation (PDE) that C must satisfy. Begin by noting that C is a function of two variables: the asset price S and time t.

Using Itô's lemma, we can express the differential of $C(S,t)$:

$$dC = \left(\frac{\partial C}{\partial t} + \mu S\frac{\partial C}{\partial S} + \frac{1}{2}\sigma^2 S^2\frac{\partial^2 C}{\partial S^2}\right) dt + \sigma S\frac{\partial C}{\partial S} dW(t)$$

Next, construct a portfolio Π composed of one short position in the option and an amount Δ of the underlying asset, such that:

$$\Pi = -C + \Delta S$$

The change in this portfolio value over a small interval dt is:

$$d\Pi = -dC + \Delta dS$$

Substituting the expressions for dC and dS:

$$\begin{aligned} d\Pi &= -\left(\frac{\partial C}{\partial t} + \mu S\frac{\partial C}{\partial S} + \frac{1}{2}\sigma^2 S^2\frac{\partial^2 C}{\partial S^2}\right) dt - \sigma S\frac{\partial C}{\partial S} dW(t) + \Delta\left(\mu S dt + \sigma S dW(t)\right) \\ &= \left[-\frac{\partial C}{\partial t} - \mu S\frac{\partial C}{\partial S} - \frac{1}{2}\sigma^2 S^2\frac{\partial^2 C}{\partial S^2} + \Delta\mu S\right] dt + \left[\Delta\sigma S - \sigma S\frac{\partial C}{\partial S}\right] dW(t) \end{aligned}$$

To eliminate the stochastic term (the term involving $dW(t)$), we set:

$$\Delta = \frac{\partial C}{\partial S}$$

This choice yields:

$$d\Pi = \left(-\frac{\partial C}{\partial t} - \frac{1}{2}\sigma^2 S^2\frac{\partial^2 C}{\partial S^2}\right) dt$$

Note that the portfolio Π is risk-free (since the stochastic term has been eliminated), implying it must earn the risk-free rate of return r. Therefore:

$$d\Pi = r\Pi dt$$

Substituting $\Pi = -C + \Delta S = -C + S\frac{\partial C}{\partial S}$:

$$\left(-\frac{\partial C}{\partial t} - \frac{1}{2}\sigma^2 S^2 \frac{\partial^2 C}{\partial S^2}\right) dt = r\left(-C + S\frac{\partial C}{\partial S}\right) dt$$

Canceling dt and rearranging terms gives the Black-Scholes PDE:

$$\frac{\partial C}{\partial t} + rS\frac{\partial C}{\partial S} + \frac{1}{2}\sigma^2 S^2 \frac{\partial^2 C}{\partial S^2} - rC = 0$$

This completes the derivation of the Black-Scholes equation. This fundamental PDE underpins much of modern financial theory and the myriad of applications in pricing European options. The final form neatly encapsulates the interplay between the option's price sensitivity to the underlying asset and the passage of time, adjusted for both volatility and the risk-free rate.

8.4 Assumptions of the Black-Scholes Model

The Black-Scholes Model, while powerful and widely utilized, is built upon a set of key assumptions that form the foundation of its theoretical framework. Understanding these assumptions is crucial for comprehending the model's strengths, its practical applications, and its limitations in real-world trading. Here, we will explore these assumptions in detail, shedding light on how they contribute to the model's structure and where they might diverge from market realities.

S(t) = Price of the underlying asset at time t

1. No Arbitrage Opportunities

The first and perhaps most fundamental assumption is that there are no arbitrage opportunities in the market. Arbitrage, the practice of exploiting price discrepancies of the same asset in different markets, is assumed to be nonexistent. If arbitrage exists, traders could potentially make risk-free profits, undermining the model's pricing outcomes. The no-arbitrage condition ensures a fair pricing environment where the relationship between the option price and the underlying asset price is maintained without external distortions.

2. Log-Normally Distributed Returns

The model assumes that the returns of the underlying asset follow a log-normal distribution. This implies that while the asset price itself can vary widely, the logarithm of the asset price is normally distributed. Mathematically, if S(t) is the price of the underlying asset at time t, then ln(S(t)) is normally distributed. The log-normality assumption ensures that the asset prices are non-negative and provides a tractable framework for modeling price dynamics.

3. Constant Volatility and Interest Rates

Volatility, which measures the asset price's tendency to fluctuate, and the risk-free interest rate are both assumed to be constant over the option's life. Volatility is denoted by σ, and the risk-free rate by r. These constants greatly simplify the analytical derivation of the Black-Scholes formula:

$$dS = \mu S dt + \sigma S dW$$

where μ is the drift rate, and dW represents a Wiener process (a form of Brownian motion).

4. Continuous Trading

The model assumes that trading occurs continuously, allowing for the continuous hedging of options positions. This means that investors can buy and sell the underlying asset and the option at any point in time without restriction. Continuous trading helps maintain the dynamic replication strategy assumed in the model, which requires frequent adjusting of the portfolio to remain delta-neutral.

5. No Dividends During Option Life

For simplicity, the original Black-Scholes model assumes that the underlying asset does not pay dividends during the option's life. This places a constraint on its immediate use for dividend-paying stocks, although modifications and extensions of the model have addressed this limitation. The dividend-adjusted model incorporates expected dividend payments to refine the pricing accuracy.

6. Efficient Markets

The efficient market hypothesis underpins the Black-Scholes model, suggesting that market prices fully reflect all available information. In such a market, price changes are driven by new information, and prices fluctuate accordingly. The asset prices follow a geometric Brownian motion, meaning they capture the stochastic nature of price movements under an efficient market framework.

7. No Transaction Costs or Taxes

Another practical simplification is the assumption that there are no transaction costs or taxes. This allows for the construction and rebalancing of a hedged portfolio without incurring additional costs, facilitating the theoretical application of the model. In practice, transaction costs and taxes do affect the profitability and replicability of trading strategies, but they are omitted here to maintain clarity in the model's core mechanics.

8. Risk-Neutral Valuation

The Black-Scholes model employs risk-neutral valuation, where it's assumed that investors are indifferent to risk. This approach simplifies the pricing by discounting expected payoffs at the risk-free rate instead of including a risk premium. Under risk-neutrality, the expected growth rate of the underlying asset equals the risk-free rate:

$$\mathbb{E}\left[\frac{\text{S(T)}}{\text{S(t)}}\right] = e^{r(T-t)}$$

Given these assumptions, the Black-Scholes model offers a robust analytical framework for pricing European-style options. However, it's essential to be aware of these underlying assumptions, especially when applying the model to real-world scenarios where deviations from the idealized conditions are likely to occur. Understanding these limitations helps traders and investors better calibrate the model to observed market conditions and adapt strategies to cater to practical constraints.

8.5 The Black-Scholes Formula

The Black-Scholes formula is an essential tool for determining the fair market value of European call and put options. This seminal model, introduced by Fischer Black and Myron Scholes in 1973, provides a closed-form solution that revolutionizes financial markets.

At its core, the Black-Scholes formula relies on several key variables:

- S – The current price of the underlying asset.
- K – The strike price of the option.
- T – The time to maturity of the option (in years).
- σ – The volatility of the underlying asset.
- r – The risk-free interest rate.

The beauty of the Black-Scholes model lies in its ability to combine these variables into a single expression that yields the theoretical price of an option. Below, we present the formulas for European call and put options:

$$C = S\Phi(d_1) - Ke^{-rT}\Phi(d_2)$$
$$P = Ke^{-rT}\Phi(-d_2) - S\Phi(-d_1)$$

Here, Φ represents the cumulative distribution function (CDF) of the standard normal distribution, and d_1 and d_2 are calculated as follows:

$$d_1 = \frac{\ln\left(\frac{S}{K}\right) + \left(r + \frac{\sigma^2}{2}\right)T}{\sigma\sqrt{T}}$$
$$d_2 = d_1 - \sigma\sqrt{T}$$

The cumulative distribution function $\Phi(d)$ gives the probability that a standard normal variable will be less than or equal to d. This use of the normal distribution is a reflection of the assumption that the returns of the underlying asset follow a geometric Brownian motion, creating a log-normal distribution of prices.

To better illustrate how the Black-Scholes formula is applied in practice, consider the following example:

Example

Let's assume an investor is interested in pricing a European call option on a stock currently priced at $S = \$50$. The strike price K is \$55, the time to maturity T is 0.5 years, the risk-free rate r is 5% (0.05 in decimal form), and the volatility σ is 20% (0.20 in decimal form).

We start by calculating d_1 and d_2:

$$\begin{aligned} d_1 &= \frac{\ln\left(\frac{50}{55}\right) + \left(0.05 + \frac{0.20^2}{2}\right) \times 0.5}{0.20\sqrt{0.5}} \\ &= \frac{\ln(0.9091) + (0.05 + 0.02) \times 0.5}{0.20 \times 0.7071} \\ &= \frac{-0.0953 + 0.035}{0.1414} \\ &= -0.4276 \end{aligned}$$

$$\begin{aligned} d_2 &= -0.4276 - 0.20 \times 0.7071 \\ &= -0.4276 - 0.1414 \\ &= -0.5690 \end{aligned}$$

Next, we find $\Phi(d_1)$ and $\Phi(d_2)$. Using standard normal distribution tables or a computational tool, we get:

$$\begin{aligned} \Phi(d_1) &\approx \Phi(-0.4276) \approx 0.334 \\ \Phi(d_2) &\approx \Phi(-0.5690) \approx 0.285 \end{aligned}$$

Finally, we substitute these values into the Black-Scholes formula for the call option price:

$$
\begin{aligned}
C &= 50 \times 0.334 - 55 \times e^{-0.05 \times 0.5} \times 0.285 \\
&= 16.70 - 55 \times 0.9753 \times 0.285 \\
&= 16.70 - 15.27 \\
&= 1.43
\end{aligned}
$$

Thus, the theoretical price of the call option is approximately $1.43.

The Black-Scholes formula is not only a cornerstone for option pricing but also serves as a foundation for further explorations into derivative markets and financial engineering. Understanding and applying this formula illuminates the dynamics of option prices, allowing for more sophisticated trading and risk management strategies.

8.6 Greeks: Sensitivity Measures

The concept of the Greeks is pivotal in the realm of option pricing and risk management. These sensitivity measures provide a deeper understanding of the various factors that influence an option's price. Named after Greek letters, the Greeks are instrumental in constructing hedging strategies and gauging risk exposure.

The primary Greeks are Delta (Δ), Gamma (Γ), Theta (Θ), Vega (ν or Λ), and Rho (ρ). Each measures a specific type of sensitivity, and together, they offer a comprehensive view of an option's behavior under different market conditions.

Delta (Δ)

Delta represents the sensitivity of an option's price to changes in the price of the underlying asset. It is defined as the first derivative of the option price with respect to the underlying asset's price:

$$
\Delta = \frac{\partial V}{\partial S}
$$

where V is the option price and S is the underlying asset's price. For call options, Delta ranges from 0 to 1, indicating the option price moves in the same direction as the underlying asset. For put options, Delta ranges from -1 to 0, reflecting an inverse relationship.

Delta is crucial for hedging, providing a direct measure of the number of units of the underlying asset needed to hedge one option. For example, a Delta of 0.5 means holding 0.5 units of the underlying asset per option to remain delta-neutral.

Gamma (Γ)

Gamma measures the rate of change of Delta with respect to the underlying asset's price, providing insight into the convexity of the option's price:

$$\Gamma = \frac{\partial \Delta}{\partial S} = \frac{\partial^2 V}{\partial S^2}$$

A higher Gamma indicates greater sensitivity of Delta to changes in the underlying asset's price. This measure is particularly important for at-the-money options, where Gamma is typically highest.

Gamma helps in understanding the stability of Delta and is crucial for designing advanced hedging strategies, as it influences the adjustments needed to maintain a delta-neutral position.

Theta (Θ)

Theta represents the sensitivity of the option's price to the passage of time, often termed as time decay. It is defined as the first derivative of the option price with respect to time:

$$\Theta = \frac{\partial V}{\partial t}$$

Theta is generally negative for options, indicating that the option loses value as it approaches expiration, all else being equal. For long option positions, a higher magnitude of negative Theta signifies greater time decay, which is a crucial consideration for traders holding options over a period.

Vega (ν or Λ)

Vega measures the sensitivity of the option's price to changes in the volatility of the underlying asset. Formally, it is the first derivative of the option price with respect to the volatility (σ):

$$\nu = \frac{\partial V}{\partial \sigma}$$

Vega is essential in understanding the impact of volatility fluctuations, which are often significant due to market events. Options with higher Vega are more sensitive to changes in volatility, making this Greek particularly relevant in volatile markets.

Rho (ρ)

Rho measures the sensitivity of the option's price to changes in the risk-free interest rate. It is defined as the first derivative of the option price with respect to the interest rate (r):

$$\rho = \frac{\partial V}{\partial r}$$

For call options, Rho is typically positive, whereas for put options, it is negative. Although Rho is often less emphasized compared to other Greeks, it becomes crucial in environments with fluctuating interest rates, affecting the pricing and strategic decisions for long-term options.

Understanding and utilizing these Greeks effectively empower traders to manage risk, develop precise hedging strategies, and make informed decisions under different market conditions. Each Greek offers distinctive insights, collectively enabling a robust framework for option valuation and strategic implementation in the financial markets.

8.7 Implied Volatility

Implied volatility is an integral concept in the realm of option pricing and is a pivotal factor for traders and investors seeking to understand the market's expectations of future volatility. Unlike historical volatility, which is calculated based on past price movements, implied volatility is forward-looking and derived from the market prices of options. It serves as an indicator of the market's consensus on the uncertainty or risk associated with the price of the underlying asset.

To delve into implied volatility, one must first recognize that it is not directly observable; rather, it must be inferred from the market prices of options using the Black-Scholes model. The Black-Scholes formula, which provides the theoretical price of option contracts, takes into account several known parameters such as the underlying asset's current price, the strike price, time to expiration, risk-free interest rate, and dividend yield. The volatility parameter in the model, however, can be adjusted to match the model's output to the actual market price of the option. The volatility value that achieves this match is known as the implied volatility.

Mathematically, determining the implied volatility involves solving the Black-Scholes equation for the volatility parameter σ. Given the complexity of the Black-Scholes formula, this is typically done using numerical methods, as there is no closed-form solution for implied volatility.

The typical approach is to use iterative techniques such as the Newton-Raphson method to converge on the implied volatility value.

The equation for a European call option under the Black-Scholes model is given by:

$$C = S_0\Phi(d_1) - Ke^{-rT}\Phi(d_2)$$

where

$$d_1 = \frac{\ln\left(\frac{S_0}{K}\right) + \left(r + \frac{\sigma^2}{2}\right)T}{\sigma\sqrt{T}}$$

$$d_2 = d_1 - \sigma\sqrt{T}$$

Φ represents the cumulative distribution function of the standard normal distribution, S_0 is the current price of the underlying asset, K is the strike price, r is the risk-free interest rate, T is the time to expiration, and σ is the volatility.

Given a market price C_m for the call option, the implied volatility σ_{imp} is the volatility input that solves:

$$S_0\Phi(d_1) - Ke^{-rT}\Phi(d_2) = C_m$$

Determining σ_{imp} can be visualized as finding the point where the actual market price intersects with the theoretical price curve, given the other known parameters.

Implied volatility is crucial because it reflects the market sentiment and can affect trading decisions. High implied volatility suggests that the market expects significant price fluctuations in the underlying asset, which could be an indicator of upcoming news events, earnings reports, or other market-moving occurrences. Conversely, low implied volatility implies that the market anticipates stable or less volatile price movements.

For practical applications, traders often refer to volatility surfaces and volatility smiles to gain deeper insights. A volatility surface is a three-dimensional plot that shows the implied volatility for different strike prices and maturities, revealing patterns and anomalies that could indicate mispricing or specific market conditions. The volatility smile, which is a cross-section of the volatility surface, plots implied volatility against strike prices for options with the same maturity. It often shows a "smile" shape, where out-of-the-money and in-the-money options exhibit higher implied volatilities compared to at-the-money options.

Understanding implied volatility helps traders make more informed decisions regarding option strategies. It allows them to gauge the relative expensiveness of options, implement strategies like volatility arbitrage, or hedge positions effectively. Moreover, changes in implied volatility can significantly impact option prices, thereby affecting the profitability of option positions.

Finally, it is important to recognize that implied volatility, while insightful, is not infallible. It encapsulates the market's expectations, which can be influenced by a myriad of factors, both rational and irrational. Hence, while it is a valuable tool, it should be considered alongside other analytical methods and market indicators to construct a well-rounded trading or investment strategy.

8.8 Applications of the Black-Scholes Model

The Black-Scholes model has transformed the landscape of financial markets by providing a standardized and theoretically sound method for pricing options. Its applications extend beyond mere academic interest, serving as a practical tool for traders, risk managers, and financial engineers. This section delves into the various applications, offering insight into how this model facilitates the understanding and exploitation of option markets.

One primary application of the Black-Scholes model is in the accurate pricing of European options. By employing the Black-Scholes formula:

$$C = S_0 N(d_1) - X e^{-rT} N(d_2)$$

where

$$d_1 = \frac{\ln(S_0/X) + (r + \sigma^2/2)T}{\sigma\sqrt{T}}, \quad d_2 = d_1 - \sigma\sqrt{T}$$

market participants can determine the theoretical fair value of a call option. Similarly, put options can be priced using:

$$P = X e^{-rT} N(-d_2) - S_0 N(-d_1)$$

These formulas consider factors like the underlying asset's current price (S_0), strike price (X), time to maturity (T), risk-free rate (r), and volatility (σ). By inputting these parameters, traders can establish the expected cost of an option, aiding in informed decision-making and effective portfolio management.

Furthermore, the Black-Scholes model is instrumental in deriving the Greeks, which are critical sensitivity measures that describe how the option's price changes in response to various factors. These include:

- Delta (Δ): Measures the rate of change of the option's price concerning the underlying asset's price.
- Gamma (Γ): Assesses the rate of change of Delta concerning the underlying asset's price.
- Theta (Θ): Represents the rate of change of the option's price concerning the passage of time.
- Vega (ν): Gauges the sensitivity of the option's price to changes in the volatility of the underlying asset.
- Rho (ρ): Evaluates the sensitivity of the option's price to changes in the risk-free interest rate.

Risk managers utilize these Greeks to hedge portfolios against market fluctuations. For instance, by understanding Delta, they can construct Delta-neutral portfolios, reducing market risk exposure. Gamma helps in managing the convexity of the portfolio, thereby ensuring a higher level of risk precision. Theta gives insights into time decay, which is particularly crucial for options nearing expiration. Vega and Rho are essential for managing volatility and interest rate risks, respectively.

Additionally, the Black-Scholes model facilitates the computation of implied volatility. Unlike historical volatility, which is backward-looking, implied volatility estimates the market's view of the underlying asset's future volatility, extrapolated from the current option prices. By rearranging the Black-Scholes formula and solving for σ, traders can infer implied volatility, aiding in the valuation of volatility trades like straddles and strangles.

Derivatives desks frequently employ the Black-Scholes framework to optimize trading strategies. For example, traders arbitrage mispriced options by comparing market prices with theoretical prices computed via Black-Scholes. Identifying discrepancies allows them to buy undervalued options or sell overvalued ones, locking in risk-free profits.

In corporate finance, the Black-Scholes model plays a pivotal role in valuing employee stock options (ESOs). These options, often part of employee compensation packages, are similar to European calls. Companies use Black-Scholes to estimate the cost and benefits accurately, ensuring fair valuation in financial statements and aiding in strategic HR policies.

Beyond plain vanilla options, the model extends to complex derivatives through various modifications. Adjusted models account for dividends, American options' early exercise feature, and other intricacies not covered by the original framework. For instance, incorporating dividends into the Black-Scholes formula involves adjusting the stock price S_0 by the present value of expected dividends.

The practical use cases of the Black-Scholes model underscore its significance in modern finance. From trading and risk management to corporate governance and strategic planning, it remains an indispensable tool for professionals striving for precision and efficiency in the dynamic world of financial markets.

8.9 Limitations and Extensions of the Black-Scholes Model

The Black-Scholes model, while revolutionary and widely used, is not without its flaws and limitations. Recognizing these limitations enables traders and financial analysts to make more informed decisions, potentially seeking alternative models or extensions to improve pricing accuracy.

One significant limitation of the Black-Scholes model is its underlying assumption of constant volatility. In reality, market volatility is not static; it fluctuates over time due to various economic and geopolitical factors. This deficiency often leads to inaccuracies in option pricing, particularly for long-dated options. To address this, practitioners may employ models such as the Stochastic Volatility Model, where volatility is treated as a random variable. The Heston model is a prime example, described by the following system of stochastic differential equations:

$$\begin{aligned} dS_t &= \mu S_t \, dt + \sqrt{v_t} S_t \, dW_t^S, \\ dv_t &= \kappa(\theta - v_t) \, dt + \sigma \sqrt{v_t} \, dW_t^v, \end{aligned} \tag{8.1}$$

where v_t represents the stochastic variance of the asset price, κ the rate at which variance reverts to its long-run level θ, and σ the volatility of the volatility.

Another key assumption is the frictionless market hypothesis, which presumes no transaction costs or taxes and the ability to trade continuously. In practical terms, trading incurs costs and markets may experience liquidity constraints. Transaction costs can significantly affect hedging strategies and option pricing. Discrete-time models or the inclusion of transaction cost terms in the continuous-time framework can provide a more realistic approach to option pricing.

The assumption of a lognormal distribution of asset returns also presents challenges. Empirical evidence suggests that asset returns often exhibit leptokurtosis – heavier tails than a normal distribution, indicating a higher probability of extreme events. Such phenomena can be modeled using jump-diffusion processes or Lévy processes. The Merton jump-diffusion model, combining a continuous diffusion process with a Poisson jump process, can be represented as:

$$dS_t = \mu S_t\,dt + \sigma S_t\,dW_t + (J_t - 1)S_{t^-}\,dN_t, \tag{8.2}$$

where J_t signifies the percentage jump size, and N_t the Poisson process counting the number of jumps by time t.

Furthermore, the model presupposes that interest rates are constant over the life of the option. This instantiation is rarely observed in real-world markets, where interest rates vary due to monetary policies and economic conditions. The Heath-Jarrow-Morton (HJM) framework and the Brace-Gatarek-Musiela (BGM) model for interest rate derivatives provide a more flexible approach, capturing the evolution of the entire yield curve over time.

To better adapt to observed market conditions, practitioners often use the notion of implied volatility, which varies across strike prices and maturities, forming what is known as the volatility surface. Techniques such as local volatility, as introduced by Dupire, refine the model by allowing volatility to be a function of both the asset price and time. The local volatility approach modifies the Black-Scholes framework as follows:

$$dS_t = \mu S_t\,dt + \sigma_{loc}(S_t, t)S_t\,dW_t, \tag{8.3}$$

where $\sigma_{loc}(S_t, t)$ is the local volatility dependent on the current asset price and time.

Additionally, the Black-Scholes model's assumption of European-style options, which can only be exercised at expiration, is limiting for American options that can be exercised at any point before expiry. The valuation of American options requires solving a more complex free-boundary problem, often addressed through numerical methods such as finite difference methods, binomial trees, or Monte Carlo simulations.

Understanding these limitations and exploring extensions are crucial for advanced practitioners who aim to achieve more accurate and responsive pricing models. Adapting the basic assumptions of the Black-Scholes model to better fit real-world scenarios mitigates risk and enhances the robustness of pricing strategies in volatile and dynamic markets.

8.10 Alternative Option Pricing Models

The Black-Scholes model, despite its groundbreaking contributions to option pricing theory, has limitations rooted in its underlying assumptions. These assumptions, while facilitating mathematical tractability, often fail to capture the complexities observed in real financial markets. As a response, alternative models have been developed to address these limitations. This section explores several notable models that extend or deviate from Black-Scholes to provide more nuanced insights and accurate pricing in diverse market conditions.

The Binomial Option Pricing Model

One of the earliest alternatives to the Black-Scholes model is the Binomial Option Pricing Model, introduced by Cox, Ross, and Rubinstein in 1979. The binomial model is a discrete-time approach that breaks the option's life into a potentially very large number of time steps. At each step, the underlying asset's price can move to one of two possible values, creating a recombining tree of potential prices. The risk-neutral valuation is then applied at each node, moving backward from the terminal nodes (option's expiration) to the present to determine the option's fair price.

The binomial model's primary advantage is its flexibility in handling a wide array of conditions including varying interest rates, dividends, and volatility structures. Moreover, because it operates in discrete time, it provides a straightforward method to incorporate American-style options, which can be exercised at any point before expiration.

Mathematically, the price evolution can be described as:

$$S_u = S \cdot u \quad \text{and} \quad S_d = S \cdot d$$

where S is the current stock price, u is the up factor, and d is the down factor. The probabilities of the up and down movements under the risk-neutral measure are:

$$p = \frac{e^{r\Delta t} - d}{u - d} \quad \text{and} \quad 1 - p$$

where r is the risk-free interest rate and Δt is the length of each time step.

Stochastic Volatility Models: The Heston Model

One key limitation of the Black-Scholes model is its assumption of constant volatility. In practice, market volatility is dynamic and can exhibit significant fluctuations. The Heston Model, proposed by Steven Heston in 1993, incorporates stochastic volatility, allowing the volatility itself to follow a random process. This model is expressed by the following set of stochastic differential equations:

$$\begin{aligned} dS_t &= \mu S_t dt + \sqrt{v_t} S_t dW_t^S \\ dv_t &= \kappa(\theta - v_t)dt + \sigma\sqrt{v_t} dW_t^v \end{aligned}$$

where μ is the drift rate of the stock price, v_t is the variance at time t, κ is the rate at which the variance reverts to its long-term mean θ, σ is the volatility of the variance (volatility of volatility), and W_t^S and W_t^v are correlated Wiener processes with correlation coefficient ρ.

The Heston model can better capture the skewness and kurtosis observed in the distribution of asset returns, providing a more accurate reflection of market behavior and improving the pricing and hedging of options, particularly those with long maturities or exotic structures.

Jump-Diffusion Models: The Merton Model

To account for sudden and significant movements in asset prices, which are not captured by the continuous paths assumed in the Black-Scholes model, Robert Merton introduced the Jump-Diffusion Model in 1976. The model adds a jump component to the diffusion process, allowing for the incorporation of both continuous price changes and discrete jumps.

The Merton model's dynamics are given by:

$$dS_t = (\mu - \lambda k)S_t dt + \sigma S_t dW_t + S_t(J - 1)dq_t$$

where λ is the jump intensity (average frequency of jumps per unit time), k is the expected percentage change in the stock price due to a jump, J is a random variable representing the jump size, and q_t is a Poisson process with intensity λ.

This hybrid model resonates better with empirical asset price behaviors, capturing phenomena like market crashes or other extraordinary events. Jump-diffusion models can thus provide more robust pricing and hedging strategies for options, especially in markets with pronounced discontinuities.

Local Volatility Models: The Dupire Model

Another alternative addressing the constant volatility constraint is the Local Volatility Model, formulated by Bruno Dupire in 1994. The model posits that volatility is not only stochastic but also a deterministic function of the asset price and time. Dupire showed that under no-arbitrage conditions, if we know the market prices of European options for all strikes and maturities, we can extract a local volatility function $\sigma_{local}(S,t)$.

The Dupire model's key equation is:

$$\sigma_{local}^2(S,t) = \frac{\frac{\partial C}{\partial t} + rS\frac{\partial C}{\partial S} + qSC}{\frac{1}{2}S^2\frac{\partial^2 C}{\partial S^2}}$$

where C is the market price of the call option, r is the risk-free rate, and q is the dividend yield.

Local volatility models are particularly useful for fitting observed market prices precisely, making them advantageous for traders who need to mark-to-market their portfolios accurately.

Monte Carlo Simulation

Underpinning several of these models, especially those incorporating stochastic processes, Monte Carlo Simulation stands out as a powerful numerical technique. This method entails generating a large number of potential future price paths for the underlying asset by simulating the stochastic differential equations governing its behavior. The option price is then obtained by averaging the discounted payoff across these simulated paths.

Monte Carlo methods are extraordinarily flexible and can accommodate a variety of complex features including path dependency, multi-dimensional assets, and intricate payoffs that are not easily treated with traditional analytical models.

Each of these models provides unique advantages and can be employed based on the specific market conditions and the nature of the options being priced. By understanding and utilizing these alternative pricing models, traders and risk managers can achieve more accurate valuations, better risk assessments, and more effective hedging strategies. This, in turn, supports more informed trading decisions and enhances overall financial market efficiency.

Chapter 9

Interest Rate Models

Interest rate models are essential for understanding and predicting the behavior of interest rates, crucial for valuing fixed-income securities and managing interest rate risk. This chapter introduces key models like the Vasicek, Cox-Ingersoll-Ross (CIR), and Hull-White models, along with the Heath-Jarrow-Morton (HJM) framework and Libor Market Model (LMM). It covers their calibration, applications, and limitations, providing comprehensive insights into their use in financial analysis and risk management.

9.1 Introduction to Interest Rate Models

Interest rate models are foundational tools in quantitative finance, serving to describe the evolution of interest rates over time. These models are used extensively in the valuation of fixed-income securities, risk management, and the pricing of interest rate derivatives. To grasp their utility, one must understand both their theoretical foundations and practical applications.

Interest rates themselves can be seen as the cost of borrowing money or the reward for lending money, typically expressed as a percentage. They are influenced by various economic factors including central bank policies, inflation expectations, and the overall supply and demand for credit. The dynamic nature of these influences requires sophisticated models to accurately predict interest rate movements and their impact on financial instruments.

- **Classification of Interest Rate Models:** Interest rate models can be broadly classified into two categories: equilibrium models and no-arbitrage models.

- **Equilibrium Models:** Equilibrium models, such as the Vasicek and Cox-Ingersoll-Ross (CIR) models, describe the stochastic process of interest rate movements by assuming that the market is in equilibrium. These models typically focus on capturing the mean-reverting behavior of interest rates, where rates tend to revert back to a long-term average over time. The mean-reversion feature is essential as it reflects the empirical observation that extremely high or low interest rates are usually temporary.

  The Vasicek model, for instance, is formulated as:

  $$dr_t = \kappa(\theta - r_t)dt + \sigma dW_t$$

  where r_t is the short-term interest rate, κ is the speed of mean reversion, θ is the long-term mean level, σ is the volatility, and W_t is a Wiener process or Brownian motion.

- **No-Arbitrage Models:** No-arbitrage models, including the Hull-White and Heath-Jarrow-Morton (HJM) frameworks, ensure that there are no arbitrage opportunities in the market. These models are aligned with the current market prices of a wide range of financial instruments and are often used for pricing complex interest rate derivatives.

  The Hull-White model, an extension of the Vasicek model to allow for time-dependent parameters, is defined as:

  $$dr_t = (\theta(t) - \kappa r_t)dt + \sigma dW_t$$

  Here, $\theta(t)$ is a deterministic function of time that ensures the model fits the current term structure of interest rates.

- **Significance and Applications:** The significance of these models lies in their application across various domains in finance. In the context of bond markets, interest rate models help in determining the appropriate discount factors to value cash flows from bonds. They are crucial in risk management for assessing the interest rate exposure of portfolios and devising strategies to hedge this risk. Derivatives like interest rate swaps, caps, and floors are priced using these models, making them indispensable for both corporate treasurers and financial institutions.

Additionally, these models play a pivotal role in the execution of Monte Carlo simulations used to estimate the future states of interest rates and evaluate the probabilistic outcomes of different financial strategies. The parameters within these models (such as mean reversion rate and volatility) are calibrated to market data to reflect prevailing economic conditions, thereby enhancing their predictive capabilities.

In practice, selecting the appropriate interest rate model is contingent upon the specific requirements of the user, the characteristics of the instruments being analyzed, and the desired accuracy of the predictions. While simpler models like Vasicek might be suitable for basic applications, more complex models such as the HJM framework cater to the needs of advanced financial engineering.

Understanding the nuances of each model and how they fit into the broader landscape of quantitative finance equips traders and investors with the skills to navigate the intricacies of the fixed-income markets efficiently.

9.2 The Term Structure of Interest Rates

The term structure of interest rates, often referred to as the yield curve, is a fundamental concept in finance that represents the relationship between interest rates and the maturity of debt securities. This relationship is critical because it helps to understand various economic conditions, informs investment decisions, and is integral to valuing fixed-income securities. The term structure is depicted graphically by plotting the yields of similar quality bonds against their maturities, presenting a curve that offers a snapshot of market expectations and prevailing economic sentiment.

To appreciate the term structure of interest rates, it's important to delve into its key characteristics and the factors influencing its shape. The yield curve can take several forms, each signaling different economic conditions:

1. Normal Yield Curve

A normal yield curve is upward sloping, indicating that longer-term securities have higher yields compared to short-term ones. This shape suggests that investors demand a risk premium for holding longer-term securities, compensating for the higher uncertainty and risk associated with a longer time horizon. Typically observed during periods of economic expansion, this curve reflects expectations of rising future interest rates and robust economic growth.

2. Inverted Yield Curve

An inverted yield curve slopes downward, with short-term yields higher than long-term yields. This anomaly occurs when investors expect future interest rates to decline, often due to anticipated economic slowdowns or recessions. An inverted yield curve is a strong predictive indicator of economic downturns, as it reflects market sentiment that the central bank may reduce interest rates to stimulate the economy.

3. Flat or Humped Yield Curve

A flat yield curve suggests that short-term and long-term yields are similar, signaling uncertainty regarding future economic conditions. A humped yield curve, on the other hand, peaks at intermediate maturities and slopes downward for longer maturities. Both configurations can occur during transitions in the economic cycle or periods of monetary policy adjustments.

The shape of the yield curve arises from the interaction of several theories:

Expectations Theory

The expectations theory posits that long-term interest rates are a geometric average of current and expected future short-term interest rates. According to this theory, if investors expect short-term rates to increase, the yield curve will slope upward. Conversely, if they anticipate a decrease, the yield curve will slope downward. The expectations theory emphasizes the role of investor beliefs about future interest movements in shaping the yield curve.

Liquidity Preference Theory

The liquidity preference theory suggests that investors demand a premium for holding longer-term securities, primarily because these securities are subject to greater interest rate risk and reduced liquidity. Therefore, the yield curve is typically upward sloping, reflecting this risk premium. Longer-term bonds are less liquid, and investors require additional compensation for committing their capital for extended periods.

Market Segmentation Theory

Market segmentation theory, sometimes known as the preferred habitat theory, asserts that the bond market is segmented based on maturity. Different institutional investors have preferences for various maturities due to their own liquidity needs, risk tolerances, and investment horizons. The yield curve's shape results from the supply and demand dynamics within these segmented markets. Under this theory, the dynamics of each maturity segment are independently driven by institutional investor preferences and regulatory or funding constraints.

Analyzing the term structure of interest rates involves understanding these theories and the factors they emphasize. An essential tool for this analysis is the zero-coupon yield curve, constructed using securities that pay no interim coupons and only their principal at maturity. These yields are crucial for discounting future cash flows in fixed-income valuation and risk management.

Mathematically, the zero-coupon yield curve can be described by the spot rate $r(t)$ for different maturities t. The relationship between spot rates and bond prices can be formulated as:

$$P(t) = \frac{F}{(1 + r(t))^t}$$

where $P(t)$ is the price of a zero-coupon bond maturing at time t, F is the bond's face value, and $r(t)$ is the spot rate for maturity time t.

Moreover, it's important to consider forward rates, which are interest rates implied by current zero-coupon rates for future periods. The one-period forward rate $f(t, t+1)$ from time t to $t+1$ is given by:

$$1 + f(t, t+1) = \frac{(1 + r(t+1))^{t+1}}{(1 + r(t))^t}$$

Spot and forward rates are critical components in the pricing and hedging of fixed-income securities and derivatives. Accurately constructing and interpreting the yield curve enables investors and financial professionals to make informed decisions regarding bond investments, interest rate risk management, and economic forecasting.

Understanding the term structure of interest rates equips investors with the knowledge to navigate financial markets effectively. Through careful analysis of the yield curve and the underlying theories, investors can gain insights into market expectations, assess interest rate risks, and develop strategies that align with their investment goals and risk tolerance.

9.3 Vasicek Model

The Vasicek model, introduced by Oldřich Vasicek in 1977, is a cornerstone in the study of term structure and the dynamics of interest rates. It is formulated as a mean-reverting stochastic process, capturing the tendency of interest rates to revert to a long-term average over time. Its mathematical formulation is given by the stochastic differential equation (SDE):

$$dr_t = \kappa(\theta - r_t)dt + \sigma dW_t$$

where r_t represents the short-term interest rate at time t, $\kappa > 0$ is the speed of reversion to the mean, θ is the long-term average interest rate, σ is the volatility of the interest rate, and W_t is a standard Wiener process.

Key characteristics of the Vasicek model include:

- **Mean Reversion**: The parameter κ determines the rate at which r_t reverts to the long-term mean θ. Higher values of κ indicate faster reversion, while lower values suggest a slower adjustment.
- **Volatility**: The parameter σ captures the extent to which r_t deviates from its mean due to random fluctuations.
- **Normal Distribution**: The model assumes that the changes in the interest rate are normally distributed, which implies that the interest rate can theoretically take any value, including negative rates. This is one limitation of the model in certain financial contexts.

To solve this SDE, we first recognize that it is a linear SDE, which permits an analytical solution. The explicit solution can be written as:

$$r_t = r_0 e^{-\kappa t} + \theta(1 - e^{-\kappa t}) + \sigma \int_0^t e^{-\kappa(t-s)} dW_s$$

By simplifying this solution, we find that r_t follows a normal distribution with mean and variance given by:

$$\mathbb{E}[r_t|r_0] = r_0e^{-\kappa t} + \theta(1 - e^{-\kappa t})$$

$$\text{Var}(r_t) = \frac{\sigma^2}{2\kappa}(1 - e^{-2\kappa t})$$

These formulations illustrate the mean-reverting nature of the model and how the variance depends on both the short-term and long-term factors.

The Vasicek model extends its utility through applications in several financial contexts. For instance:

- **Pricing Zero-Coupon Bonds**: The price $P(t, T)$ of a zero-coupon bond maturing at time T, given the short-rate model under Vasicek, can be expressed as:

  $$P(t, T) = A(t, T)e^{-B(t,T)r_t}$$

  where

  $$B(t, T) = \frac{1 - e^{-\kappa(T-t)}}{\kappa}$$

  $$A(t, T) = \exp\left(\left(\theta - \frac{\sigma^2}{2\kappa^2}\right)(B(t, T) - (T - t)) - \frac{\sigma^2}{4\kappa}B(t, T)^2\right)$$

  These formulas capture the bond's price in a tractable form, a significant advantage for implementing analytical pricing models.

- **Yield Curve Dynamics**: The ability of the Vasicek model to simulate the evolution of the yield curve over multiple periods enables traders and analysts to understand and anticipate changes in the term structure. This aspect is critical for both risk management and devising trading strategies that hinge on interest rate movements.

Despite its advantages, the Vasicek model has limitations. Primarily, its assumption that interest rates are normally distributed can sometimes be unrealistic, especially in environments where interest rates can become negative or excessively high. Additionally, the mean-reversion feature may not adequately capture the structural changes in economic regimes or market conditions over time.

In practice, calibrating the Vasicek model to market data involves estimating the parameters κ, θ, and σ. Techniques such as maximum likelihood estimation (MLE) are employed to fit the model to historical interest rate series. This process ensures that the model accurately reflects observed market behavior, enhancing its practical relevance and predictive power.

For a comprehensive understanding and practical application, traders and financial analysts must appreciate both the theoretical foundations and practical implications of the Vasicek model. This understanding enables them to leverage its strengths effectively while remaining mindful of its limitations in diverse financial contexts.

9.4 Cox-Ingersoll-Ross (CIR) Model

The Cox-Ingersoll-Ross (CIR) model is a widely used framework in the field of financial economics for modeling the evolution of interest rates. It was introduced by John Cox, Jonathan Ingersoll, and Stephen Ross in their seminal paper in 1985. The CIR model offers a realistic description of interest rate dynamics by addressing some limitations present in earlier models, such as the Vasicek model.

The CIR model belongs to the class of one-factor short-rate models. It assumes that the instantaneous short rate $r(t)$ follows a mean-reverting square root process. The stochastic differential equation (SDE) governing the CIR model is given by:

$$dr(t) = \kappa(\theta - r(t))dt + \sigma\sqrt{r(t)}dW(t),$$

where:

- κ (mean-reversion rate): This parameter determines the speed at which the interest rate reverts to its long-term mean, θ.
- θ (long-term mean rate): This is the long-term mean level to which the short rate reverts.
- σ (volatility): This parameter influences the volatility of the short rate. The volatility term $\sigma\sqrt{r(t)}$ ensures that the interest rate remains non-negative.

- $dW(t)$ represents the increment of a standard Wiener process.

One notable feature of the CIR model is the term $\sqrt{r(t)}$ in the volatility component. This specification prevents the short rate $r(t)$ from becoming negative, a desirable property that addresses a key drawback of the Vasicek model where negative rates are possible.
To understand the dynamics of the CIR model, consider the behavior of the short rate $r(t)$:

- When $r(t)$ is below θ, the drift term $\kappa(\theta - r(t))$ is positive, pulling $r(t)$ upwards towards θ.
- Conversely, when $r(t)$ is above θ, the drift term is negative, pushing $r(t)$ downwards towards θ.
- The volatility term $\sigma\sqrt{r(t)}$ introduces randomness into the process, with fluctuations increasing in magnitude as $r(t)$ increases.

The mean-reverting nature of the CIR model ensures that interest rates do not indefinitely drift away from the long-term mean, a critical aspect for the stability and realism of the model.

Calibration of the CIR Model

Calibration of the CIR model involves estimating the parameters κ, θ, and σ from market data. This process typically uses historical short-rate data or the prices of fixed-income securities such as bonds. One common technique for parameter estimation is the method of moments, which involves matching theoretical moments derived from the CIR model to sample moments from the data.
The theoretical moments of the short rate $r(t)$ in the CIR model can be expressed as:

$$\mathbb{E}[r(t)] = r(0)e^{-\kappa t} + \theta(1 - e^{-\kappa t}),$$

and

$$\text{Var}[r(t)] = \frac{\sigma^2}{2\kappa}\left(1 - e^{-2\kappa t}\right).$$

By matching these moments to their empirical counterparts, we can derive estimates for the parameters. Calibration can also be performed using maximum likelihood estimation (MLE) or through fitting market prices of instruments that are sensitive to interest rates, such as bonds or interest rate swaps.

Applications of the CIR Model

The CIR model has numerous applications in finance, particularly in the valuation of interest rate-sensitive securities and in risk management. Some key applications include:

- **Bond Pricing**: The CIR model is used to derive the term structure of interest rates and to price zero-coupon bonds. The price of a zero-coupon bond under the CIR model can be expressed as:

  $$P(t,T) = A(t,T)e^{-B(t,T)r(t)},$$

  where $P(t,T)$ is the price of the bond at time t maturing at T, and $A(t,T)$ and $B(t,T)$ are functions determined by the model parameters κ, θ, and σ.

- **Derivatives Pricing**: The CIR model is employed to price interest rate derivatives such as futures, options, and swaps. Due to its mean-reverting nature and realistic volatility structure, it provides a solid foundation for modeling the evolution of interest rates over time.

- **Risk Management**: The model is used in risk management to assess interest rate risk by simulating future short-rate paths and valuing portfolios of interest rate-sensitive assets.

- **Economic Analysis**: Economists use the CIR model to study the behavior of interest rates and to analyze monetary policy impacts.

The Cox-Ingersoll-Ross model's balance of theoretical tractability and empirical realism has made it a cornerstone of interest rate modeling. It has significantly influenced both the academic literature and practical applications in the financial industry.

9.5 Hull-White Model

The Hull-White model, also known as the Hull-White extended Vasicek model, is a popular and widely utilized framework for modeling interest rates. It builds upon the foundational concepts proposed by the Vasicek model, incorporating additional flexibility to better fit the initial term structure of interest rates. This enhancement makes the Hull-White model particularly useful for both theoretical and practical applications in finance.

The model assumes that the short-term interest rate, $r(t)$, follows the stochastic differential equation (SDE):

$$dr(t) = [\theta(t) - \alpha r(t)]\, dt + \sigma dW(t)$$

where:

- $\theta(t)$ is a time-dependent function that adjusts the drift,
- α is the mean reversion rate,
- σ is the volatility parameter,
- $W(t)$ is a standard Wiener process.

The term $\theta(t)$ is chosen such that the model is able to fit the initial term structure of interest rates perfectly. Unlike the Vasicek model, which assumes constant parameters, the time-dependent drift function $\theta(t)$ allows for a more accurate calibration to market data at time $t = 0$.

To better understand the dynamics of the Hull-White model, consider the following steps involved in the process of calibration and application:

1. Calibration

Calibrating the Hull-White model involves determining the parameters $\theta(t)$, α, and σ. The parameter $\theta(t)$ is particularly crucial as it ensures the initial term structure, $P(0, T)$, is accurately captured. The process typically involves these steps:

1. **Set Initial Conditions:** Begin with the initial yield curve derived from market data.
2. **Estimate α and σ:** These can be estimated using historical time series data of interest rates.
3. **Determine $\theta(t)$:** Solve for $\theta(t)$ to ensure the model fits the initial yield curve. This can be done by setting:

$$\theta(t) = \frac{\partial f(0,t)}{\partial t} + \alpha f(0,t) + \frac{\sigma^2}{2\alpha}\left(1 - e^{-2\alpha t}\right)$$

where $f(0,t)$ is the instantaneous forward rate at time t given at time 0.

2. Numerical Solutions and Simulation

Due to the time-dependent nature of $\theta(t)$, numerical methods and simulations are often employed to solve the SDE. Techniques such as the Euler-Maruyama method can be used to approximate the path of interest rates under this model:

$$r(t + \Delta t) \approx r(t) + [\theta(t) - \alpha r(t)]\,\Delta t + \sigma\sqrt{\Delta t}\zeta$$

where ζ is a random variable drawn from a standard normal distribution.

3. Valuation of Interest Rate Derivatives

The Hull-White model is particularly useful for pricing a wide range of interest rate derivatives, including European options on bonds, caps, floors, and swaptions. For instance, the price of a European call option on a zero-coupon bond with maturity T and strike K can be derived using:

$$C(0, T_1, T_2, K) = P(0, T_2)N(d_1) - KP(0, T_1)N(d_2)$$

where:

$$d_1 = \frac{1}{\sigma_P}\left(\ln\left(\frac{P(0,T_2)}{KP(0,T_1)}\right) + \frac{\sigma_P^2}{2}\right)$$

$$d_2 = d_1 - \sigma_P$$

$$\sigma_P^2 = \frac{\sigma^2}{2\alpha}\left(1 - e^{-2\alpha(T_2 - T_1)}\right)\left(1 - e^{-2\alpha T_1}\right)$$

where $N(\cdot)$ denotes the cumulative distribution function of the standard normal distribution.

Applications and Flexibility

One of the key strengths of the Hull-White model is its ability to adapt to different market conditions through the time-dependent drift $\theta(t)$, making it highly flexible. It is extensively used in the valuation of complex financial instruments and in risk management practices. This flexibility stands out when considering the model's capability to adjust to new market data, thus providing practitioners with a robust tool for dynamic environments.

The Hull-White model also serves as a foundational element upon which more complex models, such as the Heath-Jarrow-Morton framework and the Libor Market Model, build. These advanced models often encapsulate the core dynamics introduced by Hull-White, such as mean reversion and stochastic volatility.

Overall, the Hull-White model's incorporation of a time-dependent drift represents a significant advancement over the Vasicek model, offering enhanced calibration to the observed term structures. This adaptability ensures that the model remains a staple in interest rate modeling, underlining its importance in the field of quantitative finance.

9.6 Heath-Jarrow-Morton (HJM) Framework

The Heath-Jarrow-Morton (HJM) framework represents an advanced and noteworthy approach in the modeling of interest rates. Unlike the single-factor models such as Vasicek and Cox-Ingersoll-Ross (CIR), which directly model the instantaneous short rate, the HJM framework operates within the more general framework of modeling the entire forward rate curve. This shift provides a more flexible and comprehensive structure for capturing the dynamics of interest rates, making it particularly useful for risk management and the valuation of interest rate derivatives.

To understand the HJM framework, it's essential first to grasp the concept of forward rates. The forward rate $f(t,T)$ is the interest rate between times t and T, as seen from time t. Unlike spot rates which reflect current borrowing costs, forward rates project future interest rates, given the information available today.

The HJM model focuses on the evolution of these forward rates over time. This can be mathematically represented by the following stochastic differential equation (SDE):

$$df(t,T) = \alpha(t,T)dt + \sigma(t,T)dW(t)$$

Here, $\alpha(t,T)$ represents the drift term and $\sigma(t,T)$ represents the volatility term of the forward rate $f(t,T)$, while $W(t)$ is a standard Brownian motion. The flexibility of the HJM framework arises because $\alpha(t,T)$

and $\sigma(t,T)$ can be functions of time and the maturity T, allowing the model to describe a wide range of term structures.

A pivotal result in the HJM framework is the no-arbitrage condition, which constrains the drift term $\alpha(t,T)$ by the volatility structure $\sigma(t,T)$. The no-arbitrage condition ensures that the model is consistent with the absence of arbitrage opportunities, a fundamental principle in finance. The no-arbitrage condition can be expressed as:

$$\alpha(t,T) = \sigma(t,T)\int_t^T \sigma(t,u)du$$

The implication of this restriction is profound, as it directly ties the drift of the forward rates to the volatilities, thus simplifying the model calibration to observed market prices.

In practical terms, the HJM model is often employed with a finite number of factors to manage complexity. For example, in a two-factor HJM model, the forward rate dynamics might be driven by two sources of uncertainty, each with its volatility structure:

$$df(t,T) = \sigma_1(t,T)dW_1(t) + \sigma_2(t,T)dW_2(t)$$

Calibration of the HJM model involves estimating the volatility functions $\sigma_1(t,T)$ and $\sigma_2(t,T)$ from historical data or directly from market prices of liquid instruments such as caplets, swaptions, or bonds. The ease of incorporating market data makes the HJM framework particularly powerful in practice.

The HJM framework's ability to model the entire forward rate curve is particularly advantageous for pricing and managing the risk of exotic interest rate derivatives, whose payoffs can depend on the path of interest rates over time. For instance, callable bonds, mortgage-backed securities, and interest rate caps and floors all benefit from the forward-rate-centric approach of the HJM model.

To illustrate, consider the pricing of a caplet under the HJM model. A caplet provides insurance against rising interest rates, paying the holder when a certain reference rate exceeds a predefined strike rate. Under the HJM framework, the payoff of a caplet at maturity can be discretized and valued by simulating the entire forward rate curve and applying the risk-neutral valuation approach. This involves:

$$\text{Caplet Payoff} = \max(f(T,T+\Delta) - K, 0)$$

where K is the strike rate, T is the caplet's maturity, and Δ is the accrual period. The forward rate $f(T, T+\Delta)$ is simulated using the above SDE, factoring in the volatility structure derived during calibration.

The HJM model, through its flexible forward rate modeling, provides robust tools for comprehensive interest rate risk modeling and derivative pricing. Its primary challenge lies in the complexity of adequately capturing and calibrating the volatility structure, a task that necessitates sophisticated statistical and computational techniques. Despite these challenges, the Heath-Jarrow-Morton framework remains a cornerstone in the realm of interest rate modeling, offering practitioners a profound level of depth and adaptability in their financial toolkit.

9.7 Libor Market Model (LMM)

The Libor Market Model (LMM), also known as the Brace-Gatarek-Musiela (BGM) model, is a well-regarded framework that directly models the evolution of forward LIBOR rates. This approach is particularly useful for pricing interest rate derivatives and managing interest rate risk, offering significant advantages over alternative constructs like short-rate models.

Unlike single-factor models such as the Vasicek or Cox-Ingersoll-Ross (CIR) models, which rely on a single short rate to capture the dynamics of interest rate movements, the LMM explicitly represents the forward rates that are fundamental to the valuation of many market instruments. By doing so, it ensures consistency with the initial term structure of interest rates and volatility structures, leading to more accurate and reliable pricing of assets.

At its core, the LMM assumes that the forward LIBOR rates follow a lognormal distribution under the risk-neutral measure. Mathematically, the evolution of these rates can be described using a set of stochastic differential equations (SDEs):

$$dL_i(t) = L_i(t)\left(\mu_i(t)dt + \sigma_i(t)dW_i(t)\right)$$

where $L_i(t)$ denotes the forward rate for the period $[T_i, T_{i+1}]$, $\mu_i(t)$ denotes the drift term, $\sigma_i(t)$ the volatility term, and $W_i(t)$ is a standard Brownian motion under the risk-neutral measure.

The drift term $\mu_i(t)$ ensures the no-arbitrage condition is met and can be computed using other forward rates, while the volatility term $\sigma_i(t)$

encapsulates the stochastic nature of the model. The drift term generally takes a more complex form given the correlation between different forward rates:

$$\mu_i(t) = \sigma_i(t) \sum_{j=i+1}^{N} \frac{\delta_j L_j(t)}{1 + \delta_j L_j(t)} \rho_{i,j} \sigma_j(t)$$

Here, δ_j represents the year fraction between T_j and T_{j+1}, and $\rho_{i,j}$ is the instantaneous correlation between the forward rates $L_i(t)$ and $L_j(t)$.

One of the compelling features of the LMM is its ability to be used in a consistent framework for all maturities, which is essential when pricing swaptions, caps, floors, and other interest rate derivatives. To exemplify its practical utility, consider the pricing of a European swaption – an option granting the holder the right to enter into an interest rate swap at a specified future date.

To manage numerical integrations and avoid analytical complexities, the Monte Carlo simulation method is often employed in the context of LMM. This involves simulating a large number of potential future paths for forward rates according to the governing SDEs and averaging the resultant payoffs. The primary steps for implementing this approach include: discretizing the time intervals, simulating random samples for the forward rate increments, and computing the discounted payoff for each path.

The model's calibration process involves fitting the model's parameters to market data, ensuring the model is aligned with observed market prices of liquid instruments, such as caplets and swaption volatilities. Calibration typically includes choosing the volatility function $\sigma_i(t)$ to best match market quotes, often employing optimization techniques to minimize the difference between model prices and market prices.

Despite its advantages, the LMM is not without limitations. Its computational intensity, particularly when calibrating and simulating high-dimensional models, can be significant. Additionally, assumptions around the lognormal distribution of forward rates may not fully capture market realities, necessitating extensions or modifications to the core model, such as incorporating stochastic volatility or jumps.

The Libor Market Model remains a cornerstone in the toolkit of quantitative finance professionals, facilitating sophisticated trading and risk management strategies in interest rate markets. By mastering its intricacies, traders and investors can better navigate the complexities of financial instruments and harness market opportunities.

9.8 Calibration of Interest Rate Models

Calibration is a crucial step in the practical application of interest rate models, as it entails the estimation of model parameters that align with observed market data. This process ensures that the model accurately reflects the current interest rate environment and can make reliable predictions. Calibration involves various techniques and tools, each suited to different models and datasets. We will explore the fundamental principles of calibration, followed by practical methods used to calibrate some of the popular interest rate models discussed in previous sections.

The calibration objective is to minimize the discrepancy between model outputs and market data, typically through an optimization process. The market data usually encompasses bond prices, swap rates, cap and floor volatilities, and other relevant financial instruments. The optimization should adjust the model parameters so that the theoretical prices generated by the model match the observed market prices as closely as possible.

To illustrate the calibration process, consider an interest rate model represented by the function $P(t, T; \theta)$, where $P(t, T; \theta)$ is the model's output (such as bond prices or swap rates), t is the current time, T is the maturity date, and θ represents the set of model parameters. Define M_i as the observed market price for the i-th instrument. The calibration can be formulated as an optimization problem:

$$\text{Minimize} \quad \sum_i w_i \left(P(t, T_i; \theta) - M_i\right)^2,$$

where w_i are weights that reflect the importance or reliability of each observed market price. This least-squares problem is then solved using numerical optimization techniques such as gradient descent, the Levenberg-Marquardt algorithm, or other sophisticated methods.

Let us delve into the calibration procedures for the Vasicek, Cox-Ingersoll-Ross (CIR), Hull-White, Heath-Jarrow-Morton (HJM), and Libor Market Model (LMM).

For the **Vasicek model**, the parameters that need calibration are the mean reversion rate a, the long-term mean level b, and the volatility σ. The market data typically include zero-coupon bond prices or yield curves. A common approach involves using historical time series data of interest rates to estimate the parameters via maximum likelihood estimation (MLE). The Vasicek model's linearity properties facilitate the use of analytic expressions for MLE, making this approach both computationally efficient and robust.

In the **Cox-Ingersoll-Ross (CIR) model**, the calibration targets the mean reversion rate a, the long-term mean b, and the volatility σ, akin to the Vasicek model, but with a distinct variance structure. Calibration often employs the method of moments, matching the model's theoretical moments (mean and variance) to the empirical moments derived from historical data. Additionally, MLE can be employed, albeit with more complexity due to the nonlinearity of the CIR model's variance term.

The **Hull-White model** demands calibration of parameters such as the mean reversion rate a and the instantaneous volatility σ. Given the model's adaptability, it is often calibrated to the initial term structure by fitting the yield curve exactly and then to the volatility structure through caplets and swaptions. Optimization techniques like the least-squares minimization introduced earlier are commonly used, and when combined with numerical methods, they offer good convergence properties.

For the **Heath-Jarrow-Morton (HJM) framework**, the calibration focuses on the volatility functions $\sigma(t, T)$, which can be quite flexible. Calibrating the HJM model is more intricate due to the need to fit various market instruments, such as cap/floor/volatility surfaces and swaption volatilities. This often involves a parametric form for volatility, followed by the use of spline fitting or other sophisticated interpolation methods to ensure accurate and smooth calibration.

The **Libor Market Model (LMM)** requires calibration of the drift and volatility parameters of forward rate processes. The LMM calibration is typically performed using observed caplet volatilities and swaption volatilities. Given the LMM's complexity, advanced numerical techniques, such as bootstrapping and Monte Carlo simulations, are often employed. Calibration accuracy is paramount, as even small misestimations can significantly affect pricing and hedging outcomes.

In practice, the calibration process benefits from robust numerical libraries and software tools that enhance precision and efficiency. Tools like QuantLib, Python, R, and specialized financial software provide built-in functionalities for optimization, statistical estimation, and numerical solutions, making the calibration process more accessible and consistent.

Mastering the calibration of interest rate models equips traders and portfolio managers with the confidence to deploy these models in real-world scenarios, ensuring alignment with market conditions and improving decision-making accuracy. This meticulous process is foundational to the effective application of complex financial models in achieving market success.

9.9 Applications of Interest Rate Models

Interest rate models serve as indispensable tools for a plethora of financial operations, particularly in the realms of fixed-income securities valuation, interest rate risk management, and derivatives pricing. A thorough understanding and application of these models is not only beneficial but crucial for sophisticated traders and investors seeking to optimize their portfolios and manage risk judiciously. This section delves into key applications of interest rate models, illustrating how theoretical constructs translate into practical solutions in financial markets.

One of the most prominent applications of interest rate models is in the valuation of fixed-income securities. Bonds, being the primary constituent of fixed-income instruments, entail cash flows that are profoundly influenced by prevailing interest rates. By leveraging models such as Vasicek, Cox-Ingersoll-Ross (CIR), and Hull-White, traders can forecast the yield curve, which is instrumental in determining the present value of bond cash flows. Consider a zero-coupon bond with maturity T and face value F. The present value P can be expressed as:

$$P = \mathbb{E}\left[e^{-\int_0^T r_t\,dt}\right] F$$

where r_t denotes the instantaneous short rate modeled by the chosen interest rate model. Each model provides a unique dynamic for r_t, influencing the discounting and, consequently, the bond pricing.

In addition to bond valuation, interest rate models play a critical role in interest rate derivatives pricing. Instruments like interest rate swaps, caps, floors, and swaptions require precise modeling of interest rate movements to accurately price and hedge these derivatives. For instance, in the pricing of a European call option on a zero-coupon bond maturing at time T, with strike price K, the pricing formula under the Hull-White model can be derived through:

$$C = P(0,T)\Phi(d_1) - KP(0,S)\Phi(d_2)$$

where:

$$d_1 = \frac{\ln\left(\frac{P(0,T)}{KP(0,S)}\right) + \frac{1}{2}\sigma^2}{\sigma}$$

$$d_2 = d_1 - \sigma$$

Here, $P(0,T)$ is the price of the zero-coupon bond, Φ is the cumulative distribution function of the standard normal distribution, and σ represents the volatility derived from the interest rate model.

Risk management is another significant domain where interest rate models prove invaluable. Financial institutions and portfolio managers employ these models to quantify and mitigate interest rate risk. Through Value at Risk (VaR) and scenario analysis, these models allow practitioners to simulate adverse movements in interest rates and evaluate the potential impact on their portfolios. For instance, the simulation of portfolio values under different interest rate scenarios generated through the CIR model can help a portfolio manager understand the likelihood of substantial losses and adjust their risk exposure accordingly.

Interest rate models also assist in the strategic planning of corporate finance operations, such as selecting optimal debt structures and timing of issuing new debt. A corporation seeking to issue a fixed-rate bond would benefit from understanding future interest rate movements to lock in favorable rates. The Heath-Jarrow-Morton (HJM) framework and the Libor Market Model (LMM) are particularly useful for modeling the evolution of forward rates and managing timing effectively:

$$\frac{df(t,T)}{f(t,T)} = \mu(t,T)\,dt + \sigma(t,T)\,dW_t$$

where $f(t,T)$ represents the forward rate, $\mu(t,T)$ is the drift term, $\sigma(t,T)$ denotes volatility, and W_t is a Wiener process. Accurate modeling of $f(t,T)$ aids in forecasting favorable issuance windows and interest rate movements.

Lastly, interbank lending markets and the pricing of mortgage-backed securities (MBS) also benefit from interest rate models. The Libor Market Model (LMM), for instance, is particularly necessary for pricing interest rate caps and floors, which are integral components of MBS. Given its ability to model the dynamics of forward Libor rates, LMM facilitates the assessment of prepayment risks and cash flow variations in MBS.

Through these applications, interest rate models exemplify their utility beyond theoretical abstractions, empowering market participants to make informed and strategic decisions. By understanding and applying these models effectively, traders and investors can enhance their market acumen and achieve superior risk-adjusted returns.

9.10 Limitations and Extensions of Interest Rate Models

Interest rate models are fundamentally powerful tools in the domain of quantitative finance. While they provide substantial insights and computational frameworks for valuing fixed-income securities and managing interest rate risk, these models are not without limitations. Recognizing these limitations is crucial for effective model application, allowing traders and financial analysts to adjust their strategies accordingly. Additionally, numerous extensions and refinements have been developed to address some of these limitations, enhancing model accuracy and applicability.

One of the primary limitations of classical interest rate models, such as the Vasicek and Cox-Ingersoll-Ross (CIR) models, lies in their assumptions about the dynamics of interest rates. These models typically assume a mean-reverting process, which posits that interest rates will revert to a long-term mean. While this assumption can simplify calculations and provide a comfortable theoretical framework, it does not always align with observed market behavior. Interest rates in reality can exhibit periods of prolonged increase or decrease that do not adhere strictly to mean reversion.

Furthermore, these models often assume normally distributed interest rate changes, which fails to capture the leptokurtic nature of observed interest rate returns—essentially, the 'fat tails' wherein extreme events occur more frequently than predicted by a normal distribution. The implications of this limitation are significant for risk management, as standard models may underestimate the probability and impact of extreme interest rate movements.

Another critical limitation is the single-factor nature of many traditional models. For instance, the Vasicek and CIR models use a single factor (short-term interest rate) to describe the entire term structure of interest rates, which simplifies model calibration and application. However, this approach can be overly simplistic, as it does not account for the nuances and complexities observed in real-world interest rates, which can be influenced by numerous factors such as macroeconomic conditions, monetary policies, and market sentiment. Single-factor models may therefore fail to capture the true dynamics of the yield curve, leading to less accurate pricing and hedging of fixed-income securities.

To address these limitations, multifactor models and more sophisticated frameworks have been developed. The Heath-Jarrow-Morton (HJM) framework, for instance, significantly extends the capabilities of traditional models by modeling the entire forward rate curve rather than just a single rate. This approach can better capture the term structure dynamics and is more flexible in accommodating varying market conditions. The Libor Market Model (LMM), also known as the Brace-Gatarek-Musiela (BGM) model, further extends these concepts by modeling the evolution of forward rates directly, which is particularly useful for pricing interest rate derivatives.

$$dL(t,T_i) = L(t,T_i)\left(\sum_{j=i+1}^{M} \lambda_j \sigma_j \frac{\rho_{ij}}{1 + L(t,T_j)\delta t}\right) dt + L(t,T_i)\sigma_i dW_i(t)$$

where $L(t, T_i)$ represents the forward rate at time t for maturity T_i, σ_i is the volatility of the forward rate, ρ_{ij} is the correlation between the forward rates of T_i and T_j, and $W_i(t)$ is a Brownian motion.

Additionally, the Hull-White model introduces another layer of flexibility by allowing time-varying parameters, which can better fit observed market data and accommodate a broader range of yield curve shapes. The Hull-White model is given by:

$$dr(t) = (\theta(t) - \alpha(t)r(t))\,dt + \sigma(t)dW(t)$$

Here, $\theta(t)$ is a time-dependent mean reversion level, $\alpha(t)$ is a time-dependent reversion rate, and $\sigma(t)$ is the time-dependent volatility. The incorporation of time-varying parameters makes the model more adaptable to changing market conditions.

Moreover, stochastic volatility models, such as the GARCH (Generalized Autoregressive Conditional Heteroskedasticity) framework, can be integrated with interest rate models to better capture the observed volatility clustering in financial markets. These models assume that volatility itself follows a stochastic process, thus addressing the limitation of constant volatility assumptions in simpler models.

Finally, advanced computational techniques and machine learning methods are being increasingly employed to enhance interest rate models. Machine learning algorithms can analyze large datasets to detect patterns and correlations that may not be apparent through traditional statistical methods, offering a new dimension of insights and predictions. These techniques can be particularly beneficial in real-time applications and dynamic market environments, providing adaptive and robust models.

While interest rate models have intrinsic limitations, recognizing and addressing these constraints through model extensions and innovations significantly enhances their application and reliability. Understanding these factors enables sophisticated traders to leverage these models effectively, thus achieving more accurate pricing, better risk management, and informed investment decisions.

Chapter 10

Algorithmic Trading and Market Microstructure

Algorithmic trading leverages computer algorithms to execute trades at optimal speed and price, significantly impacting market microstructure. This chapter explores the evolution of algorithmic trading, various strategy types, and the basics of market microstructure including order types and execution strategies. It delves into high-frequency trading, transaction costs, liquidity considerations, and market impact. Additionally, the chapter covers the regulatory environment and ethical considerations, providing a holistic view of how algorithmic trading shapes today's financial markets.

10.1 Introduction to Algorithmic Trading

Algorithmic trading has emerged as a revolutionary practice in financial markets, fundamentally reshaping the landscape of trading and investing. At its core, algorithmic trading involves using computer algorithms to automate trading processes, allowing traders to execute orders with precision, speed, and efficiency that human capabilities alone cannot match. The adoption of algorithmic trading has led to significant improvements in market liquidity, efficiency, and transparency.

The essence of algorithmic trading lies in its ability to systematically follow predefined rules and strategies to execute trades. These algorithms can analyze vast datasets, identify trading opportunities, and implement orders—all within milliseconds. The speed and accuracy offered by algorithmic trading have given rise to a highly competitive environment, where profitability often hinges on microsecond advantages.

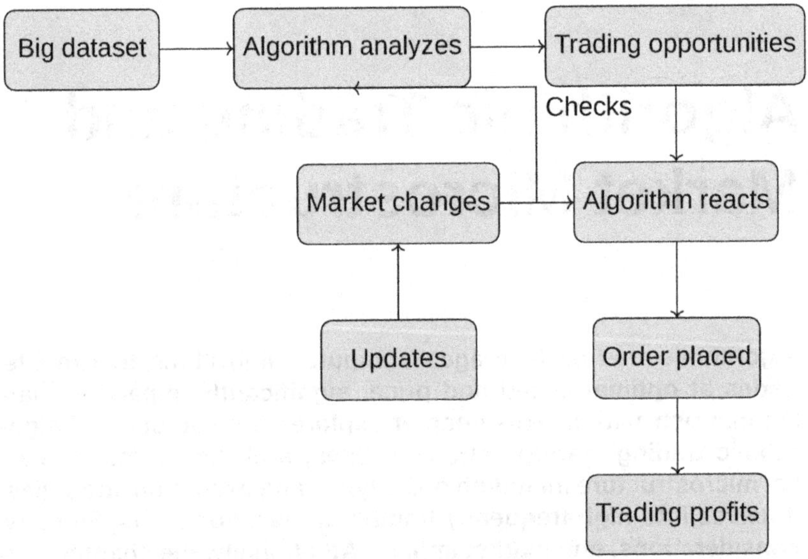

Algorithmic trading can be broadly categorized into two main types: execution algorithms and alpha-generating algorithms. Execution algorithms focus on optimizing the process of order placement, aiming to minimize market impact and transaction costs. Common execution algorithms include VWAP (Volume Weighted Average Price) and TWAP (Time Weighted Average Price), which distribute orders over time to achieve an average trading price aligned with market conditions.

On the other hand, alpha-generating algorithms are designed to identify and exploit market inefficiencies to generate profits. These algorithms incorporate advanced mathematical models, statistical analysis, and machine learning techniques to predict price movements and capitalize on trading opportunities. Examples of such strategies include statistical arbitrage, momentum trading, and market making.

To comprehensively understand algorithmic trading, one must appreciate the technological infrastructure that underpins it. This infrastructure comprises robust computer systems, high-speed internet connections, low-latency data feeds, and sophisticated trading platforms. The development and optimization of trading algorithms also necessitate significant computational resources, including powerful servers and specialized hardware such as FPGAs (Field Programmable Gate Arrays).

The data-driven nature of algorithmic trading means that historical data and real-time market information are indispensable. Traders leverage historical data to backtest their algorithms, assessing their performance over various market conditions before deploying them in live markets. Real-time data ensures that the algorithms can respond promptly to market changes, executing orders at the most opportune moments.

$$\text{TWAP} = \frac{1}{T}\int_0^T P(t)\,dt$$

One of the critical advantages of algorithmic trading is its ability to mitigate the influence of human emotions on trading decisions. By adhering to predefined rules and strategies, algorithms can maintain consistency and discipline, reducing the likelihood of trading errors driven by fear, greed, or other emotional biases. This objectivity is particularly beneficial in volatile markets, where rapid price swings can lead to impulsive decision-making.

However, the adoption of algorithmic trading also introduces new challenges and considerations. The speed and complexity of these algorithms necessitate rigorous risk management practices to prevent unintended consequences. Flash crashes, characterized by sudden and severe market declines, highlight the potential risks associated with algorithmic trading. To mitigate these risks, traders implement various safeguards, such as circuit breakers, kill switches, and real-time monitoring systems.

Furthermore, the regulatory landscape for algorithmic trading is continually evolving. Regulatory bodies aim to ensure fair and orderly markets by imposing requirements around algorithm testing, risk management, and transparency. Traders must stay abreast of these regulations and adapt their practices accordingly to maintain compliance.

The ethical implications of algorithmic trading also warrant significant attention. The potential for market manipulation, information asymmetry, and other unethical practices has led to ongoing debates about the proper role and regulation of algorithmic trading. Ethical considerations must be at the forefront of developing and deploying trading algorithms to maintain market integrity and public trust.

As algorithmic trading continues to evolve, it is reshaping the financial industry in profound ways. Its impact extends beyond traditional markets, influencing the trading of new asset classes such as cryptocurrencies. The convergence of advances in artificial intelligence, big data, and machine learning promises to further enhance the capabilities and complexity of trading algorithms in the future. For traders and investors, mastering the principles and practices of algorithmic trading is essential to navigate and succeed in this dynamic and rapidly changing market environment.

10.2 Historical Background and Evolution

The evolution of algorithmic trading is a compelling journey that highlights the intersection of technology, finance, and regulatory influences. Understanding this historical pathway provides critical context for contemporary market dynamics and the strategies that traders deploy today.

Algorithmic trading traces its roots back to the early developments in electronic trading systems during the late 20th century. The launch of the New York Stock Exchange's (NYSE) Designated Order Turnaround (DOT) system in 1976 marked one of the initial steps towards automated execution. This system allowed orders to be transmitted electronically, albeit with limited capabilities compared to today's sophisticated algorithms.

The advent of the NASDAQ in 1971, the world's first electronic exchange, further catalyzed the shift towards automation. The exchange provided more transparency and efficiency in trading, setting a precedent for the transformation that was to come. As computing power increased in the 1980s, the potential for more complex trading algorithms emerged.

One of the pivotal moments in algorithmic trading history was the development of the program trading strategies in the 1980s. Program trading refers to the execution of large orders using automated systems based on predefined conditions. This became particularly prominent with the rise of index arbitrage strategies, where computers were used to exploit price discrepancies between stock indices and their underlying securities.

The infamous market crash of October 1987, known as Black Monday, underscored the potent influence of algorithmic trading on market volatility. Program trading was heavily scrutinized, with many attributing the drastic downward spiral to the feedback loops created by these automated systems. This incident led to significant regulatory scrutiny and the implementation of circuit breakers, mechanisms designed to prevent similar occurrences by temporarily halting trading during extreme market moves.

The 1990s saw significant advancements in technology and communication infrastructure, which drastically reduced transaction costs and increased market efficiency. Algorithmic trading began to proliferate among institutional investors looking to execute large volumes of trades without impacting market prices adversely. The introduction of order matching systems and the proliferation of electronic communication networks (ECNs) allowed for after-hours trading and provided more competitive pricing structures.

During the 2000s, algorithmic trading evolved with the rise of high-frequency trading (HFT). HFT strategies exploit minute price inefficiencies across multiple markets, relying on incredibly fast execution speeds and advanced mathematical models. These strategies are characterized by high turnover rates and short holding periods, often seconds or milliseconds. The implementation of Reg NMS (Regulation National Market System) in 2007 by the U.S. Securities and Exchange Commission (SEC) aimed to enhance competition among trading venues, inadvertently providing fertile ground for HFT strategies to flourish.

As algorithmic trading became more sophisticated, so did its applications. Strategies diversified from basic execution algorithms designed to minimize market impact (e.g., VWAP—Volume Weighted Average Price or TWAP—Time Weighted Average Price) to complex strategies involving statistical arbitrage, machine learning, and artificial intelligence. These advanced techniques leverage historical data to predict future price movements and adjust trading patterns accordingly.

The flash crash of May 6, 2010, again highlighted the potential systemic risks linked to algorithmic trading. The Dow Jones Industrial Average plummeted nearly 1,000 points within minutes, only to recover a significant portion of the losses shortly afterwards. This event spurred further regulatory actions and enhancements to market safeguards, including updates to the circuit breaker rules and the implementation of the consolidated audit trail (CAT) to improve market oversight.

In recent years, the landscape of algorithmic trading continues to shift, influenced by ongoing technological innovations and evolving regulatory frameworks. The increasing use of big data and artificial intelligence has further transformed trading strategies. Algorithms now incorporate not only market data but also a wide array of alternative data sources, such as social media sentiment, satellite imagery, and even weather patterns, to inform trading decisions.

Regulatory bodies worldwide continue to refine their approaches to managing the risks associated with algorithmic and high-frequency trading, balancing the need for innovation and market efficiency with the imperative of maintaining financial stability. Concepts like co-location, where traders place their systems close to exchange servers to minimize latency, and dark pools, private trading venues for large orders, have also become integral to the current market structure, reflecting the ever-evolving technological and strategic landscape of algorithmic trading.

Understanding the historical developments and evolution of algorithmic trading not only offers insight into the current state of financial markets but also equips traders with the perspective needed to anticipate and adapt to future advancements and regulatory changes. The interplay between technological progress, market behavior, and regulatory frameworks will undoubtedly continue to shape the trajectory of algorithmic trading, demanding continual learning and adaptation from market participants.

10.3 Types of Algorithmic Trading Strategies

Algorithmic trading encompasses a broad spectrum of strategies, each tailored to exploit specific market inefficiencies or to achieve distinct investment objectives. Understanding these strategies is crucial for any investor or trader looking to leverage algorithmic trading in their financial pursuits. This section delves into some of the most prevalent algorithmic trading strategies, providing a detailed explanation of their mechanics, advantages, and potential pitfalls.

At the heart of algorithmic trading strategies lies the concept of utilizing historic and real-time data to make informed decisions. The effectiveness of each strategy relies heavily on the quality and granularity of data, as well as the sophistication of the algorithm employed.

1. Statistical Arbitrage

Statistical arbitrage, often abbreviated as stat arb, involves the simultaneous buying and selling of related financial instruments to profit from the inevitable reversion to statistical norms. This strategy hinges on the mean-reversion principle, which posits that prices and returns eventually revert to their long-term averages.

One common approach within statistical arbitrage is pairs trading, where two stocks that historically move together are identified. When the price divergence between the two exceeds a certain threshold, the algorithm triggers trades to short the overperforming stock and buy the underperforming stock, aiming to benefit from the convergence back to historical norms.

Mathematically, if S_A and S_B are the prices of two stocks, the spread X can be defined as:

$$X(t) = S_A(t) - \beta S_B(t)$$

where β is a constant derived from regression analysis. When $X(t)$ deviates significantly from its historical mean μ, positions are established per the following decision rule:

$$\text{If } X(t) > \mu + \sigma, \text{ then short } S_A \text{ and long } S_B$$

$$\text{If } X(t) < \mu - \sigma, \text{ then long } S_A \text{ and short } S_B$$

where σ is the standard deviation of $X(t)$.

2. Market Making

Market making involves providing liquidity to the market by continuously quoting both buy and sell prices for a particular financial instrument, thereby earning the spread between the bid and ask prices. This strategy requires maintaining substantial capital and computational resources to handle the rapid adjustments in prices and volumes.

The key to successful market making is the ability to manage the inventory risk effectively. An algorithmic market maker will typically adjust quotes based on quantitative models that assess short-term price dynamics and order flow. For example, an imbalance between supply and demand might prompt the algorithm to widen the spread or adjust order sizes.

3. Trend Following

Trend following strategies capitalize on the momentum of asset prices. Based on the premise that prices tend to move in trends, these algorithms aim to identify and exploit upward or downward trends over various time horizons.

One of the simplest and most widely used methods in this category is the moving average crossover strategy. Here, two moving averages (a short-term and a long-term) are tracked, and trading decisions are made based on their intersections:

$$\text{If } MA_{\text{short}}(t) > MA_{\text{long}}(t), \text{ then a long position is initiated}$$

$$\text{If } MA_{\text{short}}(t) < MA_{\text{long}}(t), \text{ then a short position is initiated}$$

where $MA_{\text{short}}(t)$ and $MA_{\text{long}}(t)$ are the moving averages over shorter and longer periods, respectively.

4. Mean Reversion

Mean reversion strategies are based on the assumption that the price of a financial instrument will revert to its historical average over time. These strategies often involve identifying assets that have deviated significantly from their average prices and taking positions contrary to the direction of the deviation.

A fundamental approach to mean reversion is through the calculation of the Z-score, which measures how many standard deviations an asset's current price is from the mean:

$$Z(t) = \frac{P(t) - \mu}{\sigma}$$

where $P(t)$ is the current price, μ is the historical mean, and σ is the historical standard deviation.

5. Momentum Strategies

Momentum strategies exploit the tendency of asset prices to exhibit momentum - the phenomenon where past performance is indicative of future performance over short to medium time horizons. Unlike trend following, which typically focuses on long-term trends, momentum strategies often function over shorter periods.

A common momentum strategy involves ranking assets based on their past performance over a specified period and forming portfolios of the top-performing assets. These assets are then bought with the expectation that their performance will continue in the same direction.

6. Arbitrage

Arbitrage strategies seek risk-free profit opportunities by exploiting price discrepancies of the same asset or related assets in different markets or forms. Pure arbitrage involves simultaneously buying and selling identical assets to profit from price differences.

A classic example is triangular arbitrage in forex markets. If the exchange rates between three currencies, A, B, and C, are not at equilibrium, an arbitrageur can convert A to B, B to C, and C back to A, thereby locking in a profit without net exposure.

As financial markets evolve and technology advances, new algorithmic trading strategies continue to emerge. Each strategy not only requires rigorous mathematical and statistical backing but also sophisticated programming and real-time execution capabilities. Ensuring a deep understanding of these strategies and their underlying principles allows traders to navigate the complexities of algorithmic trading effectively.

10.4 Market Microstructure Basics

Understanding the market microstructure is essential for effective algorithmic trading, as it governs the rules and mechanisms by which orders are processed and trades are executed. This section aims to unpack the intricacies of market microstructure, elucidating the core components that every trader must master.

At its core, market microstructure focuses on the mechanics of trading within financial markets, emphasizing the process from the time an order is placed until it is executed. This includes examining different market participants, the types of orders they use, the structure and functioning of exchanges, and the impact of these elements on liquidity and price formation. A solid grounding in these basics enables traders to develop algorithms that optimize trade execution and minimize costs.

The first component to consider is the differentiation between *order-driven* and *quote-driven* markets. In an order-driven market, trades occur through a matching process of buy and sell orders, relying heavily on the order book. In contrast, a quote-driven market involves market makers who provide continuous quotes for the buy and sell prices of a security, thus facilitating trade by ensuring liquidity.

An essential element within the order-driven market is the *order book*, a dynamic ledger where buy and sell orders are listed. Orders in the book are matched based on their prices and time of entry, following a price-time priority rule. A graphical representation of an order book for a hypothetical stock is shown in Figure 10.1.

This figure exemplifies how buy orders (demand) and sell orders (supply) are structured in an order book, presenting a visual snapshot of

Figure 10.1: Hypothetical Order Book Structure

liquidity at various price levels.

Next, we consider the various *order types* available to traders. Market orders, the simplest type, offer immediate execution at the best available price. However, they carry the risk of slippage, especially in less liquid markets, where the execution price deviates significantly from the expected price. Limit orders, on the other hand, specify the maximum price a trader is willing to pay (buy limit) or the minimum price they are willing to accept (sell limit). While they provide more control over execution price, there is a risk that the order might not be filled.

Order Type	**Description**
Market Order	Executes immediately at the best available price
Limit Order	Executes only at a specified price or better
Stop Order	Becomes a market order when a specified price is reached
Stop-Limit Order	Becomes a limit order when a specified price is reached

Table 10.1: Common Order Types and Characteristics

Table 10.1 summarizes these common order types, detailing their specific execution criteria and conditions.

Another critical concept is the *spread*, which represents the difference between the highest bid price (the maximum price a buyer is willing to pay) and the lowest ask price (the minimum price a seller is willing to accept). The spread is a fundamental indicator of market liquidity and transaction costs. In liquid markets, the spread tends to be narrow due to high competition among market participants. Conversely, in illiquid markets, spreads widen, reflecting higher uncertainty and greater risk in trade execution.

The role of *market makers* also deserves attention. These entities provide liquidity by constantly quoting bid and ask prices and standing ready to buy or sell securities. Their presence ensures that there is always a counterparty available for trade, which enhances overall market efficiency. Market makers profit from the bid-ask spread and must manage inventory risks and adverse selection to minimize losses.

The function of *transaction costs* in the context of market microstructure cannot be overlooked. These costs include explicit fees such as commissions and implicit costs like the spread and slippage. Effective algorithmic trading strategies aim to minimize these costs through optimal order execution tactics, such as using dark pools to hide large orders and reduce market impact.

Finally, one must understand the *impact of information* on market microstructure. Informed traders, who possess superior knowledge about an asset's value, can significantly affect price dynamics. The presence of asymmetrically distributed information leads to market phenomena such as adverse selection, where uninformed traders are at a disadvantage. Algorithmic strategies often seek to detect and leverage these information disparities for profitable trading opportunities.

Mastering these elements of market microstructure enables traders to engineer sophisticated algorithms that navigate the complexities of modern financial markets with precision and efficiency, ultimately leading to superior trade execution and performance.

10.5 Order Types and Execution Strategies

Understanding order types and execution strategies is crucial for effective algorithmic trading. The choice of order type can significantly influence the trading outcome, impacting both the speed and price at which trades are executed. This section explores the various types of orders available, explaining their characteristics, advantages, and potential drawbacks, and delves into execution strategies that maximize trading efficiency.

Order Types

Market Orders: A market order is the simplest type of order, instructing the broker to buy or sell a security immediately at the current market price. While market orders guarantee execution, they do not guarantee the execution price, which can lead to unfavorable fills in volatile markets.

Limit Orders: A limit order specifies the maximum price at which you are willing to buy or the minimum price at which you are willing to sell. This order is only executed if the market price meets the limit price, offering better control over execution prices but no guarantee of execution. The formula for a limit order can be expressed as:

$$\text{Execute if and only if} \quad p_{\text{market}} \leq p_{\text{limit}} \quad \text{(for buy orders)}$$
$$\text{or} \quad p_{\text{market}} \geq p_{\text{limit}} \quad \text{(for sell orders)}$$

Stop Orders: A stop order becomes a market order once the stop price is reached. For instance, a stop-loss order instructs the sale of a security if its price falls to a specified level, providing a mechanism to limit losses. Conversely, a stop-buy order is used to buy a security if its price rises to a certain level, often as a way to enter a position during a breakout.

Stop-Limit Orders: A hybrid of stop and limit orders, the stop-limit order becomes a limit order once the stop price is reached, ensuring the order is executed at a designated price or better. The execution logic is as follows:

$$\text{If} \quad p_{\text{market}} \leq p_{\text{stop}}, \quad \text{then} \quad \text{execute as} \quad p_{\text{market}} = p_{\text{limit}}$$

Trailing Stop Orders: These orders dynamically adjust the stop price based on a specified percentage or dollar amount away from the current market price. This helps lock in profits while maintaining a stop order that adapts to price movements favorably. For example, if a trailing stop percentage of 5% is set for a long position at $100, the stop price would start at $95 and move upward as the market price increases.

Execution Strategies

Slicing Algorithms: These algorithms break large orders into smaller chunks to minimize market impact and achieve better average execution prices. Examples include Time-Weighted Average Price (TWAP) and Volume-Weighted Average Price (VWAP):

$$\text{TWAP:} \quad \frac{1}{N}\sum_{i=1}^{N} p_i$$

$$\text{VWAP:} \quad \frac{\sum_{i=1}^{N} p_i \times v_i}{\sum_{i=1}^{N} v_i}$$

- **TWAP:** The aim is to execute the trade uniformly over a specified time period, reducing the risk of signaling the market about a large impending trade.
- **VWAP:** This stratagem ensures that the execution aligns with the volume profile of the market, filling more trades during high-volume periods and less during low-volume ones, which helps in achieving an average price close to the market's overall trading dynamics.

Implementation Shortfall: This strategy focuses on minimizing the trading cost relative to a pre-trade benchmark, considering both the price impact of the trade and the opportunity cost of delayed execution. This involves optimizing the trade-off between immediate execution (market impact) and potential adverse price movements (slippage).

Liquidity-Seeking Algorithms: Tailored for high-frequency traders, these algorithms rapidly scan multiple liquidity pools to execute trades with minimal market impact. They utilize real-time data and sophisticated pattern recognition to identify and exploit temporary inefficiencies or discrepancies across different venues.

Smart Order Routing (SOR): SOR algorithms route orders to various trading venues to find the best execution opportunities. They dynamically adapt to changing market conditions, seeking the best price and available liquidity while considering factors like fees, latency, and fill probabilities. The routing decision can be mathematically represented as:

$$\text{maximize} \quad E\left[P_{\text{execution}} - C_{\text{transaction}}\right]$$

where $P_{\text{execution}}$ is the expected execution price and $C_{\text{transaction}}$ is the cost of transaction, including fees and market impact.

Dark Pool Algorithms: These are designed to trade in private trading venues, or dark pools, which do not display orders to the public. Dark pools provide anonymity and larger block trading capabilities but come with the trade-off of potentially lower liquidity and less price transparency. Algorithms adapted for dark pool trading aim to minimize market impact and avoid information leakage.

Each type of order and execution strategy presents unique strengths and weaknesses, suited to different trading goals and market conditions. Mastery of these elements allows traders to fine-tune their approaches, manage risks effectively, and enhance their chances of achieving desirable trading outcomes. The intricate interplay between these components defines the landscape of algorithmic trading, offering a toolkit for navigating the complexities of modern financial markets.

10.6 High-Frequency Trading (HFT)

High-Frequency Trading (HFT) represents a highly sophisticated and speed-intensive subset of algorithmic trading that leverages powerful computing technology to execute orders at fractions of a second. HFT strategies capitalize on ultra-low latency execution, minimal transaction times, and the ability to process vast amounts of market data in real-time. This makes it a significant player in the current financial landscape, often occupying a pivotal role in the market microstructure.

At the core of HFT lies the principle of exploiting small price inefficiencies that exist for fleeting moments. These opportunities might be indiscernible to human traders due to the swiftness of price movements, but advanced algorithms can identify and act upon these inefficiencies almost instantaneously.

Foundations of HFT

The success of HFT relies heavily on several crucial components, each contributing to the overall strategy's effectiveness:

- **Latency Reduction:** Reducing time delays in sending and receiving trade orders is paramount. Firms invest in high-speed data feeds, co-location services (situating their servers physically close to exchange servers), and advanced networking hardware to shave off microseconds in trade execution.

- **Algorithm Development:** With HFT, the complexity and speed of algorithms are at the forefront. These algorithms must process large datasets, identify arbitrage opportunities, execute orders, and manage risk all within milliseconds.
- **Risk Management:** Given the high volume and rapid pace of trades, managing risk is critical. Algorithms include strict risk management protocols to prevent large losses from rapid, adverse market moves.

Common HFT Strategies

Several standardized strategies are commonly employed in HFT due to their effectiveness in capturing small, rapid price movements:

- **Market Making:** HFT firms place both buy and sell orders to profit from the bid-ask spread. By constantly adjusting these orders based on incoming market data, they provide liquidity to the market and capture small, consistent profits.
- **Statistical Arbitrage:** This involves using statistical models to identify pricing anomalies between correlated assets. When discrepancies arise, HFT algorithms execute trades to capitalize on the temporary mispricing.
- **Event Arbitrage:** Algorithms monitor news feeds, earnings releases, and other market-moving events. Rapid analysis and trading systems exploit resultant price movements before other market participants can react.
- **Momentum Ignition:** This involves initiating a large number of trades to create the illusion of increased demand or supply, thereby triggering momentum which the trader then exploits.

Challenges and Criticisms of HFT

Despite its profitability and prevalence, HFT has faced significant criticism and poses certain challenges:

- **Market Impact:** The rapid and high volume trading of HFT can lead to increased market volatility. Critics argue that HFT firms can exacerbate price swings and contribute to flash crashes.

- **Fairness Concerns:** There are arguments that HFT creates an uneven playing field, where firms with superior technology can exploit advantages that are unavailable to average investors.
- **Regulatory Scrutiny:** Due to potential market manipulation and fairness concerns, HFT is subject to stringent regulations. Governing bodies monitor trading activities closely to ensure compliance with market integrity standards.

Regulatory Environment

Various regulatory measures have been implemented to address the risks and criticisms associated with HFT:

- **Circuit Breakers:** These are automated measures that temporarily halt trading on an exchange to curb panic-selling and provide a cooling-off period during significant market declines.
- **Order-to-Trade Ratios (OTR):** Regulations may impose limits on the ratio of cancelled orders to executed trades to ensure fair use of trading systems.
- **Market Surveillance:** Advanced surveillance systems monitor trading activities for patterns of abuse, ensuring that HFT strategies comply with market manipulation laws.

High-Frequency Trading is a complex and integral part of modern markets, bringing both liquidity and potential challenges. Mastery of HFT requires understanding its foundational technologies, strategies employed, associated risks, and regulatory frameworks that govern its practice. As markets evolve, the role of HFT will likely continue to grow, necessitating constant adaptation and innovation in response to changing market dynamics.

10.7 Transaction Costs and Slippage

In algorithmic trading, understanding and managing transaction costs and slippage is paramount to optimizing performance and maximizing returns. This section aims to dissect these crucial elements, elucidating how they can influence trading strategies and overall profitability.

At its core, **transaction costs** refer to the expenses incurred during the process of buying or selling securities. These costs can be bifurcated into explicit and implicit costs. Explicit costs are direct and visible, including broker commissions, exchange fees, and taxes. On the other hand, implicit costs, though less apparent, can significantly impact the efficiency of a trade. These include bid-ask spreads, market impact costs, and delay costs.

Mathematically, the explicit transaction cost (C_e) can be formulated as:

$$C_e = \sum_{i=1}^{n} (c_i \times V_i)$$

where c_i represents the commission rate of the i-th trade, and V_i denotes the trading volume or value. The cumulative effect of these costs on a series of trades can erode the net returns significantly, hence necessitating prudent cost management strategies.

Implicit costs, particularly the bid-ask spread, can be encapsulated as:

$$\text{Spread} = \text{Ask Price} - \text{Bid Price}$$

For instance, if the ask price of a stock is $100.10 and the bid price is $100.00, the spread is $0.10. This difference, though seemingly negligible on individual trades, can cumulatively impact the overall portfolio when executing large volumes or frequent trades. Effective algorithmic trading strategies often involve optimizing trade execution timing and order placement to minimize the spread.

Slippage, another critical consideration, refers to the difference between the expected price of a trade and the actual executed price. Slippage typically occurs due to market volatility and the time taken to execute an order. While it can be positive or negative, negative slippage - where the executed price is less favorable than anticipated - can detract from the strategy's performance.

The expected slippage (S_e) can be approximated as:

$$S_e = \left(\frac{P_e - P_a}{P_a} \right) \times 100$$

where P_e is the executed price, and P_a is the anticipated price. Managing slippage involves strategic order placement and leveraging liquidity in a manner that minimizes the discrepancy between the expected and actual prices.

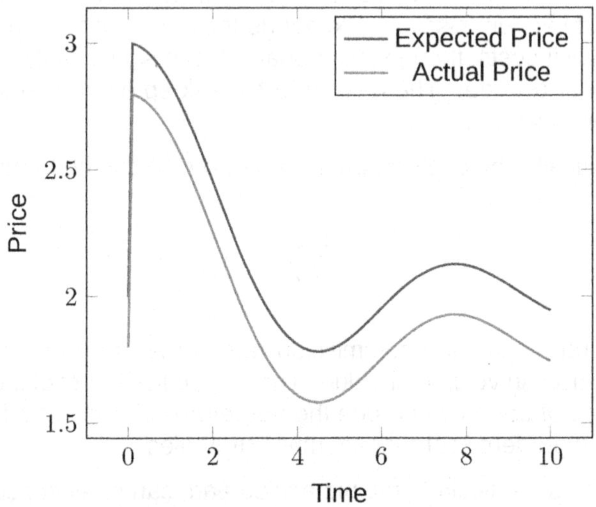

Figure 10.2: Illustration of Expected Price versus Actual Price highlighting Slippage

In high-frequency trading (HFT) environments, managing these costs becomes remarkably intricate due to the sheer volume and speed of transactions. Techniques such as **order slicing** and **order aggregation** are employed to mitigate transaction costs and slippage. Order slicing involves breaking up large orders into smaller chunks to minimize market impact, while order aggregation consolidates smaller orders to leverage better pricing.

$$P_{\text{effective}} = \frac{\sum_{i=1}^{n} P_i V_i}{\sum_{i=1}^{n} V_i}$$

where $P_{\text{effective}}$ represents the weighted average price, P_i the price of each smaller order, and V_i the respective volumes. This approach aids in achieving a more favorable execution price by balancing the trade-off between liquidity and market impact.

Market microstructure plays a significant role in the dynamics of transaction costs and slippage. Various trading venues and their associated rules, the liquidity depth, and the presence of high-frequency traders all intertwine to create a complex landscape that traders must navigate.

An in-depth understanding of these elements allows for designing algorithms that are agile and adept at responding to market signals, thereby optimizing trade execution.

Ultimately, the goal for sophisticated traders and investors is not only to recognize the existence of transaction costs and slippage but to integrate strategies that actively manage and mitigate these factors. Through careful analysis, algorithmic adjustments, and continuous monitoring of execution performance, it is possible to reduce their overall impact and enhance the efficiency and profitability of the trading strategy.

10.8 Liquidity and Market Impact

Understanding liquidity and market impact is pivotal for developing robust algorithmic trading strategies. Liquidity refers to the ability to buy or sell an asset without causing a significant change in its price. Market impact, on the other hand, encompasses the price change that occurs when an order is executed — a crucial consideration for high-frequency traders and large investors alike.

When discussing liquidity, it is essential to differentiate between two types: *trade liquidity* and *quote liquidity*. Trade liquidity indicates the ease with which trades can be executed at current market prices, characterized by high volume and tight bid-ask spreads. Quote liquidity, however, refers to the availability of buy and sell orders in the market at various prices, contributing to the depth of the order book.

Mathematically, liquidity can be quantified using various metrics. One common measure is the *Bid-Ask Spread*:

$$\text{Bid-Ask Spread} = \frac{\text{Ask Price} - \text{Bid Price}}{\text{Mid Price}}$$

where the *Mid Price* is the average of the bid and ask prices:

$$\text{Mid Price} = \frac{\text{Bid Price} + \text{Ask Price}}{2}$$

A narrower bid-ask spread indicates higher liquidity, as it suggests minimal cost for executing trades.

Another important concept is *market depth*, which illustrates the market's capacity to absorb trades without significantly affecting the price.

Market depth is often visualized using a depth chart, showing the cumulative buy and sell orders at each price level. For an analytical approach, the *Liquidity Ratio* can be used:

$$\text{Liquidity Ratio} = \frac{\text{Volume of Orders at Best Prices}}{\text{Bid-Ask Spread}}$$

A higher liquidity ratio signifies robust market depth and stability.

Market impact is typically measured using the *Price Impact Function*, which relates the size of an order to the price change it causes. A simple linear representation can be expressed as:

$$\Delta P = \eta \cdot Q$$

where ΔP is the price change, Q is the order size, and η is a coefficient representing market resilience.

Despite its simplicity, actual market behavior often exhibits non-linear dynamics. More sophisticated models, such as the *Kyle's Lambda*, provide deeper insights:

$$\Delta P = \lambda \cdot \sqrt{Q}$$

Here, λ captures market depth and liquidity resilience, indicating how sensitively prices react to trading volumes.

Algorithmic traders must carefully consider both liquidity and market impact when designing strategies. High-frequency trading (HFT) firms particularly thrive on exploiting micro-level inefficiencies in liquid markets. However, the size and frequency of trades must be managed to avoid adverse market impact.

In practical applications, traders use techniques like *iceberg orders* to mitigate visibility and thus reduce market impact. By breaking a large order into smaller chunks, iceberg orders conceal the true trade size, only showing segments of the total volume at any given time.

Liquidity also fluctuates with intraday variations, often peaking at market open and close due to heightened trading activity. Traders can leverage this knowledge by timing their orders to optimize execution quality.

Moreover, understanding *liquidity providers* and *liquidity takers* roles in the market is crucial. Liquidity providers, often market makers, post buy and sell orders to facilitate trading, benefiting from bid-ask spreads. Liquidity takers, conversely, execute trades on the available orders, potentially moving the market.

Aggregating insights from liquidity metrics and market impact models allows traders to formulate strategies that minimize costs and maximize execution efficiency. A comprehensive approach involves continuously adjusting algorithms based on real-time market conditions and historical data analysis.

One advanced technique is the implementation of *Volume Weighted Average Price (VWAP)* strategies to achieve favorable trade execution over a specified time period. The VWAP is calculated as:

$$\text{VWAP} = \frac{\sum_i P_i \cdot Q_i}{\sum_i Q_i}$$

where P_i and Q_i denote the price and quantity of trades respectively. VWAP serves as a benchmark, helping traders execute large orders in line with market conditions, thus minimizing market impact.

By understanding and harnessing liquidity and market impact, traders can optimize their algorithmic strategies to achieve better trade execution, reducing costs and enhancing overall portfolio performance.

10.9 Regulatory Environment

The regulatory environment is a critical aspect of algorithmic trading, ensuring fair and orderly markets, protecting investors, and maintaining systemic stability. Understanding the key regulatory frameworks and compliance requirements is essential for any trader, especially those leveraging automated strategies. This section explores the primary regulatory bodies, important regulations, and ongoing changes in the global landscape of algorithmic trading.

Key Regulatory Bodies

Several major regulatory bodies oversee and guide algorithmic trading and financial markets across different regions. Among these, the most influential are:

- **U.S. Securities and Exchange Commission (SEC):** The SEC is the primary regulatory body in the United States, responsible for enforcing federal securities laws and regulating the securities industry, including stock and options exchanges.

- **Commodity Futures Trading Commission (CFTC):** The CFTC regulates futures and options markets in the U.S. It oversees trading in derivatives and enforces the Commodity Exchange Act (CEA).

- **Financial Conduct Authority (FCA):** In the United Kingdom, the FCA oversees the conduct of financial firms to ensure market integrity and protect consumers.

- **European Securities and Markets Authority (ESMA):** ESMA is an independent EU authority that contributes to safeguarding the stability of the European Union's financial system by enhancing investor protection and promoting stable, orderly financial markets.

These regulatory bodies implement various rules and guidelines to govern algorithmic trading practices and mitigate risks related to market manipulation, systemic risk, and unfair trading advantages.

Significant Regulations

Several key regulations have been enacted to address the unique challenges posed by algorithmic trading:

- **Regulation NMS (National Market System):** Implemented by the SEC, Regulation NMS aims to modernize and strengthen the National Market System for equity trading. Key components include the Order Protection Rule (Rule 611), which prevents trade-throughs, and the Access Rule (Rule 610), which mandates fair access to quotations.

- **MiFID II (Markets in Financial Instruments Directive II):** MiFID II is a comprehensive regulatory framework by ESMA that came into effect in 2018. It includes provisions for algorithmic and high-frequency trading (HFT), such as requiring traders to be registered, maintaining accurate trade records, and implementing robust risk controls.

- **Dodd-Frank Wall Street Reform and Consumer Protection Act:** This U.S. federal law introduced comprehensive financial regulatory reforms, including transparency requirements and regulatory oversight of derivatives markets. It mandates pre-trade and post-trade transparency and aims to reduce systemic risk.

Compliance and Risk Management

Compliance with these regulations requires firms to implement stringent risk management systems and controls. Key compliance practices include:

- **Pre-Trade Risk Controls:** Firms must establish automated controls to prevent erroneous trades, such as price and quantity limits, maximum order size limits, and trading velocity controls.
- **Post-Trade Monitoring:** Continuous monitoring of trading activity to detect anomalies or potentially manipulative practices such as spoofing or layering.
- **Record Keeping:** Comprehensive records of all trading activities, communications, and algorithmic decision-making processes to ensure transparency and accountability.
- **Regulatory Reporting:** Timely and accurate reporting of trading activities to relevant authorities, including detailed transaction reports required under regulations like MiFID II.

Global Harmonization and Ongoing Changes

The global nature of financial markets necessitates coordination among regulatory bodies across jurisdictions. Efforts towards harmonizing regulations aim to prevent regulatory arbitrage and ensure a level playing field for market participants.

Changes in the regulatory landscape are ongoing, driven by technological advancements and emerging risks. Regulators continuously update rules and guidelines to address new challenges, such as the rise of artificial intelligence and machine learning in trading.

Engaging with regulatory bodies, staying informed about updates, and participating in industry forums are essential practices for firms to navigate the regulatory environment effectively. The ultimate goal is to foster a fair, transparent, and resilient market ecosystem where the benefits of algorithmic trading are realized while minimizing associated risks.

10.10 Ethical Considerations and Risks

In algorithmic trading, ethical considerations and associated risks are paramount topics that merit detailed exploration. As automated systems and sophisticated algorithms increasingly dominate financial markets, the potential for both significant advancements and ethical pitfalls inexorably rises.

One primary ethical consideration is the potential for market manipulation. Algorithmic trading strategies can, intentionally or unintentionally, distort market prices and liquidity. Through practices such as spoofing—where a trader places large orders with no intention of executing them to create a misleading picture of market demand—traders may unfairly influence prices to their advantage. This practice, albeit illegal, has historically posed substantial challenges to regulators due to the rapid and often opaque nature of algorithmic trade execution.

Given the capability of algorithms to execute trades at speeds far beyond human intervention, another ethical issue is the potential for flash crashes. Instances such as the 2010 Flash Crash, where a massive and rapid sell-off caused the Dow Jones Industrial Average to plummet nearly 1,000 points in minutes, underscore the systemic risks related to unanticipated algorithmic interactions. Such events not only damage market stability but also erode public trust in financial systems.

Front-running, a particularly concerning practice, involves employing algorithms to monitor and predict large, non-public buy or sell orders and then executing trades ahead of them to profit from the consequent price movements. This exploitation of informational asymmetry is not only unethical but also undermines the integrity of financial markets, disadvantaging ordinary investors.

Furthermore, the proliferation of algorithmic trading platforms brings about significant data privacy concerns. Algorithms are often designed to capture and analyze vast amounts of market data, including trade details and transactions. The improper handling or use of this data can lead to privacy breaches and conflicts of interest, where sensitive information might be exploited for personal gain or competitive advantage.

The ethical landscape is also shaped by the phenomenon of dark pools and other off-exchange trading venues. While designed to offer privacy and reduce market impact for large transactions, these platforms can reduce market transparency and potentially enable unfair trading practices. The lack of visibility into these trades can hinder price discovery and create an uneven playing field, to the detriment of retail investors and smaller market participants.

Risks also extend to the algorithms themselves. The reliance on historical data to train algorithmic models poses the risk of perpetuating past biases or overlooking rare but impactful events—often referred to as black swan events. Additionally, the complexity of these algorithms increases the difficulty of thoroughly understanding and auditing their performance, potentially leading to overreliance on flawed models.

Regulatory bodies worldwide are continually striving to keep pace with the rapid advancements in algorithmic trading. Regulations such as the European Union's Markets in Financial Instruments Directive II (MiFID II) and the U.S. Securities and Exchange Commission's (SEC) regulations require stringent oversight and operational transparency. These include mandates for pre-trade risk controls, the monitoring of algorithmic trading systems, and the maintenance of detailed trade records to prevent market abuse.

However, despite regulatory advancements, it is incumbent on firms to implement robust compliance frameworks. The development and deployment of algorithms must adhere to ethical standards that prioritize market integrity and protect investor interests. Firms should incorporate governance policies that promote ethical behavior, conduct regular audits of trading algorithms to identify potential risks, and establish crisis management protocols to address unforeseen adverse events.

Ultimately, algorithmic trading offers vast potential to enhance market efficiency and liquidity, but it is fraught with ethical complexities and risks that require vigilant management. Traders, firms, and regulators must collaborate to uphold ethical standards and fortify the robustness of financial markets against the myriad challenges posed by evolving trading technologies.

Chapter 11

Machine Learning in Quantitative Finance

Machine learning is revolutionizing quantitative finance by enabling data-driven decision-making and predictive modeling. This chapter introduces supervised and unsupervised learning techniques, emphasizing their applications in financial analysis. It covers feature engineering, data preprocessing, and model evaluation. Readers will learn how machine learning can enhance algorithmic trading, risk management, and natural language processing (NLP) for financial text analysis. The chapter also addresses ethical considerations and the importance of model interpretability in finance.

11.1 Introduction to Machine Learning

Machine learning (ML) is a subset of artificial intelligence (AI) that focuses on developing algorithms and statistical models that enable computers to perform tasks without explicit instructions. The core idea behind machine learning is to allow systems to learn from data, identify patterns, and make decisions with minimal human intervention. This capability has profound implications in quantitative finance, where the ability to rapidly and accurately analyze vast amounts of data can provide a significant edge.

At its essence, machine learning involves training algorithms on a dataset to make predictions or classify data points. The beauty of these models lies in their adaptability; as new data becomes available, the models can be retrained or updated to refine their accuracy. Machine learning can be broadly categorized into three types: supervised learning, unsupervised learning, and reinforcement learning. Each type employs different approaches to achieve the learning objective.

In supervised learning, the algorithm learns from a labeled dataset, meaning that each training example is paired with an output label. This technique is particularly powerful for predictive modeling tasks, such as predicting stock prices or classifying financial transactions. Some of the most popular supervised learning algorithms include linear regression, logistic regression, support vector machines (SVM), and neural networks.

Unsupervised learning, on the other hand, deals with unlabeled data. The objective here is to uncover hidden patterns or intrinsic structures within the dataset. This approach is useful for tasks such as clustering, anomaly detection, and association rule mining. Key unsupervised learning algorithms include k-means clustering, hierarchical clustering, and principal component analysis (PCA).

Reinforcement learning differs from both supervised and unsupervised learning in that it centers around agents that learn to make decisions by interacting with an environment. The agent receives feedback in the form of rewards or penalties based on its actions, enabling it to learn optimal strategies over time. This type of learning is especially relevant for developing trading algorithms that adapt to market conditions.

Understanding machine learning in quantitative finance begins with grasping these foundational concepts. For instance, consider the problem of predicting the future price of a stock. Using supervised learning, one might collect historical data on the stock's prices, trading volumes, and perhaps other indicators like interest rates or economic measures. With this data, a regression model can be trained to predict the stock's future price based on its past behavior.

Mathematically, if we denote the historical data as matrix $\boldsymbol{X}$ and the stock's future price as vector $\boldsymbol{y}$, a linear regression model aims to learn the weights $\boldsymbol{w}$ that minimize the prediction error:

$$\hat{\boldsymbol{y}} = \boldsymbol{X}\boldsymbol{w}$$

where $\hat{\boldsymbol{y}}$ represents the predicted prices. The common approach to finding the optimal weights is to minimize the mean squared error (MSE):

$$\text{MSE} = \frac{1}{n}\sum_{i=1}^{n}(y_i - \hat{y}_i)^2$$

Unsupervised learning, on the other hand, could be employed to identify clusters of stocks that exhibit similar price movements. Using k-means clustering, one tries to partition the dataset into k clusters, optimizing the centroids' positions to minimize the variance within clusters. The objective function for k-means clustering is:

$$\arg\min_{S}\sum_{i=1}^{k}\sum_{x\in S_i}\|x - \mu_i\|^2$$

where S represents the set of clusters, and μ_i denotes the centroid of the i-th cluster.

Moreover, reinforcement learning can be utilized for constructing adaptive trading strategies. For instance, a trading algorithm might be designed to buy or sell based on the rewards it receives from various actions it takes in a simulated market environment. Over time, the algorithm learns to maximize cumulative rewards, thereby optimizing its trading policy.

A practical example might involve a simplified environment where the agent decides whether to buy, hold, or sell a stock. The reward function R could be defined based on the profit or loss of the actions:

$$R = P_{\text{sell}} - P_{\text{buy}}$$

where P_{sell} and P_{buy} represent the selling and buying prices, respectively. The learning process thus focuses on maximizing this reward.

Ultimately, the power of machine learning in quantitative finance is amplified by the abundant data available in financial markets. Proper feature engineering and data preprocessing are crucial steps that precede the training of any machine learning model. Features such as technical indicators, macroeconomic variables, and sentiment scores from news articles can be engineered to enhance model performance.

Throughout this chapter, we will delve deeper into these machine learning techniques, exploring how they can be effectively leveraged to build robust predictive models, identify underlying structures in financial data, and develop adaptive trading strategies. The goal is to equip you with the knowledge and tools to harness the full potential of machine learning in quantitative finance, enabling informed and data-driven decision-making.

11.2 Supervised Learning Techniques

Supervised learning is a foundational aspect of machine learning, playing a pivotal role in quantitative finance. At its core, supervised learning involves training a model on labeled data, where the relationship between input features and the corresponding output is explicitly known. This method equips the model to predict outcomes or classify data based on new, unseen data. To demystify supervised learning techniques, we shall delve into key methods such as linear regression, logistic regression, decision trees, and support vector machines, elucidating their relevance and applications in financial markets.

Linear regression is the simplest form of regression analysis, aiming to model the relationship between a dependent variable Y and one or more independent variables X. The model is expressed as:

$$Y = \beta_0 + \beta_1 X_1 + \beta_2 X_2 + \cdots + \beta_n X_n + \epsilon$$

where β_0 is the intercept, β_i are the coefficients for the respective independent variables, and ϵ is the error term. In quantitative finance, linear regression can be employed to predict stock prices, returns, or volatility based on historical data. For instance, a simple linear regression might use past returns to predict future returns, aiding traders in making informed decisions.

Logistic regression, on the other hand, is used for binary classification problems. This technique predicts the probability that a given input belongs to a particular class. The logistic regression model can be represented as:

$$P(Y = 1|X) = \frac{1}{1 + e^{-(\beta_0 + \beta_1 X_1 + \beta_2 X_2 + \cdots + \beta_n X_n)}}$$

where $P(Y = 1|X)$ is the probability of the output being class 1, given the inputs X. In finance, logistic regression can be pivotal in credit scoring, predicting the likelihood of default, or classifying market movements as 'up' or 'down'.

Decision trees offer a visual and intuitive means of decision-making based on input features. They split the data into branches based on feature values, creating a tree-like structure of decisions. Each internal node represents a decision based on an attribute, each branch represents the outcome of the decision, and each leaf node represents a class label or a continuous value (in the case of regression trees). An example of this in finance might be classifying whether a day's market condition (up, down, or flat) based on various indicators such as moving averages or trading volumes.

Support Vector Machines (SVM) are powerful tools for both classification and regression tasks. SVMs operate by finding the hyperplane that best separates data points of different classes in a high-dimensional space. For classification, the goal is to maximize the margin between the closest points of the classes, known as support vectors. Mathematically, for a linearly separable dataset, this can be formulated as:

$$\boldsymbol{w} \cdot \boldsymbol{x} - b = 0$$

subject to the constraints that:

$$y_i(\boldsymbol{w} \cdot \boldsymbol{x}_i - b) \geq 1 \quad \text{for all} \quad i$$

where $\boldsymbol{w}$ is the normal vector to the hyperplane, b is the bias term, and y_i denotes the class labels. In quantitative finance, SVMs are often used for recognizing patterns in market behavior, leading to more accurate predictions.

These supervised learning techniques are not only confined to basic applications but can be sophisticatedly combined and enhanced to tackle complex financial problems. For instance, ensemble methods like Random Forest and Gradient Boosting improve predictive performance by combining the outputs of multiple learning algorithms. Random forests construct multiple decision trees and aggregate their results for classification or regression. Gradient boosting builds models sequentially, each new model correcting errors made by the previous ones.

Applying these supervised learning techniques to algorithmic trading can significantly enhance trading strategies. For example, linear regression might be used to predict future prices and place trades accordingly, while logistic regression could be applied in identifying profitable trade signals. Decision trees and SVMs can be used to classify market conditions and adjust trading strategies dynamically.

Effective implementation of supervised learning in finance requires careful attention to feature selection and engineering, appropriate model tuning, and rigorous back-testing to ensure robustness and prevent overfitting. Moreover, integrating domain knowledge aids significantly in interpreting results and formulating actionable insights, enhancing the decision-making process in trading and investment.

The progression from theoretical understanding to practical application ensures these supervised learning techniques serve as robust pillars in the arsenal of quantitative finance professionals, fostering data-driven and analytically sound strategies in the volatile landscape of financial markets.

11.3 Unsupervised Learning Techniques

Unsupervised learning is a subset of machine learning where the algorithm is fed data without explicit labels, allowing it to identify patterns and structures within the input data autonomously. This technique is essential in financial analysis where large datasets without labeled outcomes are common. By leveraging unsupervised learning, traders and investors can uncover hidden structures, detect anomalies, and segment markets, leading to new insights and strategies.

A prevalent method in unsupervised learning is clustering. Clustering algorithms group data points based on their similarities, enabling the discovery of inherent structures within the data. Two widely-used clustering techniques in finance are k-means clustering and hierarchical clustering.

k-Means Clustering

k-Means clustering aims to partition data into k clusters wherein each data point belongs to the cluster with the nearest mean. To achieve this, the algorithm follows an iterative optimization approach as outlined in the steps below:

1. Initialization: Randomly select k cluster centroids.

2. Assignment: Assign each data point to the closest centroid, forming k clusters.

3. Update: Recompute the centroids of the new clusters.

4. Repeat steps 2 and 3 until convergence (i.e., cluster assignments no longer change or the change is below a threshold).

The mathematical formulation of the k-means objective function is given by:

$$\min_{C} \sum_{i=1}^{k} \sum_{\boldsymbol{x} \in C_i} \|\boldsymbol{x} - \mu_i\|^2$$

where C_i represents the i-th cluster, $\boldsymbol{x}$ is a data point, and μ_i is the centroid of cluster C_i. This optimization minimizes the within-cluster sum of squares (WCSS).

In financial applications, k-means clustering can be utilized to segment stocks into various groups based on performance metrics, volatility, or other financial ratios, enabling investors to tailor strategies to each segment.

Hierarchical Clustering

Hierarchical clustering builds a tree-like structure, called a dendrogram, representing nested clusters at varying levels of similarity. This technique has two approaches: agglomerative (bottom-up) and divisive (top-down).

- Agglomerative: Each data point starts in its own cluster, and pairs of clusters are merged iteratively based on minimum distance until a single cluster remains.
- Divisive: The process starts with all data points in one cluster, which is recursively split into smaller clusters.

The linkage criterion defines the distance between clusters in hierarchical clustering. Common criteria include:

- Single linkage: Distance between the closest points in two clusters.
- Complete linkage: Distance between the farthest points in two clusters.
- Average linkage: Average distance between points in two clusters.

The dendrogram produced by hierarchical clustering provides a detailed view of data similarity and can help in visualizing the relationship between different stocks or financial instruments.

Dimensionality Reduction

High-dimensional data, such as financial time series or portfolio metrics, often require dimensionality reduction to facilitate analysis and visualization. Principal Component Analysis (PCA) is a powerful unsupervised technique for this purpose. PCA transforms the data into a set of orthogonal components, ranked by the amount of variance they explain.

Mathematically, PCA involves solving the eigenvalue problem:

$$Cv = \lambda v$$

where C is the covariance matrix of the data, λ are the eigenvalues, and v are the eigenvectors. The eigenvectors corresponding to the largest eigenvalues form the principal components, which capture the most significant variance in the data.

In finance, PCA can reduce complexity in high-dimensional datasets, such as factor models for asset returns, by identifying the principal factors driving market behavior.

Anomaly Detection

Detecting anomalies or outliers in financial data is crucial for risk management and fraud detection. Unsupervised learning methods excel in identifying unusual patterns in unlabeled data. Two effective techniques for anomaly detection are Isolation Forest and One-Class SVM.

Isolation Forest isolates anomalies by constructing random forests. The anomalies are few and different, which makes them easier to isolate. A lower number of required splits to isolate a point indicates an anomaly.

One-Class SVM creates a boundary around normal data points, identifying data points that fall outside this boundary as anomalies. This boundary is defined through an objective function similar to the traditional SVM but optimized for single-class classification.

By utilizing unsupervised learning techniques, financial professionals can harness the power of data to uncover hidden insights, enhance predictive capabilities, and develop sophisticated trading and investment strategies.

11.4 Feature Engineering and Data Preprocessing

Feature engineering and data preprocessing are critical steps in the machine learning pipeline, especially in quantitative finance where the quality of inputs significantly influences model performance. This section delves into the best practices and sophisticated techniques to effectively prepare financial data, ensuring robustness and accuracy in subsequent predictive modeling.

To begin with, **feature engineering** involves creating new input variables from raw data to improve model predictions. Financial datasets often contain raw features that are neither directly informative nor readily usable in their initial form. For example, raw price data or trading volume logs can be transformed into meaningful features like moving averages, momentum indicators, or relative strength indices (RSI).

Consider the moving average, a simple yet powerful technical indicator. The formula for a moving average of length n at time t is given by:

$$MA_t = \frac{1}{n} \sum_{i=0}^{n-1} P_{t-i}$$

where P_{t-i} represents the price at time $t - i$. By calculating different types of moving averages (simple, exponential), traders can smooth short-term fluctuations and identify trends.

Additionally, it's essential to engineer features that capture volatility and risk, such as the Standard Deviation or the Average True Range (ATR). The ATR, for instance, is calculated as:

$$ATR_t = \frac{1}{n} \sum_{i=0}^{n-1} TR_{t-i}$$

where TR (True Range) is the maximum of:

$$TR_t = \max\left(H_t - L_t, |H_t - C_{t-1}|, |L_t - C_{t-1}|\right)$$

Here, H_t, L_t, and C_t denote the high, low, and close prices at time t, respectively.

Once features are engineered, the next step is **data preprocessing**, which includes cleaning, normalizing, and transforming data to be in a suitable format for modeling. Raw financial data often contains noise, missing values, and inconsistencies that must be addressed through various preprocessing techniques.

Handling Missing Values: Financial time series data frequently has gaps due to non-trading days, corporate actions, or data collection issues. Strategies to impute missing values include forward filling, backward filling, and interpolation. For instance, forward filling uses the last available observation to fill in subsequent missing values:

$$P_t = P_{t-1} \quad \text{if } P_t \text{ is missing}$$

Another method is linear interpolation, particularly useful for continuous data, which estimates a value within two known values on a linear scale.

Normalization and Scaling: To ensure that features with larger scales do not dominate those with smaller scales, normalization or scaling is applied. Common techniques include min-max scaling and z-score normalization. Min-max scaling transforms features to a predefined range, typically [0, 1]:

$$X_{\text{scaled}} = \frac{X - X_{\text{min}}}{X_{\text{max}} - X_{\text{min}}}$$

where X_{min} and X_{max} are the minimum and maximum values of the feature, respectively.

Z-score normalization, on the other hand, transforms the data to zero mean and unit variance:

$$X_{\text{normalized}} = \frac{X - \mu}{\sigma}$$

where μ and σ are the mean and standard deviation of the feature, respectively.

Removing Outliers: Outliers can distort model training, particularly in models sensitive to the range and scale of data. Outlier detection methods such as the z-score method (where values with a z-score greater than a certain threshold are flagged as outliers) or the IQR (Interquartile Range) method can be employed. The IQR method defines outliers as those outside $1.5 \times IQR$ from the first and third quartiles:

$$\text{Lower Bound} = Q1 - 1.5 \times IQR$$

$$\text{Upper Bound} = Q3 + 1.5 \times IQR$$

where $Q1$ and $Q3$ are the first and third quartiles, respectively.

Another crucial preprocessing step is **data transformation**. In financial time series, it is often necessary to transform non-stationary data into a stationary form to meet the assumptions of many machine learning algorithms. Techniques such as differencing, logarithmic scaling, and seasonal decomposition are commonly used.

Differencing transforms the series by subtracting the previous observation from the current observation:

$$Y'_t = Y_t - Y_{t-1}$$

Logarithmic transformation stabilizes variance by applying the log function:

$$Y'_t = \log(Y_t)$$

By meticulously constructing new features and addressing data quality issues through preprocessing steps, the transformed dataset becomes a more powerful input for machine learning models, enabling more accurate and insightful financial analysis.

11.5 Machine Learning Model Evaluation

Evaluating a machine learning model is akin to testing the engine of a high-performance sports car before hitting the racetrack. It's an essential step that ensures the model performs reliably in real-world scenarios, especially critical within the volatile landscape of quantitative finance. We will delve into key metrics and methodologies that traders and investors can use to measure the effectiveness and reliability of their machine learning models.

The first concept to grasp is the distinction between training and testing data. A common approach in model evaluation involves splitting the dataset into training and testing subsets. Typically, the training dataset comprises 70-80% of the original data, leaving the remainder for testing.

This methodology allows us to evaluate the model's performance on unseen data, better simulating real-world applications.

Several metrics can be employed to assess a model's performance. For classification problems, accuracy, precision, recall, and the F1 score are primary metrics:

- **Accuracy**: This is the ratio of correctly predicted instances to the total instances. While useful, it may not suffice for imbalanced datasets commonly found in financial predictions.

$$\text{Accuracy} = \frac{\text{Number of Correct Predictions}}{\text{Total Number of Predictions}}$$

- **Precision**: Precision measures the number of true positive predictions out of all positive predictions. It is crucial when the cost of a false positive prediction is high.

$$\text{Precision} = \frac{\text{True Positives}}{\text{True Positives + False Positives}}$$

- **Recall**: Recall calculates the number of true positive predictions made out of all actual positives. This metric is vital when missing a positive instance has significant implications.

$$\text{Recall} = \frac{\text{True Positives}}{\text{True Positives + False Negatives}}$$

- **F1 Score**: The F1 score is the harmonic mean of precision and recall, providing a balanced metric that conveys a more comprehensive view of the model's performance.

$$\text{F1 Score} = 2 \times \frac{\text{Precision} \times \text{Recall}}{\text{Precision + Recall}}$$

For regression problems, the following metrics are often employed:

- **Mean Squared Error (MSE)**: MSE measures the average squared difference between predicted and actual values. It is highly sensitive to outliers, making it less robust in scenarios with volatile outliers.

$$\text{MSE} = \frac{1}{n}\sum_{i=1}^{n}(y_i - \hat{y}_i)^2$$

- **Mean Absolute Error (MAE)**: MAE calculates the average absolute difference between predicted and actual values, providing a more interpretable error metric that is less sensitive to outliers than MSE.

$$\text{MAE} = \frac{1}{n}\sum_{i=1}^{n}|y_i - \hat{y}_i|$$

- **R-squared (R^2)**: R^2 represents the proportion of the variance in the dependent variable that can be predicted from the independent variable(s). It's a measure of goodness of fit for regression models.

$$R^2 = 1 - \frac{\sum_{i=1}^{n}(y_i - \hat{y}_i)^2}{\sum_{i=1}^{n}(y_i - \bar{y})^2}$$

Beyond these basic metrics, advanced methodologies such as cross-validation and bootstrapping offer more robust evaluation frameworks. Cross-validation involves partitioning the dataset into k subsets (or folds), training the model on k-1 folds, and testing it on the remaining fold. This process is repeated k times with each fold serving as the test set once, and the results are averaged to produce a more reliable performance estimate. k-fold cross-validation mitigates overfitting and provides a more realistic assessment by leveraging multiple subsets of the data.

$$\text{Cross-Validation Score} = \frac{1}{k}\sum_{i=1}^{k}\text{Score}_i$$

Bootstrapping, on the other hand, involves repeatedly sampling from the dataset with replacement and evaluating the model on these samples. This method helps estimate the distribution of an estimator and is particularly useful when the dataset is too small for k-fold cross-validation.

Finally, visualization techniques can play an integral role in model evaluation. Confusion matrices offer a comprehensive view of classification model performance by displaying the true vs. predicted classifications in a matrix format. For regression models, residual plots help visualize the differences (or residuals) between predicted and actual values, emphasizing patterns that might indicate model flaws.

For algorithmic traders, integrating these evaluation techniques into the model development pipeline ensures the creation of robust, reliable models capable of performing in real-world financial markets. By systematically applying these methods, traders can gain confidence in their models, mitigate risks, and enhance their predictive power.

11.6 Applications of Machine Learning in Finance

Machine learning has become an integral part of modern finance, driving innovations and efficiencies across various domains. The vast amounts of data generated in financial markets provide a rich landscape for machine learning algorithms to identify patterns, predict outcomes, and optimize decisions. This section explores several key applications of machine learning in finance, focusing on practical strategies and clear examples to enhance understanding.

One of the foremost applications of machine learning in finance is in the area of **predictive analytics**. By analyzing historical data, machine learning models can forecast future price movements, allowing traders and investors to make informed decisions. For instance, a common approach involves using time-series models like Long Short-Term Memory (LSTM) networks, which are particularly adept at handling sequential data. The mathematical representation of an LSTM cell's operations can be expressed as follows:

$$
\begin{aligned}
\boldsymbol{f}_t &= \sigma(\boldsymbol{W}_f \cdot [\boldsymbol{h}_{t-1}, \boldsymbol{x}_t] + \boldsymbol{b}_f) \\
\boldsymbol{i}_t &= \sigma(\boldsymbol{W}_i \cdot [\boldsymbol{h}_{t-1}, \boldsymbol{x}_t] + \boldsymbol{b}_i) \\
\boldsymbol{C}_t &= \boldsymbol{f}_t * \boldsymbol{C}_{t-1} + \boldsymbol{i}_t * \tanh(\boldsymbol{W}_C \cdot [\boldsymbol{h}_{t-1}, \boldsymbol{x}_t] + \boldsymbol{b}_C) \\
\boldsymbol{o}_t &= \sigma(\boldsymbol{W}_o \cdot [\boldsymbol{h}_{t-1}, \boldsymbol{x}_t] + \boldsymbol{b}_o) \\
\boldsymbol{h}_t &= \boldsymbol{o}_t * \tanh(\boldsymbol{C}_t)
\end{aligned}
$$

Here, $\boldsymbol{f}_t$, $\boldsymbol{i}_t$, and $\boldsymbol{o}_t$ represent the forget, input, and output gates respectively, which regulate the flow of information through the LSTM cell. The effective application of such models in predicting stock prices can significantly enhance trading strategies.

Another pivotal area is **portfolio management**. Machine learning algorithms can optimize asset allocation by continuously learning from new data. Techniques such as reinforcement learning are particularly useful in this context. In reinforcement learning, an agent interacts with the environment by taking actions that maximize cumulative rewards. The value of a state under a particular policy π can be expressed using the Bellman equation:

$$V^\pi(s) = \mathbb{E}_\pi\left[R_{t+1} + \gamma V^\pi(S_{t+1}) \mid S_t = s\right]$$

where $V^\pi(s)$ denotes the expected return following policy π, starting from state s. The discount factor γ represents the importance of future rewards. Implementing reinforcement learning for dynamic portfolio optimization involves continuous learning and adaptation to market conditions, which can lead to superior risk-adjusted returns.

Additionally, machine learning plays a crucial role in **risk management**. Credit scoring, fraud detection, and market risk assessment benefit significantly from machine learning techniques. Credit scoring models, for example, can utilize classification algorithms to determine the likelihood of default. Logistic regression is a common method in credit scoring due to its simplicity and interpretability:

$$P(Y = 1 \mid \boldsymbol{X}) = \frac{1}{1 + e^{-(\beta_0 + \beta_1 X_1 + \cdots + \beta_p X_p)}}$$

where $P(Y = 1 \mid \boldsymbol{X})$ is the probability of default given predictors $\boldsymbol{X} = (X_1, \ldots, X_p)$. By assessing these probabilities, financial institutions can make informed lending decisions and manage credit risk more effectively.

Machine learning also enhances **algorithmic trading**, where automated systems execute trades based on predefined criteria. Machine learning models can identify arbitrage opportunities, predict short-term price movements, and optimize trading strategies for profitability. For example, Support Vector Machines (SVM) can classify high-probability trading signals:

$$\min_{\boldsymbol{w}, b} \frac{1}{2}\boldsymbol{w}^\top \boldsymbol{w} + C\sum_{i=1}^{N} \xi_i$$

subject to the constraints $y_i(\boldsymbol{w}^\top \phi(\boldsymbol{x}_i) + b) \geq 1 - \xi_i \quad \forall i$, where $\boldsymbol{w}$ represents the weight vector, b the bias term, ξ_i the slack variables, C the regularization parameter, and $\phi(\boldsymbol{x}_i)$ the feature mapping. By training on historical data, SVM can discern patterns that indicate profitable trades, automating the decision-making process.

In **natural language processing (NLP)**, machine learning algorithms are adept at extracting actionable insights from financial news, earnings reports, and social media. Techniques such as sentiment analysis gauge market sentiment, influencing trading strategies. A widely used NLP model is the Bidirectional Encoder Representations from Transformers (BERT), which achieves state-of-the-art performance in understanding context and sentiment in text.

Moreover, **model interpretability and ethical considerations** are paramount in financial applications. Transparent models ensure that stakeholders understand the decision-making process, fostering trust and compliance with regulatory standards. Techniques such as SHapley Additive exPlanations (SHAP) provide interpretable insights into model predictions:

$$\text{SHAP value} = \phi_i = \sum_{S \subseteq N \setminus \{i\}} \frac{|S|!(|N| - |S| - 1)!}{|N|!} [f_x(S \cup \{i\}) - f_x(S)]$$

where ϕ_i quantifies the contribution of feature i to the prediction f_x for a specific example. Ensuring ethical considerations involves avoiding biases and ensuring fairness in model development and deployment.

Machine learning's applications in finance continue to evolve, driven by advancements in algorithmic techniques and computational power. By leveraging these technologies, financial professionals can achieve greater accuracy in predictions, more efficient risk management, and innovative trading strategies, ultimately enhancing market success.

11.7 Algorithmic Trading with Machine Learning

Algorithmic trading has become a cornerstone of modern financial markets, automating trade execution and strategy implementation by leveraging advanced algorithms. Machine learning (ML) enhances algorithmic trading by providing tools to analyze and predict market movements with high precision. This section delves into how machine learning is transforming algorithmic trading, exploring various strategies, their implementation, and potential outcomes.

Algorithmic trading relies heavily on data-driven decisions. By integrating machine learning, traders can develop models that not only execute trades but also learn and adapt from historical data. These models can identify patterns and correlations across vast amounts of data that would be impractical for human traders to discern.

One fundamental strategy in algorithmic trading is statistical arbitrage. This technique involves simultaneously buying and selling correlated securities to exploit price differentials. Machine learning enhances this strategy by refining predictions of price movements and correlations. Let's consider a statistical arbitrage example using a simple model:

$$\text{Profit} = (P_i^{\text{buy}} - P_i^{\text{sell}}) \cdot N_i$$

where P_i^{buy} and P_i^{sell} are the predicted buying and selling prices respectively, and N_i is the number of shares.

To implement this with machine learning, one could use a regression model to forecast prices based on historical data, thereby predicting P_i^{buy} and P_i^{sell}. The model would need features such as historical prices, trading volumes, and other relevant market indicators.

Another popular machine learning application in algorithmic trading is the construction of adaptive market-making strategies. Market makers provide liquidity by offering to buy and sell securities at quoted prices. Machine learning models can optimize the quoting process by predicting short-term price movements and adjusting quotes accordingly.

$$Q_t = f(\text{Features}_t)$$

where Q_t is the quote at time t and f represents the machine learning model applied to features such as current market prices, bid-ask spreads, and recent order flow.

Reinforcement learning (RL) is particularly well-suited for developing such adaptive strategies. In RL, the trading system is seen as an agent that interacts with the market environment to maximize cumulative rewards over time. The agent learns optimal actions (e.g., adjusting quotes) through trial and error, balancing the trade-off between exploration (trying new strategies) and exploitation (using known profitable strategies).

Here is a simple RL reward function that could be used for market-making:

$$R_t = \sum_{i=1}^{N} P_i^{\text{sell}} \cdot N_i - \sum_{i=1}^{N} P_i^{\text{buy}} \cdot N_i - \text{Transaction Costs}$$

where R_t is the reward at time t, and N represents the number of trades executed.

Machine learning's ability to handle vast datasets also facilitates the development of predictive models for price and volume trends. This is particularly useful for momentum trading strategies, which seek to capitalize on the continuation of existing trends. Traders employ models such as Long Short-Term Memory (LSTM) networks to forecast future price movements based on sequential data:

$$y_{t+1} = \text{LSTM}(\text{Historical Prices}_{1:t})$$

where y_{t+1} is the predicted price at the next time step.

A practical implementation of LSTM in trading might involve feeding the model with not just historical prices, but also technical indicators like moving averages, relative strength index (RSI), and other momentum indicators.

Machine learning also facilitates the backtesting of trading strategies, which is crucial for assessing their viability before deployment. By simulating trades using historical data, traders can estimate the potential profit and risk associated with a given algorithm. Cross-validation techniques ensure that models generalize well to unseen data, reducing the risk of overfitting.

The integration of machine learning in algorithmic trading requires meticulous attention to data quality and preprocessing. Algorithms need clean, well-structured data to provide accurate predictions. Feature engineering plays a vital role, as the choice of features directly impacts model performance. Techniques such as normalization, outlier detection, and de-seasonalization are often employed to enhance the dataset.

Risk management is another critical aspect. Machine learning can predict not only returns but also the associated risks. Value-at-Risk (VaR) models, for instance, can be augmented with ML techniques to better estimate potential losses in volatile markets:

$$\text{VaR}_\alpha = -\text{Quantile}_\alpha(\text{Returns})$$

where Quantile$_\alpha$ is the α-quantile of the return distribution.

Machine learning models should be continuously monitored and updated to adapt to changing market conditions. Out-of-sample testing and ongoing validation help ensure that models remain robust over time.

In the rapidly evolving landscape of financial markets, algorithmic trading powered by machine learning offers a potent toolkit for sophisticated traders. Whether through predictive modeling, adaptive strategies, or enhanced risk management, the fusion of these technologies is driving unprecedented levels of efficiency and profitability.

11.8 Risk Management with Machine Learning

In financial markets, effectively managing risk is crucial to long-term success and stability. Machine learning offers innovative tools that can enhance traditional risk management frameworks, enabling more accurate predictions, real-time risk assessment, and adaptive strategies. This section delves into the integration of machine learning techniques in risk management, offering practical insights and advanced methods to mitigate financial risks.

Risk management involves identifying, assessing, and prioritizing potential adverse financial consequences, and taking actions to minimize the impact of these risks. Machine learning enhances this process through advanced data analysis, pattern recognition, and predictive modeling. Here, we explore some key machine learning applications and methodologies in the context of financial risk management.

One of the primary benefits of machine learning in risk management is its ability to handle vast amounts of data and uncover hidden patterns that traditional statistical methods may not detect. For instance, credit risk, market risk, and operational risk can all be analyzed with higher precision using machine learning models.

Credit Risk Assessment

Credit risk is the potential loss resulting from a borrower's failure to repay a loan or meet contractual obligations. Machine learning models such as logistic regression, decision trees, and gradient boosting can significantly improve credit risk assessment by accurately predicting the probability of default. The process typically involves the following steps:

- *Data Collection and Preprocessing*: Gather historical data on borrowers, including credit history, income, employment status, and other relevant factors.
- *Feature Selection*: Identify the most significant features that influence credit risk. This could include credit utilization ratios, payment history, and debt-to-income ratios.
- *Model Training*: Use a portion of the dataset to train the machine learning model, applying algorithms like logistic regression:

  $$P(\text{default}) = \frac{1}{1 + e^{-(\beta_0 + \beta_1 X_1 + \ldots + \beta_n X_n)}}$$

  where X_i represents the features, and β_i are the model coefficients.
- *Model Validation and Testing*: Validate the model on unseen data to ensure its predictive accuracy and generalizability. Metrics such as the Area Under the Curve (AUC) of the Receiver Operating Characteristic (ROC) curve and Precision-Recall curves are useful for evaluation.

The model's predictions can then be used to categorize borrowers into different risk classes, enabling more informed lending decisions and the setting of appropriate interest rates.

Market Risk Modeling

Market risk refers to the potential financial loss due to adverse movements in market prices, including stocks, bonds, commodities, and currencies. Machine learning can enhance traditional Value at Risk (VaR) models by incorporating more complex dependencies and non-linear interactions among variables. For example, techniques such as Monte Carlo simulations and GARCH (Generalized Autoregressive Conditional Heteroskedasticity) models can be combined with machine learning for more accurate market risk projections.

A machine learning approach for market risk assessment could involve:

- *Historical Data Analysis*: Study historical asset prices and volatilities.

- *Volatility Forecasting*: Implement GARCH models to estimate future volatility. A GARCH(1,1) model, for instance, can be represented as:

  $$\sigma_t^2 = \alpha_0 + \alpha_1 \epsilon_{t-1}^2 + \beta \sigma_{t-1}^2$$

  where σ_t^2 is the conditional variance, ϵ_{t-1} is the residual return from the previous period, and $\alpha_0, \alpha_1, \beta$ are constants.

- *Predictive Modeling*: Apply machine learning algorithms to predict future price movements and correlate them with volatility estimates.

By using machine learning, financial institutions can better estimate potential losses under different market conditions and take preemptive measures to safeguard their portfolios.

Operational Risk Management

Operational risk involves losses resulting from inadequate or failed internal processes, people, and systems. Machine learning provides tools to monitor operational risks in real-time by analyzing transaction data, system logs, and other operational data sources. Techniques such as anomaly detection using support vector machines (SVM) and neural networks can identify irregular patterns that might indicate potential fraud or system failures.

For example:

- *Anomaly Detection*: Implement algorithms to detect unusual behaviors. SVM-based anomaly detection can be formulated as follows:

  $$\min_{\boldsymbol{w},\xi,\rho} \frac{1}{2}\|\boldsymbol{w}\|^2 + \frac{1}{\nu l}\sum_{i=1}^{l} \xi_i - \rho$$

  subject to:

  $$(\boldsymbol{w} \cdot \phi(\boldsymbol{x}_i)) \geq \rho - \xi_i, \quad \xi_i \geq 0$$

  where $\boldsymbol{w}$ is the weight vector, ξ_i are slack variables, ρ is the margin threshold, ν is a parameter specifying the fraction of outliers, and $\phi(\boldsymbol{x}_i)$ is the feature transformation.

- *Real-time Monitoring*: Implement real-time data analytics to continuously monitor system activities and flag anomalies.

By leveraging these advanced techniques, organizations can significantly mitigate operational risks and respond more swiftly to incidents.

Machine learning, with its robust data processing and predictive capabilities, is transforming risk management in finance. It offers powerful tools that not only enhance the accuracy of risk assessments but also provide dynamic and adaptive strategies. Incorporating machine learning into risk management allows for a more proactive and holistic approach, ultimately contributing to more resilient financial operations.

11.9 Natural Language Processing (NLP) in Finance

Natural Language Processing (NLP) has emerged as a pivotal area of machine learning, especially in the finance sector where data is abundant and varied in form, ranging from financial news to corporate filings and social media sentiments. By employing NLP, financial analysts can extract valuable insights from textual data, which can significantly enhance decision-making processes. This section delves into the practical applications of NLP in finance, exploring various techniques and their implications on trading and investing strategies.

NLP techniques facilitate the analysis of unstructured data, enabling traders to gauge market sentiment, conduct sentiment analysis, and even predict market movements based on news trends. One prevalent application is sentiment analysis, which involves categorizing opinions expressed in text into positive, negative, or neutral sentiments. Sentiment analysis can be performed using lexicon-based methods, machine learning algorithms, or a combination of both.

Let us consider an example where sentiment analysis is applied to company earnings reports. When a company releases its quarterly earnings, the language used in its report can heavily influence stock prices. Using NLP, we can quantify the overall sentiment of the report. Suppose we have a dataset of earnings reports; we can use a lexicon-based approach such as the Loughran-McDonald sentiment word lists to assign sentiment scores to individual words or phrases within the reports. The sentiment score S for a document can be computed as follows:

$$S = \frac{\text{Positive Words} - \text{Negative Words}}{\text{Total Words}}$$

This score S provides a normalized sentiment measure that can be tracked over time or compared across different companies.

Another crucial application of NLP in finance is the analysis of news articles. Financial markets are highly responsive to news, and timely extraction of pertinent information can offer a significant edge in trading. Techniques such as Named Entity Recognition (NER) help identify and categorize entities (e.g., company names, financial instruments, dates) in text data. By applying NER to a stream of financial news, traders can quickly pinpoint relevant information about specific stocks or economic events and incorporate this into their trading strategies.

For example, consider an algorithm that scans real-time news feeds for mentions of specific companies. The NER system can highlight occurrences of company names and associated actions (e.g., mergers, acquisitions, product launches). These identified events can be parameterized into trading models as follows:

$$\text{News Impact} = \frac{\text{Occurrences of Entity}}{\text{Time Interval}}$$

The computed News Impact metric can then be integrated into a trading algorithm to adjust positions dynamically.

Textual data's temporal aspect also plays a fundamental role in predicting future trends. NLP techniques, combined with time series models, can forecast financial metrics based on historical text data. An example of this would be utilizing deep learning techniques such as Recurrent Neural Networks (RNNs) to model and predict stock prices based on the sentiment score history of relevant news articles.

Consider the following RNN architecture where the input x_t at time t represents a sequence of sentiment scores derived from news articles:

$$h_t = \sigma(W_h h_{t-1} + W_x x_t + b_h)$$

$$\hat{y}_t = W_y h_t + b_y$$

In this model, h_t represents the hidden state at time t, capturing the sentiment context over time, and $\hat{y}_t$ is the predicted stock price. Parameters W_h, W_x, W_y and biases b_h, b_y are learned during the training phase.

Another significant NLP application in finance is extracting insights from corporate filings, such as 10-K filings or prospectuses. These documents contain a wealth of information about a company's operations, risks, and management discussions. Topic modeling techniques like Latent Dirichlet Allocation (LDA) allow analysts to identify prevailing themes and topics within these filings. By analyzing the distribution of topics over time, one can decipher shifts in management focus or potential risk factors, which are critical for long-term investment decisions.

In practice, topic modeling can be formulated as follows. Given a corpus D of documents, LDA assumes each document is a mixture of topics, and each topic is a mixture of words. The probability of a word w occurring in a document d under topic z is given by:

$$P(w|d) = \sum_{z=1}^{K} P(w|z)P(z|d)$$

where K is the number of topics. After fitting the LDA model on financial documents, the resulting topics and their distributions can be visualized and analyzed to understand the underlying themes.

To foster the best practices in NLP applications, it is essential to address challenges such as data quality, the dynamic nature of language, and model interpretability. The dynamic nature of language in finance, where jargon and context can rapidly evolve, necessitates continuous model updates and fine-tuning. Ensuring high data quality, devoid of noise and biases, significantly enhances model accuracy and reliability. Interpretability of models is crucial in finance to convince stakeholders and meet regulatory requirements. Techniques like SHapley Additive exPlanations (SHAP) values can elucidate the contribution of each feature in the decision-making process, adding a layer of transparency.

Through the lens of NLP, vast textual data can be transformed into actionable intelligence, driving more informed trading decisions and investment strategies. By leveraging NLP tools, financial professionals can gain a nuanced understanding of market sentiments, emerging risks, and trends that are not readily apparent through numerical data alone.

11.10 Ethical Considerations and Model Interpretability

As the reliance on machine learning in quantitative finance grows, it becomes crucial to address the ethical implications and the interpretability of these models. Ethical considerations and transparency help ensure that the algorithms are fair, accountable, and do not inadvertently harm any stakeholders. Furthermore, interpretability enables practitioners to understand and trust the decision-making process of complex models, facilitating better oversight and regulatory compliance.

Ethical considerations in machine learning for finance can be broadly categorized into fairness, accountability, and transparency. Fairness involves ensuring that models do not introduce or perpetuate biases against any group or individual. For instance, a trading algorithm that disproportionately favors trades from certain demographic profiles over others could be considered biased and unethical. To mitigate such risks, it is essential to implement bias detection and correction mechanisms within the model development pipeline.

Accountability refers to the responsibility of practitioners to ensure that their models are used appropriately and that any errors or harmful outcomes are addressed promptly. This includes establishing clear guidelines for monitoring model performance and for intervening when models behave unexpectedly. A robust system for logging and auditing model decisions can further enhance accountability, making it easier to trace back and rectify any erroneous or harmful trades.

Transparency is perhaps the most challenging aspect, especially with complex models like deep learning networks. Financial institutions must strive to provide clear explanations for their model's decisions, particularly when these decisions impact investors and other stakeholders. One approach to enhance transparency is to use interpretable models wherever possible, such as linear models or decision trees, which are inherently easier to understand. When more complex models are necessary, techniques like SHAP (SHapley Additive exPlanations) values or LIME (Local Interpretable Model-agnostic Explanations) can be employed to provide insights into the model's decision-making process.

Model interpretability also plays a critical role in regulatory compliance. Regulatory bodies require that financial institutions understand and can explain the workings of their models, especially when these models are used for high-stakes decisions such as credit scoring or fraud detection. The General Data Protection Regulation (GDPR) in the European Union, for example, includes a "right to explanation" clause, which mandates that organizations must be able to explain the logic behind any automated decision made about individuals.

From a technical perspective, various methodologies can be used to improve model interpretability. For instance, partial dependence plots help visualize the relationship between a specific input variable and the model's predictions, while feature importance rankings identify which variables have the most significant impact on the model's output. These tools can provide valuable insights, allowing traders and analysts to better understand the factors driving their models' behaviors.

In practice, achieving a balance between model complexity and interpretability is often necessary. While simple models are easier to interpret, they may not capture the intricate patterns and relationships present in financial markets. Conversely, more complex models can offer superior predictive performance but at the cost of reduced transparency. Practitioners must carefully consider the trade-offs and choose an approach that aligns with their specific needs and constraints.

Moreover, ongoing model validation and backtesting are essential to ensure that models remain ethical and interpretable over time. Regular updates and recalibration are necessary to account for changes in market conditions and to prevent model drift. In addition, involving a diverse team of experts, including ethicists, domain specialists, and data scientists, can provide a more holistic perspective and help identify potential ethical issues that might be overlooked by a more homogeneous group.

By prioritizing ethical considerations and model interpretability, financial institutions can build more trustworthy and reliable machine learning systems. This, in turn, fosters confidence among investors and regulators, ultimately contributing to a healthier and more sustainable financial ecosystem.

Chapter 12

Backtesting and Implementing Trading Strategies

Backtesting is a critical process for validating the effectiveness of trading strategies using historical data before live implementation. This chapter provides an overview of data collection and preparation, constructing and testing trading strategies, and evaluating performance metrics. It emphasizes the importance of addressing overfitting and accounting for transaction costs and slippage. The chapter also explores optimization techniques, robustness checks, and the practical aspects of implementing strategies in live trading, including continuous monitoring and adaptation.

12.1 Introduction to Backtesting

Backtesting serves as the bedrock of quantitative finance, providing a methodological framework to evaluate how a trading strategy would have performed using historical data. By simulating trades with past market conditions, we gain insights into the potential profitability and risk associated with a strategy before deploying it in live trading. This section lays the foundation for understanding the intricacies and importance of backtesting, establishing a base upon which the subsequent sections will build.

At its core, backtesting involves the replication of historical trading signals to assess the viability of strategies. This process not only helps in identifying strategies that yield favorable results but also in discarding those that fail to perform under varied market conditions. The essential steps in backtesting include defining the trading rules, collecting and preparing market data, executing the strategy over this data, and evaluating the performance outcomes.

To begin with, a clear definition of the trading rules is paramount. These rules delineate the conditions under which trades are entered and exited. They must be unambiguous and easily programmable. For instance, a simple moving average crossover strategy might buy when a short-term moving average crosses above a long-term moving average and sell when the opposite occurs.

Next, collecting and preparing the data is crucial. The quality and resolution of historical data significantly influence the backtesting outcomes. Precision in data, including accurate price, volume, and time stamps, ensures the reliability of the backtest. Data from different exchanges or asset classes may need harmonization to account for disparate intervals and trading calendars.

Executing the strategy over historical data involves simulating each trade as per the defined rules. Here, incorporating realistic assumptions is essential to avoid misleading results. Matters such as transaction costs, slippage, and market impact must be factored into the simulation.

For a detailed illustration, consider a momentum strategy that buys when an asset's return over the past 12 months exceeds a certain threshold and sells otherwise. This strategy can be mathematically expressed as:

$$R_{\text{momentum}} = \left(\frac{P_t}{P_{t-252}} - 1 \right)$$

where P_t is the price at time t and P_{t-252} is the price 252 trading days earlier. If $R_{\text{momentum}} >$ threshold, a buy signal is generated, otherwise a sell signal is triggered.

Performance evaluation is the final piece of the backtesting puzzle. This encompasses analyzing key metrics such as returns, Sharpe ratio, drawdowns, and the equity curve. The Sharpe ratio, represented as:

$$\text{Sharpe Ratio} = \frac{E[R_p - R_f]}{\sigma_p}$$

where $E[R_p]$ is the expected portfolio return, R_f is the risk-free rate, and σ_p is the standard deviation of the portfolio returns, provides a normalized measure of risk-adjusted returns.

Mitigating overfitting, the peril of tailoring a strategy excessively to historical data, is a critical consideration. This necessitates using techniques like walk-forward testing and cross-validation. Moreover, understanding that past performance does not guarantee future results is a cardinal principle in backtesting.

Backtesting also involves the use of various software tools and platforms, each with its strengths and limitations. Tool selection depends on factors such as the complexity of the strategy, the asset class, and the desired speed of backtesting. Commonly used platforms include MetaTrader, QuantConnect, and proprietary systems built with languages like Python and R, equipped with powerful libraries such as Pandas and NumPy for data manipulation and analysis.

A comprehensive backtesting approach forms the backbone of systematic trading strategies, providing traders with the confidence to execute their strategies with a clear understanding of the potential risks and rewards. By mastering backtesting, traders can transform theoretical models into practical, actionable strategies that stand the test of real market conditions.

12.2 Data Collection and Preparation

Accurate and comprehensive data collection is the cornerstone of effective backtesting. Historical data serves as the foundation upon which we test our trading hypotheses and strategies. In this section, we delve into the sources of market data, the types of data required, and the meticulous process of preparing the data for analysis.

A primary source of market data is financial exchanges, which provide price histories, transaction volumes, and order book information. These data can be obtained through subscriptions to data services such as Bloomberg, Reuters, or directly from the exchanges. Another valuable source is databases curated by financial institutions or third-party vendors specializing in historical financial data. These databases often offer cleaned and pre-processed data, which can save significant time in the data preparation process.

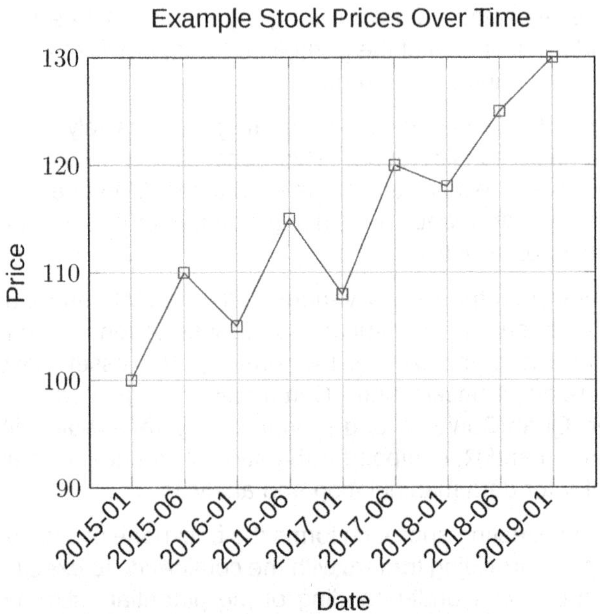

The types of data we need vary depending on the trading strategy. For a simple moving average strategy, basic daily closing prices might suffice. However, more intricate strategies, such as those involving intraday trading, require minute-by-minute or even tick-by-tick data. Additionally, data such as bid-ask spreads, liquidity measures, and market depth can greatly enhance the robustness of our strategy development.

Once collected, the data needs to be meticulously prepared. This begins with addressing missing values, which are common in financial datasets. Missing data can be handled through various imputation techniques, such as forward filling (carrying the last known price forward) or using statistical models to estimate missing values. The choice of technique can impact the strategy's performance and must be carefully considered.

Data normalization is another crucial step. This involves adjusting the data to account for events like stock splits, dividends, or major corporate actions. For instance, a stock split increases the number of shares while reducing the price per share proportionally, without changing the company's total market value. Historical prices must be adjusted to reflect such events to ensure consistency over time.

$$\text{Adjusted Price} = \text{Closing Price} \times \frac{\text{Adjustment Factor}}{\text{Factor Past Event}}$$

Another aspect of preparation is converting the data into the format required for the backtesting platform. Common formats include CSV or JSON files for simpler platforms or full SQL databases for more sophisticated systems. Properly organizing the data entails having consistent column names and formats for dates and prices. Any discrepancies in this step can lead to errors during the testing phase.

Once the data is formatted, it is essential to validate and clean it rigorously. This involves checking for outliers, ensuring that the data follows expected patterns, and confirming that there are no duplicate entries. Algorithms such as Z-score can be used to identify and manage outliers. A typical formula for Z-score is:

$$z = \frac{(X - \mu)}{\sigma}$$

Where X is the data point, μ is the mean, and σ is the standard deviation. Outliers, identified as data points with a Z-score beyond a certain threshold (typically ± 3), need to be scrutinized for data entry errors or validated as genuine anomalies.

After cleaning, the dataset should be partitioned into segments such as training, validation, and test sets. The training set is used to develop the strategy, the validation set to fine-tune it, and the test set to evaluate its out-of-sample performance. This process ensures that the strategy is not overfitted to any particular segment of the historical data and can generalize well to unseen data.

Date	Price	Volume
2015-01-02	100.5	15000
2015-01-03	101.0	16000
2015-01-04	99.8	14000
2015-01-05	100.2	15500
2015-01-06	98.5	15800

Table 12.1: Sample segment of cleaned historical data.

Finally, it is important to remember that data integrity is paramount. Continuously monitor for new data updates and maintain a systematic process for incorporating these updates into the dataset. Data should be backed up and stored in a manner that prevents loss or corruption.

By meticulously managing the data collection and preparation process, we lay a solid foundation for reliable and meaningful backtesting of trading strategies.

12.3 Constructing and Testing Trading Strategies

Constructing trading strategies involves a blend of creativity, quantitative reasoning, and a deep understanding of market mechanics. The process begins with a clear trading hypothesis: an actionable idea of how one expects the market to behave under certain conditions. The hypothesis is the foundation upon which the strategy is built, tested, and potentially improved. Whether inspired by fundamental analysis, technical signals, or statistical patterns, a strategy must exhibit a repeatable edge to be viable.

The development of a trading strategy typically follows these key steps: (1) hypothesis formulation, (2) coding the algorithm, (3) selecting the backtesting data, and (4) running the initial tests. Each step plays a critical role in ensuring the robustness and practicality of the resulting strategy.

Hypothesis Formulation

The first step in constructing a trading strategy is to define a clear, testable hypothesis. For example, one might hypothesize that stocks experiencing sharp increases in daily trading volume are likely to revert to their mean, suggesting a short-selling opportunity. A hypothesis should be grounded in market logic and ideally supported by preliminary observations or empirical data.

Coding the Algorithm

Once the hypothesis is established, the next step is to translate it into a set of rules that can be coded into an algorithm. This involves precisely defining entry and exit conditions, position sizing, and risk management rules. The strategy needs to be explicit in identifying:

- **Entry Signal**: What specific indicator or set of conditions will trigger a buy or sell order?
- **Exit Signal**: At what point, or under what conditions, will the trade be closed to realize gains or limit losses?

- **Position Sizing**: How much capital will be allocated to each trade, and how will this amount vary depending on market conditions or the portfolio's total value?

- **Risk Management**: What measures will be taken to mitigate risk, such as stop-loss orders or volatility control mechanisms?

Choosing an appropriate programming language, such as Python or R, facilitates the development of these algorithms. Below is a pseudocode example that can be adapted and coded in a specific programming language:

```
1. Initialize Parameters:
   - lookback period for moving average
   - threshold for volume increase
   - percentage for stop-loss

2. For each trading day:
   - Calculate the moving average of the stock price over the lookback period
   - Identify any days with trading volume significantly above the moving average
   - If volume exceeds the threshold, generate an entry signal
   - Monitor the stock and execute trades when exit conditions are met

3. Implement risk management and position sizing rules to adjust trades
```

Selecting Backtesting Data

The data selection process is pivotal to the credibility and applicability of the backtest. Ideally, chosen datasets need to be comprehensive, covering multiple market cycles to account for diverse market conditions. Sources such as historical price data, volume, corporate actions, and macroeconomic indicators provide a fertile ground for robust backtesting. Data should be cleaned and preprocessed to handle missing values, corporate actions like splits or dividends, and data errors.

Running Initial Tests

Running initial backtests involves applying the coded algorithm to historical data and evaluating its performance. This stage is iterative: one sets the initial parameters and runs the strategy through the backtesting engine, typically recording performance metrics on each run. Metrics to be analyzed include:

- **Cumulative Returns**: The overall gain or loss from trades over the backtesting period.

- **Sharpe Ratio**: A measure of risk-adjusted return, helping to gauge the strategy's performance relative to its volatility.

- **Max Drawdown**: The largest peak-to-valley decline, which reflects the strategy's most significant loss from a historical high point.

For instance, consider the result expressed succinctly for the Sharpe Ratio:

$$\text{Sharpe Ratio} = \frac{E[R_p - R_f]}{\sigma_p}$$

where $E[R_p - R_f]$ is the expected excess return of the portfolio over the risk-free rate, and σ_p is the standard deviation of portfolio returns.

The initial test results should be critically assessed for both profitability and robustness. A strategy that shows promising results in initial runs can be refined further, improving its parameters and logic based on the performance feedback.

Constructing and testing trading strategies is both an art and a science. It requires a systematic approach informed by market knowledge, quantitative analysis, and continuous validation through rigorous testing. Through these steps, one can develop strategies that are not only theoretically sound but also practically executable in real market conditions.

12.4 Performance Metrics and Evaluation

To assess the efficacy of any trading strategy, it is imperative to meticulously evaluate its performance using a comprehensive set of metrics. While raw returns offer a rudimentary measure of success, a multifaceted analysis provides a deeper insight into the nuances of strategy performance and risk. This section delves into various key performance metrics, elucidating their significance and application.

1. Annualized Returns Annualized returns standardize the performance of a strategy over different time periods, facilitating comparison across diverse timeframes. Given the return R over T periods, the annualized return R_a is calculated as:

$$R_a = (1 + R)^{\frac{252}{T}} - 1$$

Here, 252 represents the standard number of trading days in a year.

2. Volatility Volatility, computed as the standard deviation of returns, quantifies the risk and reliability of the strategy. A higher volatility indicates greater risk, translating to unpredictable returns. For a series of returns $r_1, r_2, \ldots, r_T$, the standard deviation σ is:

$$\sigma = \sqrt{\frac{1}{T-1}\sum_{t=1}^{T}(r_t - \bar{r})^2}$$

where $\bar{r}$ is the mean return over T periods.

3. Sharpe Ratio The Sharpe ratio evaluates the risk-adjusted return of a strategy, epitomizing the additional return per unit of risk. It is calculated as the ratio of the excess return over the risk-free rate R_f to the strategy's standard deviation σ:

$$\text{Sharpe Ratio} = \frac{R - R_f}{\sigma}$$

A higher Sharpe ratio indicates a more favorable risk-adjusted return.

4. Maximum Drawdown (MDD) Maximum Drawdown measures the greatest peak-to-trough decline during the evaluation period, reflecting potential significant losses. It is calculated as:

$$\text{MDD} = \max_{t \in [1,T]} \left(\frac{P_{peak,t} - P_{trough,t}}{P_{peak,t}} \right)$$

where $P_{peak,t}$ and $P_{trough,t}$ are the peak and trough portfolio values within the period t.

5. Sortino Ratio The Sortino Ratio refines the Sharpe Ratio by considering only downside volatility, thereby punishing only negative deviations which are more pertinent to investors. It is expressed as:

$$\text{Sortino Ratio} = \frac{R - R_f}{\sigma_d}$$

where σ_d is the standard deviation of the negative returns.

6. Calmar Ratio The Calmar Ratio measures risk-adjusted performance by comparing annualized returns to maximum drawdown, offering a clear view of returns per unit of risk. It is computed as:

$$\text{Calmar Ratio} = \frac{R_a}{\text{MDD}}$$

The higher the Calmar Ratio, the better the risk-adjusted return.

7. Risk-Return Ratios Evaluating a strategy's balance between return and risk can be effectively shown through risk-return ratios like the Treynor Ratio and Jensen's Alpha:

- *Treynor Ratio*: It adjusts returns relative to systematic risk, showing the returns earned per unit of market risk (beta β).

$$\text{Treynor Ratio} = \frac{R - R_f}{\beta}$$

- *Jensen's Alpha*: It measures the excess return generated by the strategy over the expected return predicted by the Capital Asset Pricing Model (CAPM).

$$\alpha = R - [R_f + \beta(R_m - R_f)]$$

where R_m is the market return.

8. Benchmark Comparison It's essential to compare the strategy's performance against a relevant benchmark to contextualize its efficacy. Analyzing key metrics like beta (β), alpha (α), and tracking error against an index (e.g., S&P 500) provides valuable insights into relative performance.

9. Return Distributions Investigating the distribution of returns reveals the underlying characteristics including skewness and kurtosis, indicating asymmetry and tail risks respectively. Tools such as histograms and probability density functions (PDFs) assist in visualizing these distributions.

$$\text{Skewness} = \frac{\frac{1}{T}\sum_{t=1}^{T}(r_t - \bar{r})^3}{\left(\frac{1}{T}\sum_{t=1}^{T}(r_t - \bar{r})^2\right)^{3/2}}$$

10. Monte Carlo Simulations Monte Carlo simulations project potential future performance by generating a multitude of plausible return paths based on historical data, facilitating robust risk and return estimates. This involves statistical sampling techniques applied to historical return series data.

Each of these metrics must be carefully considered within the context of the overall strategy's goals and conditions. By leveraging a combination of these performance metrics, traders and investors can obtain a well-rounded understanding of their strategies' robustness and potential in real-world scenarios.

12.5 Dealing with Overfitting

Overfitting is a common pitfall in the development of trading strategies, where a model performs exceptionally well on historical data but fails to generalize to unseen data. This happens when the model captures noise or random fluctuations rather than the underlying market dynamics. Addressing overfitting is crucial for the reliability and profitability of trading strategies. This section delves into the causes of overfitting, methods to detect it, and strategies to prevent it.

At its core, overfitting arises when a model is excessively complex, with too many parameters relative to the amount of training data. A highly complex model can fit the training data almost perfectly, but this can lead to poor performance on new, unseen data. To understand and combat overfitting, consider the following approaches:

- **1. Cross-Validation:** One of the most effective methods to detect and prevent overfitting is cross-validation. This involves partitioning the dataset into multiple subsets and validating the model on a subset not used during training. A common technique is k-fold cross-validation, where the data is divided into k subsets, and the model is trained and validated k times, each time using a different subset as the validation set and the remaining $k-1$ subsets as the training set. This helps ensure that the model performs well across different segments of the data, reducing the likelihood of overfitting.
- **2. Train-Test Split:** A simpler approach is to split the data into distinct training and testing sets. The model is trained on the training set and evaluated on the testing set. While this method is

less robust than cross-validation, it provides a quick check to see if the model can generalize to unseen data. A typical split might reserve 70-80% of the data for training and the remaining 20-30% for testing.

- **3. Regularization:** Regularization techniques add a penalty for complexity to the model's training process. Common forms of regularization include L1 regularization (Lasso), which penalizes the absolute value of coefficients, and L2 regularization (Ridge), which penalizes the square of the coefficients. The regularization term is added to the loss function, discouraging the model from becoming too complex. The regularization strength is controlled by a parameter λ, which can be tuned using cross-validation.

- **4. Simpler Models:** Adopting simpler models with fewer parameters can also mitigate overfitting. While complex models might capture more intricate patterns, they are more prone to fitting noise. Linear models, decision trees with limited depth, and other simpler techniques can often perform better in practice by focusing on the most significant patterns.

- **5. Feature Selection:** Overfitting can also occur due to the inclusion of irrelevant or redundant features. Feature selection techniques such as Recursive Feature Elimination (RFE), where features are recursively removed and model performance is evaluated, or using domain knowledge to select relevant features, can help in building more robust models.

- **6. Ensemble Methods:** Using ensemble methods like bagging, boosting, or stacking can reduce overfitting by combining multiple models to produce a more generalized result. Bagging reduces variance by averaging predictions from multiple models trained on different samples, while boosting sequentially improves the model by focusing on errors from previous stages. Stacking involves training a meta-model on the predictions of several base models.

- **7. Walk-Forward Analysis:** This technique involves retraining the model periodically with new data and testing it on subsequent out-of-sample periods, simulating a real trading situation where the model is updated over time. This not only helps detect overfitting but also assesses how the model adapts to changing market conditions.

- **8. Holding Out Recent Data:** Given that market conditions evolve, holding out the most recent data for final validation helps ensure the strategy can adapt to current market dynamics. This approach is sometimes referred to as "forward testing."

The key to dealing with overfitting lies in continuous monitoring and validation. Adjustments and refinements should be driven by out-of-sample performance, ensuring that the strategy remains robust and effective under different market conditions. By implementing these techniques, traders can develop strategies that are not just tailored to historical data but also equipped to perform reliably in live trading conditions.

$$\text{Walk-Forward Validation:} \begin{array}{cccc} \text{Training Period} & \rightarrow & \text{Testing Period} & \rightarrow \\ \text{Training Period} & \rightarrow & \text{Testing Period} & \rightarrow \\ \text{Training Period} & \rightarrow & \text{Testing Period} & \rightarrow \end{array}$$

12.6 Transaction Costs and Slippage in Backtesting

Accurately accounting for transaction costs and slippage is pivotal when backtesting trading strategies. These factors can significantly erode potential profits, and neglecting them often leads to overly optimistic performance assessments. This section will delve into understanding transaction costs and slippage, ways to model them in backtesting, and practical recommendations for traders aiming to minimize their impact.

Transaction costs encompass all expenses incurred when executing trades. These costs typically include broker commissions, spreads (the difference between the bid and ask prices), and market impact costs, which refer to the price movement caused by executing large trades. Properly incorporating transaction costs into your backtesting model is essential for a realistic evaluation of a trading strategy's profitability.

Slippage occurs when there is a difference between the expected price of a trade and the actual price at which it is executed. This typically happens in fast-moving markets or when trading illiquid assets. Slippage can be both positive and negative, but it most often works against the trader. Incorporating slippage into backtesting helps simulate real-world trading conditions more precisely.

To model transaction costs effectively, a multi-faceted approach is beneficial. For simplicity, one could start by considering fixed and variable costs:

- **Fixed Costs**: These are consistent costs per trade, such as a flat fee charged by a broker.
- **Variable Costs**: These depend on the trade size or value, such as a percentage-based commission or spread costs.

Suppose a broker charges a fixed commission of $5 per trade, and the spread for a particular stock averages 0.5% of the trade value. If a backtest involves buying and selling 100 shares of a stock priced at $100, the transaction costs can be calculated as follows:

$$\begin{aligned} \text{Commission Cost} &= \$5 \text{ (buy trade)} + \$5 \text{ (sell trade)} = \$10, \\ \text{Spread Cost} &= 0.5\% \times 100 \text{ shares} \times \$100 = \$50 \text{ (per trade)}, \\ \text{Total Transaction Costs} &= \$10 \text{ (Commission)} + 2 \times \$50 \text{ (Spread, both buy and s} \\ &= \$110. \end{aligned}$$

Incorporating slippage requires historical data and statistical methods to estimate its size. It often depends on the trade size relative to market liquidity and volatility. A fundamental approach to add slippage is to use a fixed percentage or a dynamic model based on recent trade history. For instance, if historical data suggests an average slippage of 0.1%:

$$\begin{aligned} \text{Slippage} &= 0.1\% \times 100 \text{ shares} \times \$100 \\ &= \$10 \text{ (per trade)}. \end{aligned}$$

Again considering both buy and sell trades, the total slippage costs would be:

$$\text{Total Slippage Costs} = 2 \times \$10 = \$20.$$

Therefore, incorporating both transaction costs and slippage into the backtest shows a cumulative reduction in profit of:

$$\text{Cumulative Costs} = \$110 \text{ (Transaction Costs)} + \$20 \text{ (Slippage Costs)} = \$130.$$

To make backtests more robust, it is advisable to incorporate variability and uncertainty in cost estimations. One method is to model transaction costs and slippage using random variables based on historical data distributions. For instance, if slippage varies with market conditions, simulate multiple backtesting scenarios with different slippage rates within a given range to see how sensitive the strategy's performance is to these variations.

When evaluating strategy performance, it's critical to analyze how much of the gross returns are consumed by transaction costs and slippage. Performance metrics such as *net profit* (after costs) and *cost-adjusted Sharpe ratio* provide a more accurate picture of strategy viability. Use the following net profit formula:

$$\text{Net Profit} = \text{Gross Profit} - \text{Transaction Costs} - \text{Slippage}.$$

Implementing these factors in algorithmic trading platforms often involves adding cost functions directly into the trading algorithms. Many backtesting frameworks, such as Backtrader or QuantConnect, allow users to define and integrate comprehensive transaction cost models. Here is a pseudo-code snippet demonstrating how one might include these:

```
def calculate_transaction_costs(trade_size, trade_value):
    commission = 5 # fixed cost per trade
    spread_cost = 0.005 * trade_value
    return commission + spread_cost

def calculate_slippage(trade_size, trade_value):
    slippage = 0.001 * trade_value # assuming 0.1% slippage
    return slippage

for trade in backtest_trades:
    trade_value = trade.size * trade.price
    transaction_costs = calculate_transaction_costs(trade.size, trade_value)
    slippage = calculate_slippage(trade.size, trade_value)
    total_costs = transaction_costs + slippage
    trade.profit -= total_costs # adjust the profitability based on costs
```

In sum, a comprehensive backtest must factor in transaction costs and slippage to provide realistic expectations of strategy performance. This ensures strategies are adaptive and resilient enough for live market conditions, protecting traders from unexpected losses attributable to these often underestimated components.

12.7 Backtesting Platforms and Tools

Selecting the right platform and tools for backtesting is crucial for developing effective trading strategies. A suitable platform should offer robust data handling capabilities, flexibility in implementing various trading strategies, and comprehensive performance evaluation features. Let's explore some widely-used backtesting platforms, their features, and how they can be utilized to enhance your trading strategy development process.

One prominent feature to consider is the programming language used by the platform. Python-based platforms such as QuantConnect, Zipline by Quantopian, and Backtrader are popular due to their versatility and the extensive libraries available for financial analysis. For example, QuantConnect not only supports Python but also C# and F#, making it a flexible option for diverse user preferences. These platforms often support integration with powerful libraries like NumPy, pandas, and scikit-learn, which facilitate complex data manipulations and machine learning applications.

QuantConnect: QuantConnect is a cloud-based platform that provides extensive historical data, a collaborative web-based coding environment, and a high-performance backtesting engine. It supports algorithmic trading strategies in multiple programming languages, although Python is most common. With its modular architecture, QuantConnect allows traders to simulate strategies across different asset classes, including equities, futures, forex, and cryptocurrencies. The platform offers rich APIs to retrieve historical data, execute trades, and receive market events, thus enabling the seamless development and backtesting of algorithms.

Backtrader: Backtrader is an open-source backtesting framework with vast community support. Its robust documentation and active development make it a reliable choice for traders seeking to customize their strategies. Backtrader provides features such as visualizations of equity curves, indicators, and trade entries/exits, which are crucial for thoroughly understanding strategy performance. The framework also facilitates the integration with live trading through broker APIs, allowing a seamless transition from backtesting to live execution.

Conducting backtests requires accessing reliable historical data. Platforms such as Quandl, Alpha Vantage, and Yahoo Finance offer APIs to download historical data that can be seamlessly integrated into your backtesting environment. Quandl, for example, provides not only stock price data but also various economic indicators and alternative datasets that can be used to enhance model predictions.

Zipline: Developed by Quantopian, Zipline is another robust Python-based backtesting library. Its integration with pandas for data handling makes it straightforward to manipulate and analyze historical data. Zipline handles minute-level data and provides functionalities for calculating performance metrics such as the Sharpe ratio, maximum drawdown, and other risk-adjusted return measures. This tool uses event-driven architecture to simulate real market conditions accurately, fostering the development of resilient trading algorithms.

For those preferring commercial solutions with extensive support, platforms like TradeStation, MetaTrader, and NinjaTrader offer professional-grade backtesting capabilities alongside their trading functionalities. These platforms are equipped with sophisticated charting tools, built-in technical indicators, and scripting languages for custom strategy development. For example, MetaTrader uses the MQL4 and MQL5 scripting languages, which are designed to handle complex trading conditions, custom indicators, and real-time data processing efficiently.

In addition to software platforms, consider the hardware where backtests are executed. Running high-frequency strategies or testing against extensive datasets might require substantial computational resources. Cloud computing services, such as Amazon Web Services (AWS) and Google Cloud Platform (GCP), offer scalable solutions to handle intensive backtesting tasks. By leveraging cloud resources, traders can dynamically allocate computing power to expedite backtesting processes and enhance productivity.

$$\text{ROA (Return on Assets)} = \frac{\text{Net Income}}{\text{Total Assets}}$$

Selecting a backtesting platform and tools should be aligned with the specific needs of your trading strategies. Essential considerations include the types of assets traded, the frequency of trading signals, the complexity of the algorithms, and the depth of historical data required. Utilizing the right combination of platforms and tools will streamline the backtesting process and increase the likelihood of developing robust and profitable trading strategies.

Ensuring a thorough understanding of each platform's strengths and weaknesses is vital. Experimenting with multiple platforms can provide insights into which best suits your needs and preferences.

12.8 Optimization and Robustness Checks

Optimization and robustness checks are critical components in the development and refinement of trading strategies. The goal is to identify the most effective parameters and ensure that the strategy performs consistently under varying market conditions. This section delves into the methodologies for optimizing trading strategies and conducting robustness checks to verify their reliability and resilience.

To start, optimization involves adjusting the parameters of a trading strategy to maximize its performance based on historical data. Common performance metrics used for optimization include the Sharpe ratio, net profit, maximum drawdown, and the win/loss ratio. The process typically starts with selecting a set of parameters to optimize. For example, if we are dealing with a moving average crossover strategy, we might optimize the short-term and long-term moving averages.

$$\text{Moving Average} = \frac{1}{N} \sum_{i=0}^{N-1} P_{t-i}$$

where P_{t-i} represents the price at time $t - i$ and N is the number of periods.

In practical terms, the optimization process can be performed using techniques such as grid search, random search, or more sophisticated methods like genetic algorithms and Bayesian optimization. Grid search involves evaluating the strategy's performance across a predefined grid of parameter values. Although exhaustive, it can be computationally expensive. Random search offers a more efficient alternative by sampling random combinations of parameters within specified ranges. Genetic algorithms, inspired by the principles of natural selection, evolve a population of strategies over successive iterations, selecting the best-performing individuals for reproduction and mutation. Bayesian optimization builds a probabilistic model of the objective function and uses it to select the most promising parameters to evaluate next.

As optimization progresses, it is crucial to avoid overfitting, where a strategy is tailored too closely to historical data and fails to generalize to new, unseen data. Overfitting can be identified by an unusually high performance during backtesting, which does not hold in real-world trading. One practical approach to mitigate overfitting is the use of walk-forward optimization, which involves dividing the data into multiple subsets. The strategy is optimized on one subset (the in-sample data) and then tested on another subset (the out-of-sample data). This process is repeated, shifting the data window forward, to simulate the strategy's performance over time.

Another important aspect of optimization is robustness testing. Robustness checks evaluate whether the strategy performs well across different market conditions and time periods, ensuring its reliability and adaptability. One simple method for robustness testing is the Monte Carlo simulation, where the strategy is tested across thousands of randomly generated scenarios to assess its performance variability and stability.

Additionally, parameter sensitivity analysis is performed to check how small changes in strategy parameters affect its performance. For a given strategy with parameters x and y, sensitivity analysis investigates the impact on performance from slight variations around the optimized values. If a strategy remains profitable within a range of parameter settings, it demonstrates robustness.

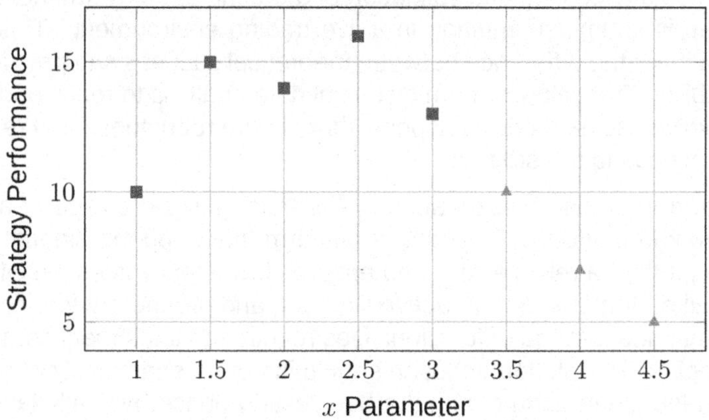

In addition to sensitivity analysis, stress testing is a valuable approach. Stress tests evaluate how a strategy performs under extreme but plausible market conditions. Scenarios such as market crashes, sudden interest rate changes, or geopolitical events are simulated to observe the strategy's behavior. For example, analyzing how the 2008 financial crisis would impact the strategy provides insights into its robustness against similar future events.

Considering both empirical and statistical measures enhances the depth and breadth of robustness checks. Portfolio heat maps, statistical tests (such as the t-test to compare means of different periods), and out-of-sample performance analysis extend beyond simple performance metrics, providing a comprehensive evaluation of a strategy's resilience.

The interplay between optimization and robustness checks forms the backbone of strategic refinement in quantitative finance. By diligently applying these techniques, traders and investors can develop strategies that are not only optimized for past performance but also robust enough to withstand the uncertainties of future market dynamics. This holistic approach builds confidence in the strategies, paving the way for their successful application in live trading.

12.9 Implementing Strategies in Live Trading

After rigorous backtesting and validation of a trading strategy, the next crucial step is its implementation in a live trading environment. This phase can mark the difference between theoretical success and practical profitability. Transitioning from historical data analysis to real-world trading involves several critical aspects that ensure robustness and reliability in executing the strategy.

The first and foremost consideration in live trading is the choice of a suitable trading platform. Selecting a platform that supports algorithmic trading, offers a reliable API, and ensures low latency is essential. Platforms like MetaTrader, Interactive Brokers, and proprietary trading platforms provide a range of functionalities required to implement complex strategies. The platform chosen should integrate seamlessly with the coding language used during the backtesting phase, typically languages such as Python, C++, or Java.

Once a platform and integration are in place, the operations must be automated to minimize human error and take advantage of market opportunities swiftly. Automation involves coding the strategy in a manner that the trading bot can execute orders based on predefined conditions.

The code must address the nuances of order types, including market orders, limit orders, stop-loss, and take-profit mechanisms. For instance, a limit order ensures you do not pay more than a specified price, while a stop-loss order helps in mitigating losses. Writing robust and precise code for these orders is crucial, and it is often beneficial to include fail-safes and error-handling routines to manage unexpected conditions in the live market.

During live implementation, real-time data feed quality and speed are critical components. Ensuring that the data provider delivers consistent and accurate market data with minimal latency can significantly impact the performance of high-frequency trading (HFT) strategies. It is advisable to contract with reputable data providers and possibly subscribe to premium, low-latency data feeds directly from exchanges if the strategy's performance is highly sensitive to speed.

Integration testing is another significant step. Before the strategy is allowed to trade with real funds, it must be tested with a simulated account. Most trading platforms offer paper trading environments where strategies can operate in live market conditions without risking actual capital. The goal of this phase is to ensure that the strategy performs as expected under real-time conditions, orders are executed correctly, and any interaction with the broker API is smooth and error-free. Simulation should run through several market cycles to validate performance across different market conditions.

Risk management cannot be overstated in live trading. Strategies must include dynamic risk controls that can adjust positions, halt trades, or systematize risk exposure based on predefined criteria. These controls could include drawdown limits, position size calculators, and volatility-based risk adjustments. For example, leveraging the concept of Value at Risk (VaR) helps in quantifying the maximum potential loss over a given period, ensuring that the strategy never exceeds the acceptable risk threshold.

Transaction costs and slippage are other critical factors that can erode profitability. While backtesting might have accounted for an average estimate, the real-world impact can be more severe, especially in volatile or low-liquidity markets. Efficient execution algorithms, such as VWAP (Volume Weighted Average Price) or TWAP (Time Weighted Average Price), can be employed to minimize market impact. These algorithms break down large orders into smaller chunks, reducing price distortions and achieving better execution prices.

A proper logging and monitoring system should be put in place to continuously track strategy performance and system health. Logging involves recording every detail of strategy decisions, market conditions, and execution outcomes. Monitoring goes hand-in-hand, enabling real-time surveillance of strategy performance metrics, risk levels, and operational status of the trading system. Alerts and notifications can be configured to inform the trader or developer about critical events like connection drops, execution delays, or performance anomalies.

Furthermore, continual adaptation and refinement of the strategy are indispensable. Financial markets are dynamic and influenced by a myriad of factors, including macroeconomic changes, geopolitical events, and technological advancements. Regular review cycles to evaluate strategy performance, the re-calibration of parameters, and enhancements based on recent data are needed to maintain a competitive edge. Mechanisms such as machine learning algorithms can be integrated for predictive analytics and self-learning capacities.

Lastly, regulatory compliance and ethical considerations must be adhered to. Ensuring that the strategy complies with the trading regulations of the jurisdiction in which it operates is crucial. This includes having proper licensing, understanding market abuse regulations, and ensuring transparency and fairness in trading activities.

Transitioning a strategy from concept to live trading is a meticulous process that involves preparation, rigorous testing, and ongoing refinements. By addressing each of these components diligently, traders can enhance the probability of achieving sustained profitability in the complex landscape of financial markets.

12.10 Continuous Monitoring and Adaptation

Trading strategies, once implemented, require diligent and continuous monitoring to ensure they remain effective and responsive to market changes. Markets are inherently dynamic, influenced by economic indicators, geopolitical events, and investor sentiments. A strategy that is profitable today might underperform tomorrow if it is not continuously refined. This section delves into the importance of ongoing strategy surveillance, the tools and techniques available for monitoring performance, and the adaptive measures necessary for sustained success.

Effective monitoring begins with establishing a robust infrastructure for real-time data collection and analysis. It is essential to track market data as well as the performance metrics of the trading strategy. This involves setting up a system that logs trades, calculates performance statistics, and generates alerts when performance deviates from expected behavior. Common metrics to monitor include percentage returns, drawdowns, the Sharpe ratio, and trade frequency. The formula for calculating the Sharpe ratio, which gauges risk-adjusted performance, is given by:

$$\text{Sharpe Ratio} = \frac{E[R_p - R_f]}{\sigma_p}$$

where $E[R_p - R_f]$ is the expected return of the portfolio minus the risk-free rate, and σ_p is the standard deviation of the portfolio's excess return. A higher Sharpe ratio indicates better risk-adjusted returns.

Moreover, automated tools such as algorithmic trading dashboards and analytics platforms enable traders to monitor these metrics in real-time. Utilizing platforms with customizable dashboards can provide insights into various dimensions of strategy performance, helping to quickly identify anomalies or trends that require attention. Many traders employ Python or R scripts to automatically fetch data and compute the necessary metrics. For instance, here is a Python code snippet using 'pandas' to calculate the Sharpe ratio:

```
import pandas as pd
import numpy as np

# Assume 'returns' is a pandas Series of strategy returns
risk_free_rate = 0.02
expected_return = returns.mean()
excess_return = returns - risk_free_rate
sharpe_ratio = np.mean(excess_return) / np.std(excess_return)
```

Staying proactive involves more than just monitoring. Adaptation necessitates making informed adjustments based on the insights gathered. This might involve reevaluating and tweaking parameters, incorporating new data, or even modifying the underlying hypothesis of the strategy. The concept of a feedback loop is critical here: systematically adjusting the strategy in light of performance metrics not only helps mitigate risks but also enhances returns.

One practical method for ensuring continuous strategy refinement is conducting rolling re-optimization. This entails periodically reassessing the parameters of the trading model using the most recent data. For example, instead of relying on a static lookback window, the model parameters can be recalibrated every month or quarter on the latest available data. This keeps the strategy aligned with current market conditions.

Pitfalls in continuous monitoring often involve ignoring the implications of transaction costs, slippage, and market impact. Each trade incurs costs that can erode net gains, especially in high-frequency strategies. It's crucial to have a realistic estimate of these factors and incorporate them into performance analysis. Regularly updating these estimates based on recent trading activity ensures more accurate assessment and decision-making.

Another key point is the psychological aspect of adapting trading strategies. Emotional biases can lead traders to either overreact to short-term losses or become complacent during winning streaks. Implementing systematic rules for strategy adjustments can help mitigate emotional biases. For example, setting predefined thresholds for key performance metrics that, once crossed, trigger a review or adjustment of the strategy.

Practical frameworks such as the Plan-Do-Check-Act (PDCA) cycle can be employed to structure the adaptation process. This iterative process involves:

- **Plan:** Identify the areas needing improvement and develop a strategy adjustment plan based on data analysis.
- **Do:** Implement the adjustment on a small scale to test its efficacy.
- **Check:** Evaluate the performance of the adjustment against predefined criteria.
- **Act:** Fully deploy the adjustment if it proves effective, or refine the plan if necessary.

Lastly, continuous education and staying abreast of market developments, technological advancements, and regulatory changes are integral to the process. Engaging with financial literature, attending webinars, and participating in trading forums can provide new perspectives and strategies, reinforcing the continuous evolution necessary in trading.

Monitoring and adapting trading strategies are as crucial as their initial development. This ongoing process demands a blend of real-time analytical capability, systematic adjustment frameworks, and emotional discipline to navigate the ever-changing market landscape effectively. By embedding these practices, traders can maintain the robustness and profitability of their strategies over time.

Made in the USA
Monee, IL
14 September 2026

63117170R00167